Nettleton and

Nettleton and His Labours

The Memoir of Dr. Asahel Nettleton

BENNET TYLER

Remodelled in some parts by

ANDREW A. BONAR

THE BANNER OF TRUTH TRUST

THE BANNER OF TRUTH TRUST
3 *Murrayfield Road, Edinburgh* EH12 6EL
P.O. Box 621, *Carlisle, Pennsylvania* 17013, *U.S.A.*

*

First published 1854
First Banner of Truth reprint 1975
Reprinted 1996

ISBN 0 85151 701 3

*

Printed in Finland by WSOY

CONTENTS.

Chapter V.

Chapter VI.

Chapter VII.

Chapter VIII.

Chapter IX.

Chapter X.

Chapter XI.

Chapter XII.

Chapter XIII.

Chapter XIV.

Appendix.

INTRODUCTION.

"I ONCE said to myself, in the foolishness of my heart: 'What sort of sermon must that have been which was preached by Peter when three thousand souls were converted at once?' What sort of sermon? Such as other sermons. There is nothing to be found in it extraordinary. The effect was not produced by eloquence, but by the mighty power of God present with the Word." How many have felt, if they have not said, what Cecil thus gives expression to!

It has been thought desirable by some who have so felt, that *Dr. Nettleton's* life and character should be better known in this country. His biographer, Dr. Bennet Tyler, has given us a most valuable and interesting memoir, with documents to attest whatever any might ascribe to partiality. It is that memoir which is here given forth again, only it has been somewhat remodelled. Not one fact has been omitted. In almost every paragraph of the narrative part, the very words of the original memoir are retained;* but some portions of the documents have been omitted, occasional remarks have been introduced by the present editor, and a few other

* Even such American phraseology as "*powerful revival,*" "*experiencing religion,*" has been retained.

changes made that seemed likely to adapt it more to this country. A considerable number of extracts, also, from Dr. Nettleton's *Remains*, have been inserted, and a few extracts from other sources, bearing on revivals, given.

We do not claim for *Dr. Nettleton* the rank of Whitefield; but yet he stands very high among those who have "converted sinners from the error of their ways, saved souls from death, and hidden a multitude of sins," (James v. 20.) There was this difference between his preaching and Whitefield's, in its substance, that while the latter proclaimed, with amazing unction and effect, the plainest and simplest truths regarding sin and the Saviour, reiterating these, in every place, all his long career,—Dr. Nettleton, on the other hand, dealt very extensively, and very perseveringly, in full doctrinal statements opened up and pressed home on the conscience.

There is a natural aversion to *authority*, even the *authority of God*, in the heart of man. And hence it has been that, both then and now, there have been zealous men who have loudly protested against those doctrines of grace usually called *Calvinistic doctrines*, pretending that the souls of men are by these doctrines lulled into sleep as far as regards their responsibility. Now, though such an abuse of these scriptural truths has often been manifested where men have grown lukewarm, yet the very opposite influence is that which they ought to exert; and whoever reads Dr. Nettleton's history, will see with what tremendous force they may be employed to awaken the conscience.

Vinet has remarked, that that very delicate psychology which goes prying into all the motives of the soul, surprising all its secrets, extorting from it confessions, ferreting into its obscure corners, giving to the soul the consciousness of all its evil, is, after all, dangerous to the soul. The knowledge of one's self is then turned into a study,—a matter of curiosity. The sorrows of repentance are unwittingly transformed into the pleasures of self-love; nay, the reproaches of conscience become the pleasures of the intellect; and so we do not enter into, but rather go out of ourselves.—(Vinet's *Homiletics.*) Such treatment of the human heart becomes mere philosophy. But not dissimilar in its result, because really carrying on an analogous process, is the method pursued by some in regard to the special doctrines of grace,—the Calvinistic doctrines. They have so preached and prelected on them, so argued and defended them, that, in their hands, these truths have become little better than dry theses; and the preachers of those truths have dropt the tone of solemn, tender, conscience-rousing Boanerges, and become merely able defenders of favourite themes. In admirable contrast with such treatment of doctrine, Dr. Nettleton's preaching, avoiding this error altogether, set these high truths before his hearers, on all occasions, in a most thoroughly practical form. They saw in them the God of majesty, glory, grace, dealing with rebels, and were bowed down before Him.

We said, that when men dislike these truths there is at the root a dislike of authority,—*God's authority.* Men forget, or willingly are ignorant, that the *will of*

God is "the Rule of rules, the Law of laws, the Justice of all justice, the Equity of all equity, the Right of all right."—(Calvin.) They think and speak *as if God had no reasons* for what He does, because *we do not know* His reasons; they will not be content to travel humbly onward until the day of Christ, when "the mystery of God shall be finished;" they insist on everything being explained to them clearly now, that they may perceive why God acts thus. But why should not we wait till the time for such explanations arrive? Why should we run the risk of losing our footing, and being drowned in those great deeps, while we insist on fathoming them ere we will believe that they are God's unfathomable depths?

It is worthy of notice, that it is *John*,—he who so fully opens up to view the love of God,—John who so expatiates on every proof of divine love, John who seems to feel the beating of the heart of God-man more than any other,—he it is whose pen is so constantly guided by the Holy Ghost to refer to the doctrines of sovereign grace. It is he who records the words: "I know whom I have chosen," and, "I have chosen you," in xiii. 18; xv. 16; and it is he who speaks so often of those whom "*the Father hath given*" to Christ; —and is not all this *Election?** It is he who records the words of Jesus: "I lay down my life *for the sheep;*" —the method of salvation, "*one* for *all;*"—and is not this *particular Redemption?*† It is he who tells how Jesus said: "No man cometh unto me, except the Father, who hath sent me, *draw him;*" and "except it

* John x 11; vi 37, 39; xvii 2, 6, 9, 11, 12.

† John vi 44, 65.

be given him of the Father,"—who relates the conversation John iii. 5; and who tells that a believer in Christ is born not by natural descent, not by his own fleshly will, not by the persuasive power of any other man's reasoning, "*but of God;*"—and is not this *Special Grace?** It is he who records, more than once, such declarations of Jesus as these: "*Every man* that hath heard and *learned of the Father, cometh unto me*"—"all that the Father giveth me *shall* come to me;"—and is not this *Irresistible Grace?* There is no free will here.† It is he who has so fully given our Lord's words about His sheep: "None shall pluck them out of my hand; they shall never perish; none shall pluck them out of my Father's hand,"—"Of those whom thou hast given me, I have lost none,"‡—and then, xiv. 16: "The Comforter shall abide with you for ever;"—and is not this the doctrine of the *Perseverance of the Saints?*§ We might add, it is he who, without attempting to reconcile the two truths, states so broadly God's "blinding the eyes, and hardening the hearts" (xii. 40) of the Jews; and yet their own sin being their ruin—"they believed not," (xii. 43,) "For they loved the praise of men more than the praise of God."

Whitefield, and Edwards, and Nettleton, never found themselves nor those they addressed, hindered by these great truths; they were helped by them, not hindered. No wonder; for do not each of these doctrines at once turn our eye on *God himself*, and cause us to hear His voice saying: "Come now, *let us reason together*, saith the Lord?"

* John i. 13. † John vi. 45; vi 37. ‡ John x 28, 29; xviii. 9. § John xiv. 16.

They lead us to the fullest and freest *Gospel*. If they teach that men naturally hate God, nay, that "*they hate Him without a cause*," (John xv. 25,) they also teach, that as truly as man is so thoroughly base and unholy that he can hate God, even God in Christ, ("Me and my Father," John xv. 24,) although there is not one reason in God that gives occasion to this hatred, yet, on the other hand, God is so gloriously gracious, that He can love man "*without a cause*." He can, out of merest grace, without there being one single quality in man to call it forth, freely love the sinner, and freely provide justification. If the man hated "without a cause," (δωρεαν,) the Lord justifies "without a cause" in us, (δωρεαν,) (Rom. iii. 25.) The warrant to the sinner goes forth in these terms: "Whosoever will, let him come and take of the water of life freely," (δωρεαν,) without waiting till there is in him one excellence that might seem likely to induce God to give it (Rev. xxii. 17). You sinned *gratuitously*, you may be saved *gratuitously*. And if it seem a strange preface to a free Gospel call, in the eyes of some, to tell sinful men that it remains with God to leave their eyes closed, or to open them on the things announced and proffered to their acceptance, still it is the very method pursued by our Lord in Matth. xi. 25, 28: "I thank thee, O Father, Lord of heaven and earth, *that thou hast hid these things from the wise and prudent, and hast revealed them unto babes.*" "*Come unto me, all ye that labour and are heavy laden!*" It is His method, too, in John vi. 37, and in iii. 5, 15. And no wonder after all! For, see, it declares that this Gospel-call, this invitation of rich, boundless love, need never fall on any man's ear in vain, however depraved, hardened, desperately wicked he may be, since the same God of holy love who sends it has the power to turn that heart in the very moment the invitation comes to it. Love is *so unlimited* that it can sweep away the very unwillingness of the sinner to whom it addresses its message of grace! Is not this glad tidings?—free unlimited love, a flood that is not turned aside into another channel by meeting the rock in its way, but that rises behind it till its waters pour over it in a cataract!

Nor let us fail to notice, that all the doctrines of grace are beams from the glorious *person of Christ.* There we may see them in their centre: (1.) The person of God-man is a proclamation of *election*—the *principle* of election—inasmuch as it is an everlasting monument of His having passed by angels, and come, in mere grace, to the help of *man.* (2.) The person of God-man is a proclamation of *particular redemption*, and all the completeness of atonement involved therein; for who is He but the one man who dies for the people, for "*all the children of God,*" (John xi. 52,)—the second Adam, who tastes death for every man of His family, His many sons, (Heb. ii. 9.) Again, (3.) The person of Christ is a proclamation of the doctrine of *special grace;* for from that fountain cometh the regenerating Spirit to man; so that if you see the stream of "repentance" in any one, you trace it up to its source in "the Prince and Saviour exalted to *give repentance,*" (Acts v. 31,) and "quickening whom He will," (John v. 21.) Then, (4.) The person of Christ proclaims *irresistible grace,* inasmuch as it is after the pattern of His resurrection from the dead that every believing one was raised from the grave of sin, (Eph. i. 20,) "according to the *energy of the might of God's power*, *wrought in Christ*, when raised from the dead;" and inasmuch as we can never fail to connect with His person such remembrances, as that He on earth called men and they came, — whether it were a Lazarus out of his grave, or a Matthew out of his tomb of corruption. (5.) The person of Christ proclaims the *perseverance of the saints;* for we never can forget His own representation of himself as *bearing home* the sheep on His own shoulders, and causing new joy in heaven by its safe arrival.

And let us add on this subject, that *the person of Christ* (associated, of course, with what He wrought) being to us the centre and core of all the doctrines of grace, we have a brief and satisfactory answer therein to those who allege that they cannot disentangle the sinner's free access to the offered salvation from the difficulties that beset some of these doctrines. We point, in this case, to the centre doctrine of all,—*the person of Christ*,—"the great mystery of godliness," and tell that this, at least, is clear, and plain, and indisputable,—viz., that God *commands you to go to Him.* Go, then, and He will be to you what the woman of Syrophenicia found Him to be, (when she could not unravel the apparent frown contained in His words,) —a bottomless fountain of grace; and every child of Adam is warranted at once to approach to this and use it. Deal with *himself* here, if other truths perplex you; and solve all questions as to whether or not *you* were specially intended when this fountain was opened for sinners, by drinking of it; or, in other words, by willingly receiving Christ himself, and putting your soul at His disposal.

We must assert one other truth in connexion with these doctrines of grace. Most assuredly they are fitted to lead a man and a minister of Christ (witness Dr. Nettleton) to be zealous of good works, and zealous for souls,—bent upon God's glory, and bent upon the salvation of men. As to the latter, which specially some call in question, how plain it is that, believing what we do, we can despair of no man so long as he lives, and so long as there is the Spirit of grace to convert men. Besides, we know that our Lord desires us, and expects us to travail as in birth for the souls of men, apart from what success we may have. This is *His will;* and to know this aright makes ministers anxious, earnest, holy, prayerful, intensely covetous of souls. There may be nothing present to excite; still the same high duty, and the same ever-remaining hope of the Holy Spirit's working, furnish sufficient motives to produce steady and fervent effort. And thus (with holy Bradford, who, in prison, before going to the stake, defended these doctrines of grace) they can yearn over men, and expostulate with them: "I pray you, I desire you, I crave it at your hands with all my very heart; I ask of you with hand, pen, tongue, and mind, in Christ, for Christ, through Christ, for the sake of His name, blood, mercy, power, truth, my most entirely beloved, that you admit no doubt of God's mercies toward you!" Yes; *we work*, and pray, and travail for souls, *because God worketh* to will and to do of His good pleasure; and holds over our head the crown of glory, which shepherds who have the Shepherd's heart receive at the day when the chief Shepherd shall appear.

COLLACE, *April* 1854.

Nettleton and his Labours.

CHAPTER I.

HIS AWAKENING AND CONVERSION.

IT cannot be otherwise than interesting to read how the Lord led one whom some believed to have been the means of AWAKENING *no less than thirty thousand souls.*

ASAHEL NETTLETON was born in North Killingworth, Connecticut, April 21, 1783. He was the eldest son, and second child, of a family of six children, consisting of three sons and three daughters. His parents, though but little known to the world, were esteemed and respected by their neighbours. His father was a farmer, in moderate, but comfortable circumstances; and in this employment Asahel was mostly engaged until he entered college, in 1805.

His childhood and youth, so far as is known to the writer, were characterized by nothing very peculiar. His early advantages of education were only such as are furnished by the common district school. That he made a good use of these advantages, we may infer from the thirst for knowledge which he evinced at a later period, and from the fact that, while a young man, he was employed, several winters, in the capacity of a school teacher.

His parents, according to the custom which prevailed at that period in some parts of New England, were professors of religion, on what was called the half-way covenant plan,—that is, they were not admitted to full communion, but having publicly assented to the covenant of the Church, they were permitted to offer their children in baptism.* Asahel was, of course, baptized in his infancy; and, while a child, received some religious instruction from his parents. He was, in particular, required to commit to memory the *Assembly's Catechism*, which, as he often remarked, was of great use to him when his attention was awakened to the concerns of his soul. His morals were also strictly guarded by his parents; and they had the satisfaction to know, that, during the period of youth, he was not addicted to any vicious habits, but sustained, in the eyes of the world, an unblemished moral character.

While a child, he was occasionally the subject of religious impressions. At one time, in particular, while alone in the field, and looking at the setting sun, he was powerfully impressed with the thought,

* This custom, according to Dr. Bellamy, was first introduced by the recommendation of a synod which met in Boston, 1662. Many ministers and churches zealously opposed it at the time; and although it gained extensive prevalence, it was never universally adopted. It began to be discontinued in the days of Edwards and Bellamy; for the latter remarks: "Of late a considerable number of churches which had adopted the practice, have laid it aside." The revivals at the beginning of the present century, put a period to it in most of the churches, and, at present, it is scarcely known in any part of New England. It is the very state of things still prevailing in many parts of our Scottish Highlands; and nothing but an outpouring of the Spirit, such as was vouchsafed to these congregations in America, is likely to remedy it.

that he and all men must die. He was so affected by this thought, that he stood for some time and wept aloud. But these feelings were transitory, and he seems to have had no permanent religious impressions till the autumn of 1800, when he was in the eighteenth year of his age. This was at the period so memorable in the history of American churches as a time of refreshing from the presence of the Lord. For half a century the influences of the divine Spirit had been, in a great measure, withdrawn from the churches. Revivals were few. But during a period of four or five years, commencing with 1798, not less than one hundred and fifty churches in New England were favoured with the special effusions of the Holy Spirit; and thousands of souls, in the judgment of charity, were translated from the kingdom of Satan into the kingdom of God's dear Son.

In the blessings of this general outpouring of the Spirit, North Killingworth shared. A narrative of the revival of religion in this town was published in the fourth and fifth volumes of the *Connecticut Evangelical Magazine*. A few individuals, whose conversion was considered particularly interesting, were requested by their pastor to give him, in writing, an account of their religious exercises. Mr. Nettleton was one of the number; and his account, with that of two or three others, is incorporated in the printed narrative, and is as follows:—

"Knowing, by experience, the deplorable state of a sinner,—that he is, by nature, totally destitute of love and conformity to God, and that he cannot be saved but by a special act of sovereign grace, induceth me to ask for further instruction upon this all-important subject, and to communicate, in a summary manner, the state of my mind, and the feelings with which it has been exercised.

"From my earliest age I endeavoured to lead a moral life, being often taught that God would punish sinners; but I did not believe that I should suffer for the few offences of which I had been guilty. Having avoided many sins which I saw in others, I imagined all was well with me, till I was about eighteen years old, when I heard a sermon preached upon the necessity of regeneration, which put me upon thinking of the need of a change of heart in myself. I did not, however, well receive the discourse at the time; for I was sensible I knew nothing about such a change; neither did I wish to know, for I believed myself as good as others without it; and to be equal with them, I thought would be sufficient. However, the thought troubled me considerably from day to day, and caused me to think of praying, which I had never done, except repeating some form as a little child, and doing it to remove the stings of a guilty conscience, when I considered myself in imminent danger. Some time after this I heard another sermon, that convinced me I had quenched the Spirit, which occasioned me the most alarming fears, that I should for ever be left to eat the fruit of my own ways. Supposing I was alone in the thoughts of eternity, I separated myself from all company, and determined to seek an interest in Christ. I concluded something must be done to appease God's anger. I read, and prayed, and strove in every possible way to prepare myself to go to God, that I might be saved from His wrath. The more I strove in this selfish way, the more anxious I was; and no hope was given. Soon I began to murmur and repine, and accused God of the greatest injustice in requiring me to return to Him; and while I was striving with all my might, as I supposed, He appeared not to regard me. I considered God obligated to love me, because I had done so much for Him; and finding no relief, I wished that He might not be, and began really to doubt the truths of His Holy Word, and to disbelieve His existence; for if there was a God, I perfectly hated Him. I searched the Scriptures daily, hoping to find inconsistencies in them, to condemn the Bible, because it was against me; and while I was diligently pursuing my purpose, everything I read, and every sermon I heard, condemned me. Christian conversation gave me the most painful sensations.

"I tried to repent, but I could not feel the least sorrow for my innumerable sins. By endeavouring to repent, I saw my heart still remained impenitent. Although I knew I hated everything serious, yet I determined to habituate myself to the duties which God required, and see if I could not, by that means, be made to love Him; and I continued in this state some months. The fear of having committed the unpardonable sin, now began to rise in my mind, and I could find no rest day nor night. When my weary limbs demanded sleep, the fear of awaking in a miserable eternity prevented the closing of my eyes; and nothing gave me ease. No voice of mirth, or sound whatever, was heard, but what reminded me of the awful day when God shall bring every work into judgment. All self-righteousness failed me; and, having no confidence in God, I was left in deep despondency.

"After awhile, a surprising tremor seized all my limbs, and death appeared to have taken hold upon me. Eternity—the word *Eternity*—sounded louder than any voice I ever heard; and every moment of time seemed more valuable than all the wealth of the world. Not long after this, an unusual calmness pervaded my soul, which I thought little of at first, except that I was freed from my awful convictions; and this sometimes grieved me, fearing I had lost all conviction. Soon after, hearing the feelings of a Christian described, I took courage, and thought I knew, by experience, what they were. The character of God, and the doctrines of the Bible, which I could not meditate upon before without hatred, especially those of election and free grace, now appear delightful, and the only means by which, through grace, dead sinners can be made the living sons of God. My heart feels its sinfulness. To confess my sins to God, gives me that peace which before I knew nothing of. To sorrow for it, affords that joy which my tongue cannot express. Were I sensible that, at death, my hope would perish, yet it seemeth to me now, that I could not willingly quit the service of God, nor the company of Christians. But my unfaithfulness often makes me fear my sincerity; and should I at last be raised to glory, all the praise will be to God for the exhibition of His sovereign grace."

In giving this account, he remarked, that the foregoing printed statement is not exactly as he wrote it. "When I heard a sermon preached upon the necessity of regeneration, which put me upon thinking of the need of a change of heart in myself,"—this, as it now reads, seems to convey the idea, that his attention was first awakened to the concerns of his soul by a particular sermon. But this was not true, nor was such an idea expressed in the original manuscript. His first permanent religious impressions occurred in the following manner:—

On the night of the annual Thanksgiving, in the Fall or autumn of 1800, he attended a ball. The next morning, while alone, and thinking, with pleasure, on the scenes of the preceding night, and of the manner in which he had proposed to spend the day, in company with some of his young companions, the thought suddenly rushed upon his mind: We must all die, and go to the judgment; and with what feelings shall we then reflect upon these scenes? This thought was, for the moment, overwhelming; and it left an impression on his mind which he could not efface. His pleasing reflections on the past, and anticipations of the future, vanished at once, and gave place to feelings of a very different kind. These feelings he concealed; but he could not entirely banish them from his mind. The world had lost its charms. All those amusements in which he had taken delight were overcast with gloom. His thoughts dwelt much on the scenes of death, judgment, and eternity. He knew that he had an immortal soul, that must be happy or miserable in the future world; and although he had consoled himself with the thought, that he was as good as others around him, and that his condition was, of course, as safe as theirs; yet he now felt conscious that he was unprepared to meet his God. He, at the same time, perceived that he was liable every moment to be cut down by the stroke of death, and summoned to his last account. He had no peace of mind by day or by night. Although, at this time, he had no very just conceptions of the divine law, or of the depravity of his heart; yet he was sensible that he was a sinner, and that his sins must be pardoned, or he could not be saved.

The duty of prayer was now forcibly impressed upon his mind,—a duty which he had almost entirely neglected; and it was not without a great struggle in his feelings, that he was brought to bend the knee to Jehovah. At the same time, he gave himself much to the reading of the Scriptures and other religious books, and separated himself as much as possible from thoughtless companions. So far as he knew, and so far as is now known, there was, at that time, no other person in the town under serious impressions.* The young people with whom he had been most intimate, were exceedingly thoughtless, and given to vain and sinful amusements. They were, at this time, making arrangements for the establishment of a dancing school, and they expected his aid and co-operation in the measure. But, to their astonishment, he utterly refused to have anything to do with it. He had made up his mind to quit for ever all such amusements, and to seek the salvation of his soul. But as he did not reveal his feelings to any of his associates, they knew not how to account for this sudden change in his appearance and conduct. Some, perhaps, suspected the true cause; while others supposed, that, for some reason unknown to them, his affections had become alienated from his former friends.

Thus, for months, he mourned in secret, and did not communicate his feelings to a single individual.

* This was in the autumn of 1800. The revival did not become visible till the following spring.

During this period he had a strong desire that some of his young companions would set out with him in pursuit of religion; and although his proud heart would not permit him to make known to them the state of his mind, yet he occasionally ventured to expostulate with them on the folly and sinfulness of their conduct; and to some few individuals he addressed short letters on the same subject. These warnings were treated by some with ridicule and contempt. On the minds of others they made an impression, which, as he afterwards learned, was never effaced. This was particularly the case with Philander Parmele, who was afterwards his class-mate in college, and intimate friend through life.*

When Mr. Nettleton first became anxious respecting the salvation of his soul, he had not, as has been remarked, any very just conceptions of the depravity of his heart. He was sensible that he was not in a safe condition. He knew that he needed something which he did not possess, to prepare him for heaven. He had a general vague idea that he was a sinner; but he saw not the fountain of iniquity within him. As is common with persons when awakened to a sense of their danger, he went about to establish his own righteousness. He vainly presumed, that by diligent and persevering efforts, he should recommend himself to the favour of God. He was, accordingly, very abundant in his religious services. He not only abandoned those amusements in which he had delighted, and forsook, in a great measure, the society

* Mr. Parmele became pastor of the church in Bolton, Conn. At his house Mr. Nettleton was sick with the typhus fever, in 1822. Mr. Parmele caught the fever of him, and died.

of those who took no interest in the subject of religion, but he spent much time in retirement, earnestly crying to God for mercy. He would often repair to the field and forests for this purpose; and he sometimes spent a large part of the night in prayer. In this way he expected to obtain the forgiveness of his sins, and the peace and consolation which God has promised to His people. But after labouring for some time in this manner, he became alarmed at his want of success. God seemed to pay no regard to his prayers; and how to account for this fact he knew not. At this crisis he was assailed by infidel doubts. The question arose in his mind, whether he had not proved the Bible to be false? It is written: *Ask, and ye shall receive; seek, and ye shall find.* He said to himself: I have asked, but I have not received; I have sought, but I have not found. How, then, can these promises be true? And how can the book which contains them be the Word of God? He found himself disposed to cherish these doubts, and to seek for further proof that the Bible is not true. He searched the Scriptures on purpose to find contradictions in them; and he even went so far as to begin to doubt the existence of a God. Like the fool, he said in his heart, There is no God,—that is, he wished there were none; for he was sensible, that, if there was a God, he was not reconciled to His character; and he wished the Bible to be false, because he saw that it condemned him. But his efforts to satisfy himself that religion is not a reality, did not succeed. The thought would sometimes arise: "What if the Bible should prove to be true! Then I am lost for ever." This would fill him with inconceivable horror.

These struggles in his mind led him to a more just knowledge of his character and condition. He began to see the plague of his own heart. His doubts respecting the truth of the promises which God has made to those who ask and seek, were dispelled by the painful conviction, that he never had asked and sought as God requires. The commandment came, sin revived, and he died. He saw that God looks on the heart, and that He requires holy and spiritual service of His creatures; that *He seeketh such to worship Him as worship Him in spirit and in truth.* He saw, at the same time, that in all his religious services he had been prompted by selfish motives. He saw that in all which he had done, he had had no love to God, and no regard to His glory; but that he had been influenced solely by a desire to promote his own personal interest and happiness. He saw that in all the distress which he had experienced on account of his sin, there was no godly sorrow—no true contrition. He had not hated sin because it was committed against God, but had merely dreaded its consequences.

During this period he read President Edwards' narrative of the revival of religion in Northampton, and the memoir of Brainerd. These served very much to deepen the conviction of his utterly lost condition. The preaching which he heard from time to time also greatly distressed him. As he says in his narrative, every sermon condemned him. Nothing gave him any relief. He seemed to be sinking daily deeper and deeper in guilt and wretchedness. One day, while alone in the field, engaged in prayer, his heart rose against God, because He did not hear and answer his prayers. Then the words of the apostle:

"*The carnal mind is enmity against God,*" came to his mind with such overwhelming power, as to deprive him of strength, and he fell prostrate on the earth. The doctrines of the Gospel—particularly the doctrines of divine sovereignty and election—were sources of great distress to him. There was much talk respecting these doctrines, at that time, in North Killingworth. Some disbelieved and openly opposed them. He searched the Scriptures with great diligence, to ascertain whether they are there taught; and although his heart was unreconciled to them, he dared not deny them, for he was convinced that they were taught in the Bible. He would sometimes say to himself: "If I am not elected I shall not be saved, even if I do repent." Then the thought would arise: "If I am not elected I never shall repent." This would cut him to the heart, and dash to the ground all his self-righteous hopes. For a long time he endured these conflicts in his mind.

Meanwhile, he became fully convinced that the commands of God are perfectly just—that it was his immediate duty to repent—and that he had no excuse for continuing another moment a rebel against God. At the same time, he saw that such was the wickedness of his heart—that he never should repent unless God should subdue his heart by an act of sovereign grace. With these views of his condition, his distress was sometimes almost insupportable. At one time he really supposed himself to be dying, and sinking into hell. This was the time of which he speaks in his narrative, when he says: "An unusual tremor seized all my limbs, and death appeared to have taken hold upon me." For several hours his horror of mind was inexpressible. Not long after this, there was a change in his feelings. He felt a calmness for which he knew not how to account. He thought, at first, that he had lost his convictions, and was going back to stupidity. This alarmed him; but still he could not recall his former feelings. A sweet peace pervaded his soul. The objects which had given him so much distress, he now contemplated with delight. He did not, however, for several days, suppose that he had experienced a change of heart; but finding, at length, that his views and feelings accorded with those expressed by others, whom he regarded as the friends of Christ, he began to think it possible that he might have passed from death unto life. The more he examined himself, the more evidence he found that a great change had been wrought in his views and feelings respecting divine things. Old things had passed away—all things had become new. The character of God now appeared lovely. The Saviour was exceedingly precious; and the doctrines of grace, towards which he had felt such bitter opposition, he contemplated with delight, and had now no doubt of their truth. He saw clearly, that if there was any good thing in him towards the Lord God of Israel, it was not the result of any effort of his own, but of the sovereign and distinguishing will of God.

It was about ten months, as has been already intimated, from the time when Mr. Nettleton's attention was first seriously turned to the subject of religion, before he obtained peace in believing. With him, what the old divines termed the *law-work* was deep and thorough. This protracted season of conviction gave him a knowledge of the human heart which few possess; and which was doubtless intended by God to prepare him for his peculiar labours as a minister of Christ. As one observes: "God prepares for himself the souls which He destines to some important work. We must prepare the vessel before we launch it on the mighty deep. If education is necessary for every man, then is a particular education necessary for those who are to influence the generations in which they live."

But although he enjoyed great peace of mind, he never expressed to others a very high degree of confidence that he was a child of God. He had such a deep and abiding sense of the deceitfulness of the human heart, and of the danger of self-deception, that not only at this period, but ever afterwards, he was exceedingly cautious in speaking about his belief that he was accepted of God. At one time, being asked whether he had any doubts respecting his interest in the promises, he replied: "I have no doubt that I have religious enjoyment; but the question is, whether it is of the right kind?" At another time he said: "The most that I have ventured to say respecting myself is, that I think it possible I may get to heaven." It was always painful to him to hear persons express great confidence of their interest in the divine favour. He feared they did not realize how deceitful the human heart is. This cautious reserve proceeded from godly jealousy over himself, and over others, in regard to inferring an interest in Christ, from superficial and partial change of feeling. It did not interfere with his own enjoyment of God, nor did it prevent him urging on others the calm joy that arises from beholding what God has given us in His Son; but it led him always to direct special attention to what was fitted at once to give true views and deepen all right feelings.

In after years, in a sermon on Psalm li. 12, we find him speaking in the following manner, of what the soul finds on first believing:—"The first joy of the new born soul does not arise from the belief that his sins are pardoned; for his sins are not pardoned until the love of God is shed abroad in his heart. He can, of course, have no evidence that he is pardoned, until he finds himself rejoicing in the contemplation of the divine character. But the joy of God's salvation may be realized when the individual has no idea that his sins are pardoned. The renewed soul, while contemplating the loveliness of Christ, and other divine objects, forgets himself, and his mind is absorbed in the delightful contemplation of these objects."

In passages like these, there seems to be some reminiscence of his own experience at the time of conversion. Indeed, in the revivals of that period, souls convinced of sin were very generally relieved and brought to rest in that manner. In the revival at New Hartford, we are told,* that the subjects of it, when asked what was the first thing that composed their minds, were often found to answer: "The thought that I was in the hands of God. It seems to me that, whatever becomes of me, I cannot bear to be out of His hands." When asked, what they had discovered of God to engage their affections? they have replied: "I think I love Him because He hates sin—because He hates my sin." One said in confidence to a friend, that she had been so taken up all day in rejoicing in God's perfections, and the certain accomplishment of His glory, that she had scarcely thought what would

* See *New England Revivals*, at the close of 18th, and beginning of the 19th century. By Benet Tyler, D.D., the writer of the *Memoir of Nettleton*.

be her own destiny. In the revival at Goshen, Connecticut, "the comfort and joy of the subjects of it seemed to rise primarily, not from an apprehension that they were brought into a safe state, but from new and delightful views of God, of the Redeemer, and the great truths that pertain to His kingdom. They lost sight of themselves, and their own particular interest, while contemplating the glory of God in the face of Jesus Christ." Nay, what is more remarkable still, in the awakening at Torrington a conspicuous feature of the work was, that those who got relief had, at first, no idea of their having got their hearts renewed as they desired. They were rather alarmed, thinking they were becoming secure and unfeeling; but when asked, how *the character of God* appeared to them? they would reply: "Great, excellent, glorious! There is none like Him! God is such a glorious being, that methinks I could praise Him even if He should cast me off." And another at Bloomfield is mentioned, who, being in deep distress, was engaged in prayer, when her mind was at once filled with a delightful view of the holiness, justice, and goodness of God, so that she felt unspeakable love to Him, and was brought, as she hoped, to resign herself wholly to His sovereign disposal. Without thinking of this being regeneration, her soul, which had hitherto been unsubdued, experienced sweet peace. "In a moment," said she, "the heavy load in my breast was removed. I burst out in rapture: 'I will for ever vow and resign myself to Thee, sinner as I am.' But while thus humble and vile in my own eyes, my soul was filled with unspeakable joy, with such happiness as I never experienced. My heart was filled with love and gratitude to God. Oh! I never knew what happiness was before." Were not these cases in which that passage of the Word of God was illustrated: "*They that know thy name* will put their trust in thee;" (Psalm ix. 10)—and where the Lord fulfilled, in its first instalment, that promise: "I will set him on high, because *he hath known my name*?" (Psalm xci. 14.) It was in this form that Mr. Nettleton's soul tasted joy and peace in believing. And is not this the most desirable way? The soul forgets all self, even self's own interests—thinking nothing even of its own act of faith—looks directly on the Lord in the face of Jesus—takes its encouragement from God alone, God revealed to sinners in His Son; and, ere ever it is aware, its serpent-bites are healed; for it has looked on the brazen serpent.

In such days, and amid such scenes in the churches all around, Mr. Nettleton was born again, and received power to become one of the sons of God.

CHAPTER II.

HIS COLLEGE LIFE AND MISSIONARY YEARNINGS.

In the year 1801, the father of Mr. Nettleton died. As he was the eldest son, the care of the family, and the management of the farm, devolved upon him. It had been his expectation to spend his days in agricultural pursuits; but God had designed him for a different course of life. After the change in his feelings described in the preceding chapter, his mind dwelt much on the worth of the soul, and the deplorable condition of those who have no interest in Christ; and he had the most intense desires to be instrumental in the salvation of his fellowmen. While labouring in the field, he would often say to himself: "If I might be the means of saving one soul, I should prefer it to all the riches and honours of this world." He would frequently look forward to eternity, and put to himself the question: "What shall I wish I had done thousands and millions of years hence?"

About this time he became exceedingly interested in the short accounts which were published in the *Connecticut Evangelical Magazine*, of the operations of the London Missionary Society, and of the Baptist Missionary Society in England. These awakened in his breast a strong desire to become a missionary to the heathen; and he decided to devote his life to the missionary service, if God, in His providence, should prepare the way. This purpose was afterwards greatly strengthened by the perusal of *Horne's Letters on Missions.* The feelings which Samuel J. Mills expressed to his father soon after his conversion, were precisely the feelings of young Nettleton at this period,—viz., "*That he could not conceive of any course of life in which to pass the rest of his days, that would prove so pleasant, as to go and communicate the Gospel-salvation to the poor heathen.*"

Samuel J. Mills and Asahel Nettleton were born on the same day. It is a remarkable fact, that their *new and spiritual birth* occurred very nearly at the same time*—that the conversion of both was signally marked—and that from the commencement of their Christian course, they seem to have been imbued with the same spirit, and to have devoted themselves to the same employment. The biographer of Mills remarks, that though a youth of but eighteen, "he discovered a zeal in the missionary cause, an eagerness in the pursuit of missionary intelligence, and an enlargement of thought in his plans to become acquainted with the unevangelized world, which left little doubt that he was chained to his purpose by a superior power. It was a heart yearning over the miseries of perishing millions, that first led him to think of acquiring an education with a view to the Gospel ministry. The Spirit of God came over him, like Elisha in the field. While toiling at the plough, his heart was touched with compassion for the heathen world; and he bade adieu

* The conversion of Mills occurred in November 1801; that of Nettleton, about two months earlier.

to his farm to obtain an education, on purpose to carry the Gospel to millions who were perishing for lack of knowledge. Thus, in a retired field in Litchfield county, was the King of Zion beginning that grand course of operations, which have produced such a revolution in the American churches, and which bear so intimate a relation to the progressive glories of His kingdom." All this, excepting the name of the county, was as true of Nettleton as of Mills, and very nearly at the same time.

It is a striking fact, that while these two individuals seem to have been the first in their own country, in recent days, to devote themselves to the missionary work, neither of them was permitted to enter upon it. It happened to them as to David, in relation to the building of the temple. They did well that it was in their hearts to go to the heathen; but the honour of actually going was reserved for others. The reasons which prevented Mills from becoming a missionary to the heathen are already before the public. Those which prevented Nettleton, will be given in the sequel.

In acquiring a collegiate education, he had many difficulties and discouragements to encounter. His pecuniary means were entirely inadequate; and, in those days, there were no education societies, and no funds for the support of indigent students. Such, also, were the circumstances of the family, recently deprived of its head, as to render his presence and labour at home apparently indispensable. So strong, however, was his desire to become a minister of the Gospel, and a missionary to the heathen, that he resolved to make the attempt to obtain an education.

He procured some books; and while labouring on the farm, devoted his leisure moments to study. In the winter he taught a school, and spent his evenings in study, occasionally reciting to his pastor. Thus, in the course of two or three years, with very little instruction, and while labouring most of the time on the farm, except when engaged in school-keeping, he mastered the preparatory studies, and entered the Freshman Class in Yale College, about the middle of the first term, in the Fall of 1805.

When Mr. Nettleton entered college, he was the only professor of religion in his class. Some others, however, entered before the close of the year,—one of whom was his friend and fellow-townsman, Philander Parmele. Some part of the time, while a member of college, he taught a school in New Haven, to procure the means of defraying his expenses. He felt a deep interest in the spiritual welfare of the children committed to his care; and had the happiness to know, that many of them became the hopeful subjects of divine grace, under his preaching, in the revival of 1815.

The Rev. Jonathan Lee, who studied with him, gives the following interesting account of his college life:—

"I was class-mate with Mr. Nettleton during the two last years of our college life, and roomed with him through the junior year. Providence brought us in contact in new and unanticipated circumstances. I was standing in melancholy mood, in the south door of the then middle or old College, disheartened at the loss of a year in standing, a stranger to the class, and with no room or room-mate engaged, reluctant to make application to any one, supposing their arrangements had been already made. Nettleton passing by, seemed attracted by my sombre attitude and downcast aspect, and approaching, kindly inquired whether I had obtained a room-mate; and learning by my reply that I had not, offered himself to room with me. The circumstances of this proffer, and the manner of its being made, gave a new and peculiar impression to my mind in regard to him, as it shewed a readiness to relinquish his previous designs on the subject, to relieve my anxiety, and shew me a kindness. I thankfully accepted his overture, which removed a heavy burden from my spirit, and carried conviction to my heart, that I had found a friend in whom it was safe to confide. From that day to this, greatly as I was grieved to leave my former class, to which I felt strongly attached, I have regarded the hand of Providence in bringing me into intimacy with that godly young man, as claiming my liveliest gratitude. It was the good hand of God upon me; it was the sovereignty of His love that chastened the aspirations for literary distinction; and after calling me, in the day of adversity, to consider, led me to daily converse with one who shewed the nature and superlative value of unostentatious, consistent piety,—and this at the most solemn crisis in my individual history.

"On becoming more particularly acquainted with Nettleton, I perceived that he was one who feared God. Ever kind, courteous, conscientious and exemplary, unassuming and unostentatious, his words and actions bore the most powerful testimony in my conscience to the genuineness of his religious principles. He evidently had a taste for the spiritual themes and exercises pertaining to religion, so predominant and controlling as to leave small space for merely literary ambition. His best-loved place was the chapel, listening with devout solemnity to the prayers and preaching of the venerated Dwight. His best-loved book was the Bible. His best-loved day was the Sabbath; and his best-loved friends were those who knew the joys and sorrows of a pious heart. He was intimate with only a few select companions, of congenial spirit, and who felt most interested in communing together upon the topics of doctrinal and experimental religion."

The same college friend tells of his studies, during which he was led through a trying spiritual experience of great severity:—

"In regard to his standing as a scholar, he was not distinguished, as he never rose above the ordinary rank in the common course of classical studies. This I attribute, not to a defect of native talent, but to the following causes:—1. He was remarkably diffident of his own powers, so far as to be restrained and embarrassed in his recitations and literary performances before the class; and the same state of feeling prevented that resolute, persevering application necessary for eminence. 2. The state of his health, through a part of the year when he roomed with me, was much impaired; and, in connexion with this, he passed through a protracted season of deep mental anxiety and depression in the spring of 1808, in which he greatly questioned the genuineness of his Christian experience. So severe were his mental trials of this nature, as to unfit him for study for some time; and he was excused and permitted to return home on account of the state of his health. Before returning home, he was wont to repair to the President for instruction and counsel; and he directed him to the perusal of *Edwards on Religious Affections*, and loaned him, also, his manuscript sermons on the *Evidences of Regeneration*. With them he went into the most intensely earnest and sifting self-examination that I ever witnessed; and in the course of it, passed through such agony of spirit, as was suited to awaken the liveliest sympathy in those who could best understand and appreciate the nature of his distress. The all-absorbing question resting on his mind by day and by night, mingled with many sighs, tears, and groans, was, Am I a child of God? Before the next term, he gained peace, and enjoyed a better state of health; but it is evident, that this interruption of his progress in regular study, had a retarding effect upon his scholarship, though it may have had a momentous influence in giving him uncommon spiritual discernment, and in fitting him for that sphere of distinguished usefulness on which he afterwards entered. 3. The peculiar taste and tendencies of Nettleton's mind, led him to bestow his intellectual energies, not upon physical sciences and elegant literature, but upon those subjects in mental and moral philosophy which stood most closely connected with the truths of theology. In topics of this nature, he ever manifested an uncommon interest and quickness of thought, with clearness of perception and power of discrimination. It was evidently a favourite employment to engage in friendly discussions upon such themes with those who were disposed to investigate them; particularly with students in theology then residing at Yale College.

At such times, his countenance, though not specially expressive in ordinary circumstances, would light up with animation, and his eye sparkle with brilliance, plainly indicating that then his mind was in its chosen element. In whatever enlisted his feelings, he was manifestly capable of close and successful investigation. But aiming at a higher mark than mere literary or scientific distinction, he sought to furnish his mind with that knowledge which relates directly to the great ends of human existence—the present and immortal interests of the soul. During his last year in college, he roomed with his beloved Christian brother, Philander Parmele; and it is my impression, that, with him, he devoted what time could be spared from customary classical studies, to the study of theology. In the exercises of the class, he took a higher rank than in the preceding year, and acquitted himself with respectability."

Mr. Lee goes on to say: "Truth compels me to admit, that I had not then discovered in him any such traits of intellectual character as led to anticipations in any measure correspondent with the well known facts of his subsequent history." And yet, even then, President Dwight is reported to have said of him: "He will make one of the most useful men this country has ever seen."

"Nettleton was held in respect by all in college; but peculiarly loved and highly esteemed by Christian professors. His spirit was excellent, and his example unexceptionable. If any affected to look superciliously upon him on account of the plainness and simplicity of his manners, still they knew and felt his superior moral worth. He was a vigilant observer of the indications of religious seriousness and anxiety among the students, and took the earliest and liveliest interest in all such cases. Burdened as I myself was with the danger and misery of my impenitent state, in the fore part of the year, when I roomed with him, he was not slow to discover the fact, though not officious to insist upon a disclosure of my feelings. As he was a professor of religion, I proposed, soon after he became my room-mate, to unite with Him in prayer, after the close of the studies of each evening, expecting only to read the Scriptures as my part of the exercise. He agreed to pray, *if I also would.* Fearing to decline, though trembling at the solemnity of such an engagement, I felt necessitated by my conscience to comply with the condition, and take my turn in prayer; and it was thus that I was first led to utter the words of supplication in the audience of any human being. It was a mighty effort, and made with faltering tongue and aching heart. He found that I had gone farther than he expected, and afterwards once asked me: 'If I considered myself a Christian?' and, upon my replying 'No,' he inquired: 'Why, then, do you pray?' His object, I have supposed, was to deepen my conviction of guilt; and it had that effect. To my answer: 'I feel it my duty to pray,' he added no remark, discovering, probably, that my wretched prayers gave me no comfort, but increased the heavy burden pressing upon my heart. More than once, after these seasons, when I have been weeping over my lost condition, that kind friend has approached my pillow, upon retiring to his own bed, and has gently endeavoured to elicit an expression of my feelings. When seeing me afraid to disclose my state of mind, he has withdrawn, sometimes, as I have reason to believe, to unite with some Christian brother in prayer on my behalf; and thus committed my case, and that of others, to that God who had taken me in hand, and who alone could renew my heart.

"At this time, in the winter of 1807-8, a revival of religion began in New Haven, and in Yale College. The first subjects of it among the students were in the Freshman Class. Nettleton was no indifferent spectator, but among the first to discover indications of special religious impressions, and to seek out persons in a state of religious anxiety. Often did I see him, with one or two heart-burdened youth of the youngest class, walking arm in arm in the college yard, before evening prayers, conversing upon the great interests of the soul. I observed that, so soon as he became acquainted with a student under religious impressions, his company and counsel were sought and greatly prized; and it was manifest that his conversation with such individuals, his silent and unostentatious labours, in connexion with his Christian brethren in their meeting for prayer and conference, held a very prominent and important place in that memorable and joyful season. His feelings were most deeply interested in the whole progress of the revival, and it seemed almost to absorb his mind by day and by night."

In the *American Quarterly Register* for February 1838, there is a history of revivals in Yale College. In the account of the revival in 1808, is the following statement:—

"There was one case in this revival which awakened very general sympathy, and to which I shall advert for a moment, because it shews how God sometimes makes use of the sufferings of one, to subdue the obstinacy of another. A member of one of the lower Classes became deeply anxious for his spiritual welfare at the commencement of the seriousness. He was, indeed, the first person in college, probably, who was under conviction of sin. As the work went on, others who were awakened at a much later period, were apparently brought into the kingdom, and were rejoicing in hope, while he was left in the bitterness of despair, with the arrows of the Almighty drinking up his spirit. His health rapidly declined under his sufferings. He was confined, in a great measure, to his bed; and it was feared that, with a feeble constitution, he must soon sink under the weight of his distress, unless relief should be obtained. In an adjoining room, there lived an avowed disbeliever in spiritual religion, who denied the reality of a divine influence in revivals, and from the commencement of the present work, had regarded those who were concerned in it with scorn. A Christian friend, who knew his sentiments, asked him to visit the sufferer, and led him toward the bed-side. He stood for a moment looking at the emaciated form before him, listened to the exclamations which told the distress and horror of an awakened conscience, and then, turning, went back to his room, to weep there under a sense of his own sin. Not long after, to the wonder of all his companions, it was said of him, as of Saul of Tarsus, 'Behold, he prayeth.' He became at once a decided and exemplary Christian. He afterwards entered into the ministry, and devoted himself to the cause of missions; and has been, for more than twenty years, an active and successful labourer upon heathen ground."

The reader may be interested to learn the issue of those sufferings which led to this happy result. I shall give the relation in the words of one who is best able to speak on this subject. "It was just at the close of the term, and late at night. A few Christian friends lingered about the bed of the agonized and despairing sinner; and many were the prayers offered, that the balm of Gilead might be applied to his wounded spirit. At length a messenger was dispatched to summon the President, as it seemed to those in attendance, that unless relief were had, death must close the scene. The hour was late; but he promptly attended the call, and came emphatically, as one sent of God, as the bearer of good tidings of great joy. For a short time he seemed overwhelmed, so deeply did he share in the agony of the agonized. At length, however, taking a seat by the bedside, he gradually directed the anxious inquirer unto the divine sufficiency, the infinite fulness of the Lord Jesus, recited the invitations of the Gospel, and then followed his paternal counsel by prayer to God. That prayer, it is believed, was heard; and the words which he spake were a healing balm from on high. A sweet serenity seemed to steal over the agitated sinner's mind—a serenity which was the harbinger of a joy that came in a short time after, and was 'unspeakable and full of glory.'"

In a letter from the individual whose case is described in the foregoing statement, it is stated: "The Christian friend there mentioned, was Mr. Nettleton. The infidel was Mr. ——, now a missionary of the American Board. The messenger, too, who went for

President Dwight, was Mr. Nettleton. He remained with me all night. He was besieging the throne of grace. His whole soul seemed bent on my deliverance. Man never pleaded with more fervency, and I cannot doubt that I was more indebted to him for my relief than to any other person. He took such an interest in my salvation, as evinced the deepest love for my soul. I think he was a professor of religion before he entered college. What was the character of his piety up to the spring of 1808, of course I know not. But I well recollect that, soon after I was brought under conviction, he found me out, and became one of my spiritual guides. I am not quite certain whether his exercises, which I am about to mention, existed in the earlier part of the revival, or a little later. My impression is, that the revival found him, in common with other professors, comparatively asleep. But he was soon enlisted, and evinced great interest in the work. In a little time, however, he fell into a melancholy and desponding state, which at length bordered upon despair. He gave up his hope, and, to me, appeared to be a most miserable man. I have known him to weep, I may say, by the hour, under an overwhelming sense of his vileness. He would often say: 'I seem to love Christians; but I am so unworthy. I hope they will not cast me off. Do you think they will allow such a poor sinner as I am to keep company with them?' Whatever peculiarity there was in his case, (and I think his exercises were singular,) there was involved in it a deep conviction of sin; such a loathing of himself, as I scarcely remember to have heard any other man express. It was difficult to convince him that God could have mercy on one so vile. Yet he was all this time manifesting a deep interest in the cause of Christ and the salvation of souls."

The mind of Mr. Nettleton was much turned to theological studies during his collegiate course. Theology, indeed, had been his favourite study, ever since his attention was turned to the subject of religion. Even before he entered college, he had read with attention a large part of the writings of Edwards, Hopkins, and Bellamy; and before he graduated, he was better acquainted with systematic theology than many young men are who are licensed to preach the Gospel. He took a deep interest in doctrinal discussions, and ably vindicated the doctrines of grace against the objections which were urged against them. During his senior year, there was much discussion among the professors of religion and theological students in college, respecting the means of grace. This was occasioned by the sermons which were preached at that time by President Dwight on that subject, and which are published in the fourth volume of his theological discourses. In these sermons, the idea is advanced, that the prayers and strivings of awakened sinners, although they possess no moral goodness, are not to be regarded, in all cases, as positively sinful. In other words, he thinks that really awakened sinners, like the publican, may offer up prayer that has in it nothing to provoke God's anger.

Mr. Nettleton entertained a high respect for Dr. Dwight. On almost all subjects, he received his views without hesitation, and considered it a great privilege to sit under his instructive preaching. But on this point he differed from him, as did also a large part of the pious students in college. He believed, with Hopkins and the New England divines generally, that sinners, properly speaking, never use, but always abuse the means of grace—that in all their efforts to escape future misery and secure future happiness, they are influenced by unholy motives—and that their religious services are mercenary and sinful. In this opinion, which appeared to him to be clearly taught in the Scriptures, he was greatly confirmed by his own religious experience. While under conviction of sin, he had such discoveries of his own heart, as to impress indelibly upon his mind a conviction of the entire sinfulness of the religious services of unrenewed men. There was no one point in theology on which his mind was more fully established than this; or on which he more strenuously insisted, during his life, both in the pulpit, and in his conversation with awakened sinners. He considered it a point of great practical importance, and particularly useful in destroying the self-righteous hopes of sinners, and in shewing them their utterly lost condition, and entire dependence on the grace of God. This was a weapon which he wielded with great power, and which seemed to be, in his hands, pre-eminently the sword of the Spirit.

The following extract of a letter written to his friend Parmele, soon after he graduated, will shew, not only what were his views on this subject at that period, but also how capable he was of defending them:—

"With respect to the works of the unregenerate, of those especially who think they understand the way of salvation by Christ, I would answer a few things. My friend, you know there are various ways (if I may so speak) of painting truth to the understanding. The actions of the body, in the first place, are neither good nor bad in themselves, any more than the rustling of a leaf, or the motions of any other matter. What, then? Why, the motions or operations of the heart are the only good or bad actions in the sight of God. God looks on the heart. And it is impossible that anything should be morally good or bad in any other sense than as God regards it. True, men may call all manner of wickedness good; but does giving it the name, by any wonderful process infuse into it the nature of good? If not, then let us inquire what God calls good, and what evil. Now, I can conceive of only three states in which it is possible for the mind to be in respect to any object—*Love*, *Hatred*, or *Indifference*. Now, these are not nice distinctions—finely spun out; they are distinctions which we must understand, or we cannot know what is good or what is evil in a moral sense. Love, hatred, or indifference to God as the object, either directly or indirectly, in ways unnumbered, are the only possible ways of sinning, or doing moral good.

"1. Do unregenerate men love God? If so, then reason says there is no regeneration. 'Every one that loveth is born of God.' 'God is love; and he that dwelleth in love dwelleth in God, and God in him.' It is intuitively evident, then, that if *all* who love God are regenerated, or born of God, all who are *not* born of God do not love Him. Besides, all who are not born of God, the Scriptures say, are in the flesh. 'That which is born of the flesh is flesh, and that which is born of the Spirit is spirit.' 'They that are in the flesh,' or are not born of the Spirit, the apostle says, '*cannot* please God.' I would ask, then, for an answer to this plain question: Can he who *cannot please God*, do anything acceptable to Him? Or, does God *require* him to do what is not acceptable to Him? Should it be said, It may be accepted on account of the merits of Christ; I would answer: What have those to do with the merits of Christ, or *even the name* of Christ, who reject Him, and who '*will not come unto Him?*'—who are, the very moment when they pray, in heart, His betrayers and murderers! But it will be said: Although they are not regenerate, yet they are wellwishers—they are *seeking* earnestly to become Christians—they know that, without Christ, they must for ever perish; it would, therefore, not only be cruel, but very unjust, to give them the lie, by telling them they reject Christ, and are His enemies. Let Christ answer: 'He that is not with me is *against* me.' And besides, that they are not regarded for their own doings, nor their doings on account of the merits of Christ, is evident; for it would be as much inconsistent with the moral perfections of God, to regard the doings of the unregenerate, as it would be if Christ had never died. It is the same thing with regard to the unregenerate, while they remain thus, as if Christ had never died.

"If, then, nothing is done acceptable to God where love is absent, it needs no proof to shew that what is done in the exercise of hatred or in indifference, is neither acceptable nor required. But, to leave this mode of reasoning, Whence is it that those who have good evidence that they are born again, and enjoy the consolations of the Divine Spirit, renounce the opinion against which I am now contending, and begin to adopt the very language of the blind man when restored to sight: 'Now we know that God heareth not sinners?'

"The reason why the genuine Gospel is not received by the unrenewed, is as plain as the sun in the heavens. You remember what it is that 'is not subject to the law of God, neither indeed can be.' The genuine Gospel has ever been considered an insult to the public taste. I care not for correctness of sentiment—for natural amiableness, or suavity of disposition, and for the whole host of natural affections—wherever the true Gospel comes—wherever it is explained and understood, if it be not cordially received and embraced, it will assuredly awaken disgust, and provoke abhorrence. Nor can it be otherwise; for its principal design is to mortify the pride of man, and to display the glory of sovereign grace—to level all human excellence in the dust, and to elevate, even to thrones of glory, the needy and the wretched—to resist the proud, and give grace to the humble. The true Gospel pays no respect to the academic, because of his profound learning; nor to the moralist, on account of his upright conduct. It pays not the least regard to the courtier, because of his pompous honours; nor to the devotee, on account of his zeal or his righteousness. No; the potent prince and the abject slave—the wise philosopher and the ignorant rustic—the virtuous lady and the infamous prostitute—*all stand on the same level in its comprehensive sight.* Its business is with the worthless and miserable wherever it finds them. If these be relieved, its end is accomplished—its work is done. To reward these is its supreme delight. But the self-sufficient of every rank are treated by it with the utmost reserve, and beheld by it with a *constant and most steady contempt.* The hungry it filleth with good things, but the rich it sendeth empty away. In short, all the fine words which are spoken—the sociability and extreme politeness with which she is treated, and the high commendations ['good Master,' 'Lord, Lord'] with which she is loaded from the *good-hearted, well-wishing world,* can never provoke her stern and angry countenance into a smile, or a single look of complacency. But on the truly contrite, she looks with a cheering smile and a heavenly countenance, to revive and cheer the drooping heart of the contrite ones.

"Oh! glorious Gospel—heavenly messenger of good tidings! Welcome, sweet messenger of peace! Friend, I believe that the Christian who sees his own heart in the light of the Gospel, is really and heartily ashamed of his very best performances. Grace hath laid the foundation of the sinner's hope. Grace erects the building; and the head-stone thereof shall be brought forth with shoutings, crying: Grace, grace unto it!"

During his junior year in college, he became acquainted with Samuel J. Mills. This was brought about in the following manner: Simeon Woodruff, a class-mate and intimate friend of Nettleton, happened, one vacation, to fall in company with Mills, and heard him converse on the subject of missions, and his plans of life. "You talk," said Woodruff, "just like one of my class-mates. He says he intends never to be settled, but to be a missionary to the heathen." Mills was so much interested in this intelligence, that he took a journey to New Haven, on purpose to become acquainted with Nettleton. They spent much time in consultation, and were happy to find a perfect coincidence of views on the subject of missions. Mills informed him of Hall, and others of his acquaintance, who entertained similar views. The next year, Mills having graduated at Williams' College, spent a few months as a resident graduate at Yale. "His ostensible object," says his biographer, "was the study of theology; but his real object was to ascertain whether there were not some kindred spirits in this institution, who could be excited and encouraged in this glorious enterprise." There was one kindred spirit in that institution, with whom he had already become acquainted, and with whom he wished to hold further intercourse. He and Nettleton conferred much on the subject, and entered into an agreement to avoid all entangling alliances, and to hold themselves in readiness to go to the heathen, whenever God, in His providence, should prepare the way. They also formed the purpose of meeting the next year at Andover, and, while pursuing their theological studies, to mature their plans of future action. This purpose, Mr. Nettleton found himself under the painful necessity of abandoning, on account of a debt which he had contracted while obtaining his education, and which he wished to discharge as soon as possible. Both he and Mills felt the disappointment deeply. Mills advised him to make application to some friends to liquidate the debt for him; but this he was unwilling to do; and soon after he graduated, at the earnest solicitation of Dr. Dwight, he accepted the office of Butler in college. This office he held nearly a year, devoting what leisure time he could command to theological studies. He then repaired to Milford, and put himself under the instruction of the Rev. Bezaleel Pinneo, with whom he remained until he received license to preach the Gospel.

Mr. Nettleton was licensed to preach by the West Association of New Haven county, at the house of the Rev. Dr. Trumbull, in North Haven, 28th May, 1811. It was not till the summer of 1817 that he was ordained as an Evangelist by the South Consociation of Litchfield county.

In June 1810, Messrs. Judson, Nott, Mills, and Newell, at that time members of the Theological Seminary at Andover, presented themselves before the General Association of Massachusetts, in Bradford, and made known their convictions of the duty and importance of personally attempting a mission to the heathen, and requested the advice of the Association. This movement, it is well known, led to the organization of the American Board of Commissioners for Foreign Missions. Mr. Nettleton was at this time Butler in Yale College. Had he gone to Andover after he graduated, as he intended, he would, doubtless, have been one of the company. When he heard what had been done, he lamented, with tears, that he could not have been there. He feared that it was an indication of Providence, that he was not to be permitted to become a missionary. His purpose, however, remained stedfast.

The reader is, doubtless, anxious, by this time, to know why Mr. Nettleton did not become a missionary, as he intended. The reasons can be stated in few words. Soon after he began to preach, his labours were crowned with signal success. Wherever he went, the Spirit of God seemed to accompany his preaching. His brethren in the ministry, witnessing the success of his labours, were of opinion that he ought to delay, at least, the execution of his purpose to leave the country. In deference to their opinion, he consented to delay; and as his labours became increasingly successful, his brethren were more and more convinced that God had called him to labour as an evangelist at home. Still, he never entirely abandoned the idea of a foreign mission, until his health failed in 1822.

We have seen, in our own day, a similar dealing of God with one in Scotland, honoured to be the instrument of many revivals—Mr. William Burns. He, too, had fully purposed in his heart, if the Lord should open a door, to go forth as a missionary to the Jews, if the door opened in that direction; or, at all events, to some foreign field. But unusual and singular success, soon after he was licensed to preach the Gospel, detained him at home. And so truly was it success alone that hindered him, that no sooner did that abate, than he sought out a foreign field,—first in Canada, and then permanently as missionary for the Presbyterian Synod in England to China. Prepared at home by seeing there—at Dundee, Kilsyth, and many other places—the arm of the Lord revealed, he now labours among the millions of that strange people, at a moment when every eye is turned toward them.

CHAPTER III.

THE LEADINGS OF PROVIDENCE THAT PREPARED HIM FOR HIS FUTURE WORK AS AN EVANGELIST.

AFTER receiving license to preach, Mr. Nettleton refused to consider himself a candidate for settlement; because he intended, and expected to engage in missionary service, as soon as the providence of God should prepare the way. He chose, therefore, to commence his labours in waste places, and in some of the most desolate parts of the Lord's vineyard. With this view he went to the eastern part of Connecticut, on the borders of Rhode Island. Here he preached for some months, in several places which had long been overrun by fanatical sects of various descriptions.

In some of these places there had once been flourishing churches, with excellent pastors; but they had been desolated, more than half a century before, by the measures which *Davenport*,* and other evangelists of that period, introduced. He became acquainted with some aged people, who gave him an account of the proceedings of that day, and of their results as they had been developed in the course of half a century. He found also some pamphlets and books, from which he obtained much important information respecting

* See Appendix, No. I.

the disorders which prevailed after the Revival of 1740. Often did he speak with deep interest of this period of his labours, and of the advantage he derived, in after life, from the information which he at that time obtained. Indeed, his residence here was, beyond doubt, ordered of the Lord for preparing him for future scenes.

Here he learned, that those who labour as evangelists, even if they have the best intentions, are in peculiar danger of mistaking false for true zeal, and of being betrayed into great indiscretions. He learned, also, that the imprudences of the evangelist may produce incalculable evils—evils which will extend through many generations. And while surveying these fields of moral desolation, he became deeply impressed with the importance of a settled ministry. He saw, that where there is no settled ministry, the minds of the people become unsettled in regard to religious truth, and they are easily carried about by every wind of doctrine,—that errorists of every description come in and occupy the ground,—and that, when there is any religious excitement among them, it is peculiarly liable to run into the wildest fanaticism. Indeed, in the minds of a people thus situated, religion and fanaticism become identified; they know of no other kind of religion, and, of course, they seek and expect no other. He found, that the churches which had been made desolate by the labours of Davenport and his coadjutors, half a century before, had remained desolate until that time; and that there existed still among the people the most violent prejudices against settled pastors, and all regular ecclesiastical organizations. He saw, that the same self-righteous and denunciatory spirit which first rent and scattered the churches, was still prevalent, and that the measures which accompany and promote fanaticism were still rife among them,—such as calling persons to the *anxious seat*, requesting them to rise to be prayed for, or to signify that they had given their hearts to God; encouraging females to exhort and pray in promiscuous assemblies, &c. These measures were adopted in these waste districts, not only by Methodists, Free-Will Baptists, and *Christ-ians,* but by Congregationalists.

Some evangelists of the Presbyterian denomination, also, were in the habit of visiting these places, who imbibed and encouraged the spirit above described. Of these, some appeared to be good men; but they were greatly deficient in prudence, and often impelled by a false zeal. They were usually found arrayed against settled pastors; and their influence went to promote the interests of the fanatical sects, with which they were in the habit of co-operating in their religious meetings. These evangelists, and those with whom they associated, perceiving that Mr. Nettleton was a young man of zeal, took great pains to draw him into their views, and to infuse into his mind prejudices against settled pastors, by insinuating that they were enemies to revivals, expecting thus to secure his co-operation in their radical movements. But he at once perceived that they were actuated by a wrong spirit, and that the course which they were pursuing, was adapted, not to promote, but to injure the cause of religion. He saw that the whole weight of their influence was employed to increase and perpetuate the prejudices of the people against sound doctrine and ecclesiastical order; and that, so far from repairing the wastes of Zion, they were only making them more desolate.

The knowledge which he obtained while labouring in this region, led him to entertain great respect for the pastoral office. He was convinced, that without a settled ministry, there could be no rational prospect of building up churches, or of enjoying genuine revivals of religion; that flocks scattered upon the mountains with no faithful shepherd to watch and feed them, would become the prey of "ravening wolves." He became, also, convinced that a tremendous responsibility rests upon those who labour as evangelists; and that it is their duty not to weaken the hands of settled pastors, but to do all in their power to strengthen them. This lesson was of immense importance to him, in preparing him for that course of labour to which he was destined; and it is doubtless one reason why he was enabled to shun those indiscretions into which most evangelists have fallen.

We have seen how Mr. Nettleton came to be an evangelist. His brethren persuaded him to relinquish, for a season, his favourite and long-cherished purpose of becoming a missionary to the heathen; and the time never came, while he had health and strength to labour as an evangelist, when they thought it would be right for him to relinquish an employment in which God was favouring him with such signal success. While engaged in this employment, it was his desire to confine his labours to waste places, and destitute congregations; and it was not without great reluctance, and much solicitation, that he consented to labour as an assistant to settled pastors. He was never complained of for thrusting himself into parishes where his assistance was not desired; but the complaint continually was, that it was so difficult to obtain him. The late Dr. Porter of Andover thus speaks of him in his letters on revivals:—

"About the close of the period which I attempted to describe in former letters, the Rev. Asahel Nettleton devoted himself to the work of an evangelist. With his eminent qualifications for this work, and usefulness in it, I presume you are well acquainted. The fact, however, which it is especially to my present purpose to mention, and which, probably, many of you do not know, is, that this distinguished itinerant found no difficulty in labouring with stated pastors without making himself their *rival*. If, in any instance, he could not conscientiously coincide in the views, or co-operate in the measures of a pastor, among whose charge he was invited to labour, he did not sow dissension in that church, nor seek to detach their affections from their minister; but quietly withdrew to another place. The consequence was, that the visits of this devoted servant of Christ *were always sought*, and never dreaded, nor regretted, by ministers or churches."

An instance, probably, cannot be mentioned, in which the influence of Mr. Nettleton led to the dismission of a pastor; but many instances might be mentioned, in which he was instrumental in strengthening the hands of pastors. He would treat ministers with such kindness, and speak of them with such respect, as to make the impression on the minds of their people, that they were worthy of their confidence; and thus not a few, who had almost lost their influence, were firmly reinstated in the affections of their people. In this course he exhibited great wisdom; and when, in connexion with this fact, we take into consideration the success of his labours, it is not surprising that his visits were so highly prized by ministers and churches.

Having already somewhat anticipated the course of events, it may not, perhaps, be improper to mention, in this place, that although the labours of Mr. Nettleton, as an evangelist, were instrumental of such abounding good—unmingled, so far as could be seen, with any evil—yet he himself became convinced, that it would be unwise for the churches to adopt the system of supporting an order of evangelists as assistants to settled pastors. He remembered what he had learned respecting the operations of Davenport and their results; also the false zeal and improper spirit manifested by certain itinerants with whom he became acquainted when he began to preach; and in addition to these things, he found that certain zealous young men were coming forward every year as evangelists, who, by rashness and imprudence, were doing injury to the cause of religion. These things convinced him, that if this description of labourers were systematically employed, more evil than good might confidently be expected as the result.

He has often been heard to say, that a few might be very usefully employed as evangelists, if we could be sure of obtaining men of the right character,—men of discretion, who would co-operate with settled pastors, and aid them in putting down irregularities and promoting order. But believing that most who engage in this service would be men of a different character, he discouraged the idea of bringing forward and supporting an order of such labourers. This accounts for the stand which he took on this subject in 1820. In that year the General Association of Connecticut appointed a committee to take into consideration the subject of increasing ministerial labour in the several congregations in our connexion. When that committee met, they invited Mr. Nettleton to meet with them, and requested his opinion as to the expediency of introducing and supporting an order of evangelists. He was told, that if he would consent to act as an evangelist for the State, and locate himself in New Haven, in that capacity the churches would undoubtedly give him an ample support. He remarked, that he had never yet received a dollar from any benevolent society, or public association; and that he did not choose to labour in this way. He, moreover, gave it as his opinion, that it would be expedient to introduce and support an order of evangelists. He foresaw the evils that would be likely to grow out of the system if it were made permanent; and they were the very evils which were afterwards so strikingly realized in some parts of the country. Through his influence the project was abandoned.

In a letter to the Rev. Lavius Hyde, dated August 24, 1829, he thus alludes to the facts above stated:—

"The course which I have pursued as an evangelist is one that I never dreamed of, as, I suppose, you know. Having designed to be a foreign missionary from the time I first thought of entering the ministry, I feel grieved and sick when I think of some who wish to be evangelists, because they are unfit for settled pastors. I have long seen and deplored the evil. Did I inform you that, at a meeting of a committee of the General Association of Connecticut, in 1820, a proposition was made to send out a number of evangelists as the best means of promoting revivals of religion, and that I objected?—that they proposed to give me a salary of one thousand dollars annually, and that I declined receiving anything in that line?"

CHAPTER IV.

HIS FIRST SUCCESS: FIFTEEN CONGREGATIONS IN CONNECTICUT VISITED WITH THE SPIRIT.—SOME DETAILS.

"Of the effects of Mr. Nettleton's labours during the few months which he spent in the eastern part of Connecticut, I am not able," says his biographer, "to speak particularly. I have understood, generally, that they were not altogether in vain,—that some souls were awakened, and hopefully converted to Christ. But, for reasons stated in the preceding chapter, he found it to be an unpromising field of labour."

He afterwards preached several Sabbaths in *Derby* with some success. A few individuals received impressions which issued, as was believed, in a saving conversion to God.

In the Fall of 1812, having received an invitation to preach in South Salem, New York, he stopped, on his way thither, at *South Britain*, Conn., where his after-biographer, Dr. Bennet Tyler, resided. This was the commencement of their acquaintance,—an acquaintance which soon ripened into an endeared friendship, that lasted through life. There was, at that time, a very interesting revival of religion in South Britain. This induced him to prolong his visit for one week. He preached on the Sabbath, and attended several other religious meetings, besides visiting, with the pastor, from house to house, and conversing with those who were anxious for their souls. His labours were very acceptable to the people; and there is reason to believe that they were blessed to the saving of some souls.

His manner at this time was somewhat peculiar; but not so much so as to injure his usefulness. His address, at the first meeting which he attended, will not soon be forgotten by those who heard it. It was in a schoolhouse crowded with people, not a few of whom were under deep conviction of sin. As he arose, being an entire stranger, every eye was fixed upon him, and a breathless silence pervaded the assembly. With great solemnity he looked upon the congregation, and thus began: "What is that murmur which I hear?—I wish I had a new heart. What shall I do?—They tell me to repent—I can't repent; I wish they would give me some other direction." He thus went on for a short time, personating the awakened sinner, and bringing out the feelings of his heart. He then changed the form of his address, and, in a solemn and affectionate manner, appealed to the consciences of his hearers, and shewed them that they must repent or perish,—that it was their reasonable duty to repent immediately,—and that ministers could not direct them to anything short of repentance without being unfaithful to their souls. The address produced a thrilling effect, and served greatly to deepen the convictions of those who were anxious.

During the week that he remained in South Britain, he took a lively interest in the revival which was in progress; and he left the place with his heart glowing with love to souls, and with ardent desires that God would give him grace to be faithful to the people among whom he was going to labour. From that time, for ten years, it was his happy lot to be employed, almost constantly, in revivals of religion.

He went on to *South Salem.* The church was destitute of a pastor, and was in a cold and backslidden state. Great spiritual apathy existed in the congregation. He preached on the Sabbath, and appointed one or two evening meetings in the course of the week. His preaching produced an immediate solemnity on the minds of the people; and in the course of a fortnight, there was a development of feeling which made it apparent that the Spirit of God was operating on many minds. At the close of one of his evening meetings, several youths repaired to his lodgings, in deep distress, to inquire what they must do to be saved. He pointed them to Christ; and, with affectionate earnestness, urged them immediately to repent and believe the Gospel. The next day, in visiting from house to house, he found others under deep religious impressions. The seriousness soon spread through the place, and the subject of religion became the engrossing topic of conversation. In the course of one or two weeks from this time, several were found rejoicing in hope. He was exceedingly afraid lest they should take up with a false and spurious hope. He warned them of the danger of self-deception, reminded them of the deceitfulness of the human heart, and pointed out the various ways in which persons are liable to deceive themselves. He also exhibited, with great plainness, the distinguishing marks of genuine conversion. The work increased with rapidity;

and, in the course of a few weeks, a large number gave pleasing evidence of having passed from death unto life.

After about two months, he left the place. He did this, in part, because the people began to take measures to give him a call to settle with them as their pastor. Having devoted himself to a missionary life, he was determined to listen to no such call. But another reason which induced him to leave, was the presumption that the work, after having made such progress, might be expected to continue as well without his labours as with them. In this respect he committed an error, as he was afterwards convinced. In the early part of his ministry, he thought that he might accomplish the most good by labouring only a short time in a place; and that when a revival had commenced, he might safely commit it to the care of others, and retire to a new field. But experience taught him that this was not the way to be most useful. He found it important to prolong his labours, when God was rendering them effectual to the salvation of souls.

After he left South Salem, he preached a few Sabbaths in *Danbury*, a town in the western part of Connecticut. Here a work of grace immediately commenced, and several interesting cases of conversion occurred. Here, too, the people began to adopt measures to obtain him for their pastor, which induced him to leave sooner than he otherwise would have done. He afterwards expressed his regret that he did not remain longer in Danbury, as there was every appearance of the commencement of a great and glorious revival. The work made but little progress after his departure.

From Danbury he went to *Monroe*. Here, also, success attended his labours. To what extent, his biographer is not able to state; nor could he learn how long he laboured in this place. It was, however, but a short time. He preached there occasionally afterwards, and often spoke with interest of the young converts, and particularly of one whose triumphant death he was called to witness.

In the spring of 1813 he visited *North Lyme*, a parish near the mouth of the Connecticut river. The church was destitute of a pastor. There was no special seriousness when he commenced his labours. But a deep solemnity soon pervaded the congregation; and in three or four weeks a large number were anxiously inquiring what they must do to be saved. He remained in this place longer than in any of the places in which he had previously resided; and "much people," in the judgment of charity, were "added unto the Lord."

While in North Lyme, he spent considerable time in assisting the Rev. Mr. Vail, pastor of the church in *Hadlyme*. Here, too, his labours were greatly blessed to the quickening of God's people, and to the awakening and conversion of sinners.

In the summer of 1813, he preached four Sabbaths in *Bloomfield*. In this place, as in the others, the Spirit of God accompanied his labours, and several interesting cases of hopeful conversion occurred.

In the autumn of 1813, he commenced his labours in *Milton*, a parish in the west part of the town of *Litchfield*. This was a waste place. The people were not only without a pastor, but had become so weakened by divisions, and by the loss of their parish fund, that they almost despaired of ever enjoying again the privilege of a preached Gospel. Dr. Beecher, who was at that time pastor of the church in Litchfield, and another neighbouring minister, agreed to solicit funds in their respective congregations, to support a preacher, for a season, in Milton. Having entered into this arrangement, they made application to Mr. Nettleton. In the meantime, the churches in the vicinity were requested specially to remember that people in their prayers. In conformity with the arrangement, Mr. Nettleton came and called on Dr. Beecher. It was the first time that they had met. "Thou hast well done," said Dr. Beecher, "that thou art come." "I ask," said Mr. Nettleton, "for what intent ye have sent for me?" "To hear all things that are commanded thee of God," said Dr. Beecher. On Friday, by the direction of Dr. Beecher, Mr. Nettleton took lodgings at the house of one of the members of his church, who lived on the borders of Milton. The next day, notice was sent to the people that they might expect preaching on the Sabbath. This was entirely unexpected by the people, as they were ignorant of the efforts which had been made in their behalf. On Sabbath morning, Mr. Nettleton repaired to the place, and preached to a very small congregation. There were but few professors of religion in the place, and these were in a lukewarm state, and very great indifference to the subject of religion prevailed among the people at large. At the close of public worship, one of the people, very reluctantly, as he afterwards confessed, invited Mr. Nettleton to his house, because there was no other individual who was disposed to do it. In this house he found a pleasant home; and it proved to be like the house of Obededom, which God blessed. Salvation came indeed to this house, and the family were much more unwilling to part with their guest, than they had been to receive him.

The curiosity of the people was soon excited; they flocked together to hear the stranger who had come so unexpectedly among them. At the close of one of his evening meetings he informed them, that he had been requested to come and labour with them for a season, and he wished them to pray for a revival of religion, adding: "Whether you do or not, it is possible there may be one; for Christians in other places have agreed to pray for you." This produced great solemnity. Several went from that meeting in deep distress. It was soon manifest that God was in the place of a truth. The work increased rapidly, and became very powerful. It was characterized by remarkably clear and distressing convictions of sin. The subjects of it had a vivid sense of the opposition of their hearts to God; and, in some instances, their distress was overwhelming.

On one evening, two or three individuals were in such horror of mind, that it became necessary to remove them from the meeting to a neighbouring house. This, for a moment, created some confusion, but order was soon restored, when Mr. N. addressed the people in the following manner: "It may, perhaps, be new to some of you, that there should be such distress for sin. But there was great distress on the day of Pentecost, when thousands were pricked in the heart, and cried out: 'Men and brethren, what shall we do?' Some of you may, perhaps, be ready to say: If this is religion, we wish to have nothing to do with it. My friends, this is not religion. Religion does not cause its subjects to feel and act thus. These individuals are thus distressed, not because they have religion, but because they have no religion, and have found this out. It was so on the day of Pentecost. The thousands who were pricked in their heart, had found that they had no religion, and were unprepared to meet their God. They had made the discovery, that they were lost sinners, and that their souls were in jeopardy every hour." These may not be the precise words, but such was the substance of his address. It produced a salutary effect. It served to check what would be the natural result of mere sympathy on such an occasion, and also to stop the mouths of those who might be disposed to cavil. It is worthy of remark, that, in most of the revivals under Mr. Nettleton's preaching, there were cases of overwhelming distress. But this distress was not the result of mere sympathy, but of clear conviction of sin; and, in almost all cases, it soon terminated in a peaceful and joyful hope of salvation.

Mr. Nettleton laboured in Milton three or four months, during which time a large number became hopefully subjects of renewing grace. The wastes of Zion were repaired. The things which were ready to die were strengthened, and there was great joy in that place. It has been mentioned that Dr. Beecher and another neighbouring minister agreed to collect funds for the support of Mr. N., while preaching in Milton. Some money was collected for this purpose, but he refused to receive it. The people had made him some presents in clothing; and with this he was satisfied. "Having food and raiment," he was "therewith content."*

While he was at Milton, some young people from *South Farms* (a parish in the south part of Litchfield) attended his meetings, and were awakened by his preaching. This prepared the way for him to visit that place, which he did in the latter part of the winter. He continued there, labouring with great success, for several months.

An account of this revival was written by James Morris, Esq., an intelligent and pious gentleman, who resided in that place, and who, for many years, sustained a high reputation as a teacher of youth. The account was never published; but the manuscript has been carefully preserved, and has been kindly submitted to my inspection. The narrative is very particular. It gives the names and age of eighty individuals, the time of each one's hopeful conversion, and some account of the religious exercises of almost all of them.

A few extracts will be interesting to the reader.

"The revival of religion began in *South Farms* in February or March 1814. Praised be God for His glorious work of redeeming love in the ingathering of His elect. The following persons are hopefully brought out of darkness into God's marvellous light, and are made heirs of God, and joint-heirs of Jesus Christ, the dear Redeemer. How astonishing is the work of the Divine Spirit, the Sanctifier and Comforter, in bringing God's chosen from the bondage of sin and Satan, and prostrating them at the foot of the Cross!

* Indeed, as opportunity will occur of noticing afterwards, during the ten years that Mr N. was labouring in revivals, he received, as a compensation for his services, barely sufficient to defray his expenses When he was taken sick, in 1822, he was found to be entirely destitute; and money was collected by his friends, in different places, to defray the expenses of his sickness.

Some have been called from among the most dissipated, thoughtless, and gay; and from seventy years of age down to school children: some from the haunts of sensuality, profaneness, and intemperance, now apparently sing with understanding the songs of redeeming love.

"The first was A—— S——, a young female, eighteen years of age. She had her first impressions, in Milton, in the month of January or February. She continued in a state of anxious inquiry until the last of February, when she entertained a hope that she had met with a change of heart. She professes to enjoy religion. This was the first instance of awakening in this place."

"R—— H——, aged nineteen years, after a conflict of serious impressions and opposition of heart, for about six weeks, was apparently, on the 20th of April, renewed in heart. The first evangelical exercise that she had any knowledge of, according to her own account, was benevolence to her fellow-men. She would that all men might be saved, even if she was lost. The divine law appeared to her holy, just, and good. She felt submissive to the divine will—a disposition to resign herself into the hands of God, feeling that the Judge of all the earth would do right. She thus continued till Friday, the 22d, when, returning from a religious meeting, she felt a love to God on account of the excellency of His character. She loved holiness for holiness' sake. She then hated sin, because, in its own nature, it is odious. This was the first time that she had those consolations that the world cannot give nor take away. Here she dates her hope, and rejoices in God her Saviour."

"B—— C——, aged twenty years, having had

frequent chidings of conscience at times for more than a year past, hopes that, on the 14th of April, she was born of the Spirit, and that she is now reconciled to God. Christ appears to her altogether lovely, and the chiefest among ten thousand. Her first gracious exercises appeared to be, love to the brethren, love to God, and faith in the Lord Jesus Christ. She hates sin, because it is exceeding sinful. She appears to have clear views of her own native depravity, and of the obstinacy of her will. She wonders at and adores the patience and long-suffering of God, that she had not been long ago consigned to everlasting despair."

"N—— L——, aged fourteen years, after sundry weeks of opposition of heart to all moral good, and hating the truth, and avoiding all good people, was made to yield up her wilful perverseness of heart to God, and to submit to the terms of the Gospel. The first exercise of her mind was that of love to all good people."

"R—— C——, aged twenty, having experienced distressing convictions of sin, with an uncommon load on her heart, and with a high sense of the malignant nature of sin, experienced, as she believed, divine consolations on the evening of the 15th of April. It was while returning home from a conference, that the burden of sin was removed, as she hopes, and the love of God was shed abroad in her soul. She retired to her chamber, and took her Bible, and opened it at the 103d Psalm, and read: '*Bless the Lord, O my soul; and all that is within me, bless His holy name. Bless the Lord, O my soul, and forget not all His benefits,*' &c. She poured out her soul to God in gratitude and praise. She perseveres in her grateful remembrance of the goodness of God, and hopes that she shall live to His honour and glory the remainder of her life."

"J—— S——, aged thirty-seven years, was naturally a passionate man. He lived in open sin and profaneness from his youth. He hated to read the Bible, and to attend meeting on the Sabbath. He hated to hear religious conversation, and avoided religious instruction. He was of an independent spirit, and impiously heaven-daring. Yet the religious instruction he had received from his mother could not be wholly effaced from his memory. He often had chidings of conscience, and was often filled with remorse; but to drive all this from his mind, he would throw himself into vain, sensual, and dissipated company. He never offered a prayer in his family. His mouth was often filled with profane oaths, and the most impious imprecations on himself. His torments of mind increasing upon him, he resolved to put an end to his dreadfully profane and wicked life. He accordingly procured a large dose of arsenic, and laid it up for that purpose. In the meantime, he had a dreadful struggle in his mind. His purpose, he thought, must be put in execution; and it seemed to him that the torments of a future world for sin could not exceed the pain of mind which he felt. In this dreadful struggle, the pride of his heart was subdued, and he was made to bow at the footstool of Sovereign grace, on the 10th day of March. Traits of humility, self-abasement, and abhorrence of sin, in no man appear more conspicuous. He admires, and adores, that such an awful, heaven-daring and heaven-despising wretch, should be plucked as a brand out of the fire. He is altogether submissive, and his life is a life of prayer."

"L—— O—— W——, aged twelve years, on the 10th day of May was hopefully delivered from the thraldom of sin and Satan. She experienced a singular conflict and conviction of sin for about a week. Her distress was seemingly too great to be long endured. Her cry was: 'Oh! what a dreadful hard heart!' 'Oh! it seems as if I was in hell.' Her conflict wore down her bodily frame like a violent attack of fever. In this youth it was clearly manifested, that when the Holy Ghost, the Comforter, is come, He will convince the world of sin, of righteousness, and of judgment. A person who had experienced a change of heart, and who had seen this child through all her trials and conflicts, would be led to conclude that the change in her is a real one. She possessed less guile than those of maturer years. There was no dissembling. And when grace was planted in her soul, she did not seem to know it. The first effect that it produced, was a calm serenity of mind. She did not know why she felt so. She continued so for some hours, not knowing but her dreadful distress would return upon her. She took her Bible and perused it, which, the day before, she perfectly hated, because looking into it increased her torments. This calm serenity appeared in the morning when she arose. She thus continued till towards noon, when she informed me that she loved God; that the Bible was a new book to her; that she loved to read it; that the world did not appear to her as it did before; that *all* was new. She took me by the hand, and said she loved me, and loved all God's creatures because God made them. She said she knew that she was a great sinner. She wondered how she could sowilfully oppose God so long. God was right and reasonable, and she was altogether wrong in being so stubborn and perverse. She said she was willing to submit herself into the hands of God, for God would do right with her. She knew that it would be just if God should send her to hell. Here submission seemed to be her first evangelical exercise, and then love to the brethren."

"Widow A—— C——, aged fifty, fixes on the 3d day of May as the time when she hopes that her heart was renewed by the Spirit of grace. She had long before entertained a hope founded on her good works. She had never before believed in total depravity. She believed, that to live uprightly, and deal fairly and honestly with mankind, was sufficient to entitle her to salvation. But at this time she found that her former hopes were nothing, and that her righteousness was but filthy rags. She now feels that all her hope is in Christ. She is full in her belief of all the great doctrines of grace. She places her confidence in God through Christ, relying on the promises."

"Widow S—— H——, aged seventy years, after having lived to the common age of man without the fear of God before her eyes, was, at this period of life, hopefully brought out of darkness into God's marvellous light. She was of French descent, and came into this State at the age of twelve years. She never was taught to read or write. She married at the age of twenty years, a man of the world, a stranger to common morality. She is the mother of four children, who grew up without any religious instruction. But this aged woman now gives evidence of a change of heart, even at the last part of the eleventh hour. She appears to rejoice exceedingly in the wonderful display of God's benevolence in the ingathering of His elect. Her last days appear to be emphatically her best days, and her last comforts the sweetest comforts of her life."

"F—— E——, aged twenty years, after quarrelling with the doctrines of grace, and having heart-risings against the Divine sovereignty and the doctrine of God's electing grace, hopes that, some time in the latter part of June, his stubborn heart was subdued. He still continues resigned and submissive, and appears to enjoy the consolations of religion. But he rejoices with fear and trembling, lest his heart should deceive him."

"S—— W——, aged twenty-six years, hopes that he is reconciled to God and His law. His heart has been much opposed to the great doctrines of grace; but now, he says, things appear right and reasonable. These views of divine things have happened to him since the revival commenced, in March; but he cannot tell the time when the change took place. But he can say, 'Whereas I was once blind, now I see.'"

"J—— B——, son of E—— B——, aged nearly thirteen years. On the last Sabbath in May, or the first Sabbath in June, his mother went to meeting, and charged him and her other child to be good children, and not to play, but read their books. His father went to a distant field to see about his cattle. Before noon, this J—— was smitten with deep conviction of sin. He continued in a distressed state about twenty-four hours, without food or sleep. His mind seemed to be overwhelmed with a sense of the dreadful nature of sin, as committed against God. Something happened to him at the end of twenty-four hours, which caused him to wipe away his tears, to wash himself, and cheerfully to partake of some food. It is now about two months since this happened. He has been, from that time to this, remarkably calm and serene in his mind. He answers questions rationally—says that he loves God and hates sin. He fails not of his daily devotions and reading the Bible, and has altogether a change of deportment. He appears to have a sense of the evil nature of sin. The duties of the Sabbath and the sanctuary appear to be his delight. It is apparent to all who know this youth, that a great change has taken place in him. From being passionate, petulant, perverse, and stubborn, he is now humble, meek, patient, forbearing, and forgiving."

These few instances, taken from many similar to them recorded in this narrative, will serve to give the reader some idea of the character, not only of this revival, but of the revivals generally thirty years ago. The subjects of this revival, so far as I have been able to learn, with few exceptions, continued to adorn the Christian profession.

Some time in the spring of 1814, Mr. Nettleton left South Farms, and repaired to North Killingworth, greatly exhausted by his labours, and intending to rest for a season. At this time, the people of *Chester*, a neighbouring parish, were destitute of a minister,—their pastor, the Rev. Mr. Mills, having died a short time before. It being known in Chester that Mr. Nettleton was at home, application was made to him to attend a funeral in that place. He at first declined, assigning as the reason, that he was greatly exhausted by his labours, and needed rest. The man who came after him, as he turned to go away, burst into tears. This so affected Mr. Nettleton that he concluded to go

He attended the funeral, and, at the close of it, he gave notice that he would meet the young people in the evening, at the house of their late pastor. A large number assembled, and the meeting was very solemn. Such were the indications of the special presence of God among the people, that he was induced, notwithstanding the state of his health, to continue with them a considerable time, and had the satisfaction to witness a very interesting work of divine grace.

In the autumn of 1814, Mr. Nettleton commenced his labours in *East Granby*. This was a waste place. The moral condition of the people was exceedingly deplorable. But God saw fit to turn again the captivity of Zion. Under Mr. Nettleton's preaching there was a very interesting revival of religion. He preached here till some time in the winter, when he was obliged to suspend his labours for several months by an attack of hemorrhage from the lungs. The Rev. J. B. Clark, the present pastor of the church in East Granby, in a letter, dated November 17, 1843, thus speaks of the effects of Mr. Nettleton's labours in that place :—

"Most of those who were connected with the church as the result of that revival, have worn remarkably well, so far as is or can be known. Many of them have been, and are still, bright and shining lights in the Church of Christ. One of the subjects, Miss C. Thrall, died as a missionary among the Western Indians.

"The effect of that revival upon the church, and upon the community, was most happy and lasting.

"The interest of Christ's kingdom had suffered much from an erroneous ministry. The church lost all spirituality and fervency. The community were buried in sinful indifference. When Mr. Nettleton came among them, stupidity and slothfulness prevailed among all classes and all ages. The effect of his entrance into the place was electric. The schoolhouse and private rooms were filled with trembling worshippers. A solemnity and seriousness pervaded the community, which had not been experienced for years before. There was no bustle—no array of means. All was orderly, quiet, and scriptural. There seems to have been an increasing solemnity while the work continued.

"I am told that his sermons were, in a high degree, practical. Doctrinal sermons were frequent; but these had a practical turn. They were eminently scriptural and plain, and made men feel that *they* were the men addressed, and not their neighbours. He sometimes preached on the severer doctrines with great power, and apparent good effect. At this day we can hardly imagine the effect which his visit had upon this waste place. This seems to have been Satan's chief seat. Infidelity had been infused into the very bosom of the church. Of course, sin in every form abounded.

"There were no spiritual hymn-books in use till Mr. Nettleton laboured here; and then those hymns, in his hands, became most solemn sermons.

"Mr. Nettleton is remembered with much interest and peculiar affection by most of those advanced in life. When I have been speaking of him in my pastoral visits, the most intense interest is excited. From many expressions used, as the old people speak of him, one may know that his labours are still remembered with affection."

Early in the spring of 1815, Mr. Nettleton having so far recovered from his illness as to be able to preach, laboured for a season in *Bolton* with signal success. Here the people gave him a call to settle as their pastor, which he immediately declined, and recommended to them his friend and class-mate, the Rev. Philander Parmele. Mr. Parmele was installed November 8, 1815.

From Bolton he went to *Manchester*, to assist the Rev. Mr. Cook, whose people were enjoying a time of "refreshing from the presence of the Lord." By the divine blessing on his labours, the work was greatly promoted and extended.

After this he spent a few weeks in *Granby*, (west parish,) where his preaching was crowned with very signal success. Peculiar circumstances prevented him from continuing long with this people; but there is reason to believe that many souls were savingly benefitted by his labours. There were but few places in which he laboured where so much apparent good was effected in so short a time.

Of the revivals mentioned in this chapter, excepting the one in South Britain, no account was published at the time; and, with the exception of that and the one in South Farms, so far as is now known, no particular account was ever written. As Mr. Nettleton kept no journal of his labours at that period, it is impossible, at this late day, to give any more than a very general account of most of these revivals. Some of the facts which have been mentioned fell under the observation of his biographer, and some of them were obtained in private conversation from Mr. Nettleton himself.

CHAPTER V.

INCREASING SUCCESS: TEN CONGREGATIONS BLESSED. HIS MODE OF PROCEEDING.

IN the spring of 1815, at the request of the pastors of the Congregational churches in *New Haven*, Mr. Nettleton repaired to that city. Soon after his arrival, he was invited to visit the school of young ladies taught by the Rev. Mr. Herrick. He gave them some account of the revivals in Litchfield county, and particularly of the revival in Mrs. Pierce's school in Litchfield. Many of the scholars were deeply affected by this account, and, in the course of a few days, a large proportion of the members of the school were anxiously inquiring what they must do to be saved. The seriousness spread, and a great and glorious work of divine grace was witnessed in the city, and, to some extent, in Yale College. Mr. Nettleton continued to labour in New Haven two or three months, to the great satisfaction of his brethren there, and with the same success which had crowned his labours in country parishes.

In the summer of 1815 he visited *Salisbury*, a town in the north part of Litchfield county. In this town was one of the most remarkable revivals which ever occurred under his preaching. No account of it was ever published. In a letter written by him, in 1827, to the Rev. John Frost, there is the following brief notice of it:—

"In 1815, in the town of Salisbury, Conn., after labouring awhile under great discouragement, there were some favourable appearances. A number were anxious, and a few in awful distress of soul in one village. It was taken hold of by some ignorant, officious hands; and they were set to groaning and screaming, and alarmed all the village in my absence. Having heard the tidings, I hastened to the spot, and, with kind but decided severity, called them to order. My attempts, by those who had given the work that turn, were considered as very obtrusive and daring. It was reported all over town, that a revival had begun in Salisbury, and that I had put a stop to it. They seemed to be very much grieved and shocked at my conduct. It took a number of days to restore order; but when it was done, the work of God advanced, silently and powerfully, until all classes, old and young, were moved all over town. The language was: 'The fountains of the great deep are broken up.' Not far from three hundred were numbered as the hopeful subjects of divine grace in that revival."

The Rev. Jonathan Lee, a native of Salisbury, and residing there, has furnished the following brief account of this revival:—

"The first and greatest revival of religion which has taken place in Salisbury, Conn., stood connected with the labours of Mr. Nettleton, and began in the summer of 1815, and extended through the autumn and winter following. The church was destitute of a pastor, and reduced to a small number, there being but seventeen male members. Having been unsuccessful in their efforts to obtain a pastor, and seeing no accessions, the few members remaining felt a deep conviction of the necessity of the effusions of the Spirit, to strengthen the things that were ready to die; and an unusual spirit of prayer was felt, as they sought the blessing at the throne of grace. In these circumstances, they applied to Mr. Nettleton to come and labour among them. After they had waited with doubt and solicitude for some time, he at length came, without previously having sent any promise or notice; and, as was ascertained, without informing the friends with whom he had been, what was his place of destination. He arrived at the house of one of the deacons of the church and lodged. He made such inquiries as were designed to ascertain whether his coming had been much looked for and relied upon in order to a revival of religion. For some cause, his fears were excited; perhaps from the fact, that Deacon S—— had that day been riding in unsuccessful pursuit of him; and he at once declined staying or making any effort, saying: 'I can do no good here.' Endeavours were made to convince him, that he had not been the object of reliance, and to persuade him to stay till the following Sabbath, and preach and take opportunity to get acquainted with the state of Christian feeling. Yielding, for the present, to importunity, he prayed and conversed with the family, the labourers being called in for the purpose from the field; and offered to meet at the same place, at a particular hour, on the next day, any young people who, when invited by the deacon, should be disposed to come in. He next visited the other deacon, and pursued the same course; and, at his second visit, met with a company of young persons at each place. He began talking to them in the most simple and solemn manner, with the view to fix upon their minds some plain important truth, suited to awaken and impress the conscience. There was no dilation of thought, but one weighty idea—such as the worth of the soul, or the necessity of true religion—dwelt upon and reiterated, and left in its naked reality and solemnity on each individual's mind. This noiseless commencement of his labours was followed by visiting the families of Christian professors, and by stated religious meetings in connexion with the labours of the Sabbath. A primary object was to find the state of feeling in Christians, and to promote a humble, praying spirit.

"At an early date, after being convinced of his duty to stay and labour, he called together the church, and, with great earnestness, besought them to lay aside all expectations from him, and pray with humility and fervency that the work of the Lord might be revived. At the same time, he gave such counsels and cautions, particularly with regard to the instruction and treatment of persons under conviction, as he judged necessary to guard against unhappy results.

"The Lord was with him in very deed. Meetings became crowded and deeply solemn, and many obtained hope in Christ. He conversed individually with the anxious, and met, at certain times, at his boarding place, all who were disposed to be conversed with on the state of the heart, and the salvation of the soul. In addressing meetings, he was wont to seize on some point of interest, bearing directly upon the state of mind in which his hearers were, and then press it with a rare degree of directness, plainness, and force.

"Without attempting further details, I feel assured, (though absent, and closely occupied in a revival among the people of my charge,) that this revival was distinguished for its stillness and solemnity, for deep conviction of conscience, for discriminating views of divine truth, for humility and subsequent stability of Christian character. The subjects were of different ages, but generally youth. As fruits of the revival, about two hundred were admitted into the Congregational church, besides several who united with other churches. Many of these young professors intermarried, and became heads of families, and have lived to train up many children for Christ. Not a few, in the twenty-seven years since elapsed, have died in the Lord. Those remaining still constitute the strength of the church; for although some other favoured seasons of ingathering have been enjoyed, none have borne comparison with this, for permanent influence upon the state of the community, for enlightened piety, and stedfastness of Christian principle and character. Many still look back to that date with the deepest interest, and liveliest gratitude, as the blest period of their espousal to Christ—as the memorable year of the right hand of the Lord. The name of Asahel Nettleton, the humble, skilful labourer in this field, at that season employed in directing so many to Christ, is embalmed in many a heart. It stands associated with their dearest hopes and purest joys, and will call forth praises never ending to the chief Shepherd, who employed him in leading so many of this flock into His spiritual fold, to stand at His right hand at the great decisive day, to the praise of His own unfathomable grace."

Mr. Nettleton himself furnished the following facts regarding this revival:—

In the commencement of it, much opposition was manifested on the part of the enemies of religion. But God overruled it to the furtherance of the Gospel. As the people assembled one evening, at a large school-house, in which they had been accustomed to meet, it was found that all the seats had been removed from the house and concealed. A large congregation having assembled in and around the house, Mr. Nettleton observed to them, that he had believed that the Spirit of God was operating on the minds of the people, and that he was now confirmed in the belief. The people then repaired to the meeting-house, where the religious services were conducted with most evident tokens of the divine presence. The work, though still, was very deep and powerful, and it spread into every part of the town. It at first prevailed mostly among the youth; but it soon began to appear among heads of families; and some who were quite advanced in life were numbered among the subjects. The conversion of a man from fifty to sixty years of age, who had been a violent opposer, seemed to be the means of arresting the attention of many. This individual was a man of considerable influence, and, like Paul before his conversion, was exceedingly mad against the Church. But God, as there is reason to believe, subdued his heart, and he became as ardent in his attachment to the cause of Christ as he had been violent in his opposition. "What a glorious work of grace is this in Salisbury!" said he one morning to Mr. Nettleton; "I hope that all my family, and all the people of the town, will become interested in it, even if I am cast off for ever." This was the first manifestation of a change in his feelings. The change in him was so striking, that many who had been sceptical were convinced that it must be the work of God. He took every opportunity to converse with his acquaintance, and to recommend to them the religion which he had formerly despised; and God made him the instrument in awakening many to a sense of their lost condition as sinners. The interest became so intense in every part of the town, that whenever Mr. Nettleton was seen to enter a house, almost the whole neighbourhood would immediately assemble to hear from his lips the word of life. Husbandmen would leave their fields, mechanics their shops, and females their domestic concerns, to inquire the way to eternal life. Religion was the great and all-absorbing theme in almost all companies, and on almost all occasions. Mr. Nettleton laboured in Salisbury through the winter.

In the spring of 1816, he commenced his labours in *Bridgewater*. This is a parish in the town of New Milford, in the south-western part of Litchfield county. Here was a small church destitute of a pastor. The state of religion was very low. Unhappy dissensions existed in the church, and great stupidity prevailed among the people at large. Soon after he commenced his labours, there seemed to be a solemn attention to the Word preached, but no cases of deep conviction of sin. He soon became convinced that there could be but little hope of a revival of religion, until a better state of feeling prevailed in the church. He endeavoured to impress upon the minds of the brethren the importance of settling their difficulties, and of uniting their prayers and their efforts for the promotion of Christ's kingdom. But his exhortations seemed to have but little effect, and perceiving that they had no proper sense of their dependence on God, but were placing undue reliance on him, he thought it best to withdraw. Accordingly, without the knowledge of any but the family in which he boarded, he suddenly left the place. The next day was the annual State Fast. The people assembled, expecting to hear him preach; when, to their astonishment, they found the pulpit vacant. The disappointment was great; but it produced the intended effect. The members of the church were deeply affected. They spent the day in prayer and mutual confession of sin. All their difficulties were healed, and brotherly love was restored. It was with them a day of deep repentance and humiliation before God. Numbers of the youth, whose minds had been somewhat impressed by Mr. Nettleton's preaching, when they found that he had left them, were brought into great distress of mind. Meanwhile, he was spending the day with a brother in the ministry in a neighbouring town. On the Saturday following, he proposed to this brother to go and spend the Sabbath in Bridgewater, and permit him to supply his pulpit. The arrangement was accordingly made. This brother found a most interesting state of things. A deep solemnity pervaded the congregation, and a considerable number were found anxiously inquiring what they must do to be saved. When Mr. Nettleton learned the state of things, he returned to Bridgewater, and laboured there with great success for several months.

In this revival there was one case of peculiar interest. Mr. C—— was a most violent opposer of religion. He had not been seen in the house of God for many years. He went one evening to hear Mr. Nettleton in a schoolhouse; but being ashamed to be seen, he stopped at the door. While standing in this situation, an arrow from the Almighty's quiver pierced his heart. He went away with a troubled spirit. He was convinced that he was a sinner, and exposed to the wrath of Heaven. But he resisted the conviction, and endeavoured to banish the subject from his mind. It was, however, impossible. The thought was impressed upon his mind, as he afterwards confessed, "You must repent—you must pray, or you will perish." His heart replied, "*I* pray!—no, never. I'll perish first." Thus he struggled till his distress became intolerable. He was one night in such horror of mind, that it seemed to him that he could not live till morning. The scene was awfully solemn. To see this bold blasphemer bewailing his sinfulness, and crying for mercy, in distress and anguish which seemed too great for human nature to sustain, was a most affecting sight. The next day he obtained peace, and seemed to be in a new world. This man became a preacher of righteousness to his former associates. On the next Sabbath morning he was seen on the steps of the church, conversing with deep interest on the subject of religion, and recommending to his fellow-sinners that Saviour whom he had found so precious to his soul. Such was the change in this individual, that it extorted the confession from the mouths of gainsayers, that it must be the finger of God; and thus this striking display of divine grace was made instrumental in promoting and extending the work.

The Rev. Fosdic Harrison of Bethlem, who was at the time pastor of the church in Roxbury, a town adjoining Bridgewater, writes:—

"In the spring of 1816, when Mr. Nettleton was labouring at Bridgewater, he was frequently at my house. On one occasion, having been with me a day or two, I was expecting his assistance at an evening meeting; but a short time before the hour of meeting he manifested his intention to return to Bridgewater. I urged him to stay and attend the meeting; but he still declined. We went together from the study into Mrs. Harrison's room. She was then in feeble health. On learning his determination to leave, she most earnestly entreated him to remain. Among other things she said: 'Do stay, Mr. Nettleton, I am unable to attend the meeting myself; but if you will stay, I will pray for you all the time.' We went out together, and he left; but her earnest entreaties went with him, and troubled him. Soon after this he heard she was dangerously ill. He came directly over and said: 'Brother, learning that you were in deep affliction, I have come to pray with you.' We retired, and bowed down together before God. Some of his earnest petitions I still remember, commencing thus: 'O Lord Jesus, she whom thou lovest is sick.' Soon after this he came to attend her funeral. He remembered his refusal to yield to her importunate solicitations to attend the meeting; and that he might comply with her entreaties as far as he then could, he requested that a meeting might be appointed for that evening at the house where she died. While the other brethren went from the funeral to a monthly meeting of ministers in New Milford, and urged him to go with them, he remained, and attended the meeting in *Roxbury*. The last conversation he had with Mrs. Harrison, the solicitude she manifested in the spiritual welfare of the people, her promise to pray for him and them, were the theme of his discourse. He reminded the people that her prayers for them were ended. His appeals were powerful. Impressions were made which, I trust, resulted in the saving conversion of some souls. He remained with me a day or two, and his counsels and prayers were truly refreshing."

In the summer of 1816, Mr. Nettleton spent some time in *Torrington*, assisting the Rev. Mr. Gillet. There was some special seriousness among the people previous to his arrival; but it greatly increased afterwards. He remained in Torrington about three months. His labours were highly appreciated by the pastor and members of the church, and were manifestly attended by a divine blessing. The Rev. John A. M'Kinstry, pastor of the church, in a letter dated June 12, 1844, says: "How long the revival continued, I cannot definitely state. At the communion in November, the first-fruits were gathered into the church; and in the January following, several more were added. The number that joined at these seasons was about fifty. Others were added at subsequent seasons; but the precise number cannot be stated. It is reported, however, by those acquainted, that the number of hopeful conversions was about seventy.

"In regard to the revival, I may say, that it extended through the parish, and was very powerful. Even at this period, when first impressions have gone, the revival of 1816 is called *the revival in Torrington*, there having been none since of equal extent and power. The subjects of that work, with few exceptions, have adorned their profession, and some of them have been, and still are, pillars in the church. The influence of this revival upon the church, and upon the community, was in a high degree salutary.

"The work was solemn, and the truths presented plain and searching. The true character and condition of the sinner was clearly set before him; and he was shewn, that his only hope was in the sovereign mercy of God through a crucified Saviour.

"The measures adopted were such as were common in this region at that time; such as the ministry of the Word on the Sabbath—frequent visitation, connected with personal conversation on the subject of religion—and more or less prayer meetings during the week. In personal conversation Mr Nettleton is said to have abounded, and many attributed their religious impressions to the truth presented at such times."

"From Torrington Mr. Nettleton went to *Waterbury*, a town in the north part of New Haven county. Here a revival had already commenced. There is an account of this revival in the second volume of the *Religious Intelligencer*, from which the following is an extract:—

"Towards the close of the summer (1816) it was the will of God that our pastor should be laid on a bed of sickness, and for some time little hopes were entertained of his recovery. He was, however, spared, and his health so far restored, as to enable him to commence preaching towards the close of the succeeding winter; and though still feeble, we enjoyed his labours, with some interruption, till some time in June following, when he was obliged to desist, from returning and increasing debility.

"Thus it pleased the great Head of the Church to deprive us of the services of our teacher, at a time when, to human appearance, they seemed to be most needed. In the meantime, whatever impressions were made by former meetings, and whatever serious effects might be expected to arise from the heavy judgments with which we, as a people, had been visited,* they appeared to be lost upon us. Vice, immorality, and irreligion, appeared to gain additional strength; and the cloud that overshadowed us in a moral point of view, appeared fraught with tenfold darkness.

"But in the midst of all these scenes of discouragement, this day of trouble, rebuke, and blasphemy, God's children did not despair. They stayed themselves on the God of Jacob; and, while waiting for an answer to their prayers, knew that He had also said: 'Fear not, little flock, it is your Father's good pleasure to give you the kingdom.' He was about to appear to build up the waste places of Zion; and in such a way as to convince us, that the work was His, and that the glory alone was due to Him. He hath said: 'Mine honour is mine own, and my glory I will not give to another.' 'I will work, and who shall let it?'

"In the month of February, a small society of young

* A mortal sickness in the spring and summer of 1815

ladies commenced a weekly meeting for the purpose of reading the Scriptures and religious conversation; and one or two soon became hopefully pious.

"On the 7th of April, 1816, our hearts were cheered by seeing four young persons come out from the world, unite with the church, own Christ before men, and covenant to walk with Him in newness of spirit.

"About the forepart of May, one general spirit of zeal appeared to actuate a great proportion of the church. The spirit of grace and supplication appeared to be poured upon them. A concert of prayer for the revival of God's work in this place was agreed on, in which all the members were to be engaged in secret, between the hours of eight and nine o'clock on Saturday evening. The monthly prayer meetings for the success of missions began to be more generally attended, and became more deeply interesting.

"A serious and solemn attention on the Sabbath now appeared to pervade the whole assembly; and though sometimes deprived of the regular administration of the Word, our meetings were interesting and instructive.

"Some time in the latter part of June, it had been stated to the writer of this, that a Mr. ——, (who had formerly been an open opposer of vital religion,) and some few others, had manifested a desire to commence a weekly meeting for religious conversation and prayer. He accordingly called on one or two of the persons named, and a meeting, consisting of four only, was held on Sabbath evening.

"In this meeting, the person alluded to above declared what God had done for his soul, mourned over his past conduct, and expressed his determination to devote himself to the service of God in future.

"The meeting was opened and closed with prayer. A stated meeting was agreed on. The next evening about twelve attended. Information began now to get abroad; and on the third evening about sixty were present. On the fourth evening (so great was the crowd that attended) they could not all be accommodated, though the house was large and convenient; and it became necessary, after this, to accommodate them at the meeting-house.

"This, I think, may be fairly stated as the first visible commencement of the work.

"Numbers now appeared to be under deep conviction in almost every part of the society. The Rev. Mr. Beecher, of Litchfield, and the Rev. Mr. Nettleton, (at that time preaching at Torrington,) were present on the next Lord's day; and at a meeting appointed for the purpose on Monday morning, a considerable number appeared to ask the all-important question, 'What must I do to be saved?' Mr Nettleton was, with some difficulty, prevailed upon to come and assist us in our then destitute situation, and returned here on the Saturday following.

"From this time his labours became incessant, and his diligence unwearied. When not attending a public conference, the house was generally thronged by numbers who were anxiously inquiring the way to Zion, and to whom he was ever ready to impart instruction.

"Our worthy pastor, though unable to attend on public duties, had the cheering prospect of seeing the work of the Lord prospering among the people of his charge, and the fields ripening for a rich harvest of souls to be gathered into Christ's spiritual kingdom. The work had now become very extensive and powerful; and one remarkably characteristic feature was, it seemed to attack and subdue the very champions of infidelity the first, and to operate in such a way as to silence the most daring opposers.

"In some instances, one or two of a family seemed to be taken, and the others left. But in many, almost whole families (or, at least, all who had arrived at years of discretion) were under deep conviction, and have since subscribed, with their own right hands, to be the Lord's, and surnamed themselves by the God of Jacob."

"This work, in its general features, has been similar to what has been in other places. It has embraced all the variety of operations, from the still small voice to the most powerful threatenings of a broken law, and the vindictive justice of a justly offended God; and has embraced all ages, from youth to grey hairs—though of the youth and middle aged by far the greatest number have been brought to see their need of an interest in Christ, and led to embrace Him as their only Saviour.

"In the month of August, some of the first-fruits of the revival (together with some few who had entertained a hope before) were gathered into the church. On this occasion seventeen were added; nine more in the month of October; and on the first Sabbath in February 1817, seventy-one publicly professed their faith in Christ, and took the vows of God upon them; and seventeen received the ordinance of baptism. Twenty-one have united themselves with the church at different times since,—making one hundred and eighteen since the first of August 1816; about one hundred and ten of whom may be considered as fruits of the revival. Many more remain yet to be gathered in; and so far as the writer of this has been able to discover, no instance of apostacy has yet appeared.*

"The doctrines taught are those considered as the grand leading truths of the Gospel,—viz., the strict spirituality of the moral law—the total depravity of the natural heart—its enmity to God—the necessity of regeneration by the Spirit of His grace—an entire dependence on the merits of Jesus Christ for justification, pardon, and acceptance—our obligations to own Him before men, and to manifest our faith in Him by a holy walk and conversation—the divine sovereignty—the electing love of God—and the final perseverance of the saints, as the only ground of the sinner's hope, and the anchor of the Christian's soul."

Mr. Nettleton continued his labours in *Waterbury*, amid scenes of thrilling interest, for several months.

After he left Waterbury, he spent some time in Bolton, taking care of his friend, the Rev. Mr. Parmele, who was labouring under mental derangement, and supplying his pulpit.

In the Fall of 1817, he was requested to preach at *Upper Middleton* for the Rev. Mr. Williams, who was sick. There was no special seriousness in this place; on the contrary, great spiritual apathy prevailed. The youth were exceedingly thoughtless, and addicted to vain amusements. Soon after he commenced his labours, he became acquainted with a very intelligent young lady, who had long been seriously in-

* This account was written in July 1817.

clined, and who was thought by many to be truly pious. She handed him *Marshall on Sanctification*, and said: "If I dared believe that book, I should think I was a Christian." "I am glad," said Mr. Nettleton, "you dare not believe it."* These words went to her heart. She immediately became exceedingly anxious, and was soon brought to rejoice in hope of the glory of God.

After he had preached in this place two or three Sabbaths, there were some cases of special seriousness; but understanding that the young people had appointed a ball on the day after the Annual Thanksgiving, he expressed the purpose of leaving the place. The young people, hearing of his purpose, concluded to give up their ball, and sent a committee to invite him to preach to them on that evening. He very readily accepted the invitation. The meeting was appointed in the academy. A large congregation of youth assembled; some came from other towns. This meeting was one of thrilling interest. Some who had been previously awakened were brought to rejoice in hope, and great numbers were brought under deep and powerful conviction. God made the Word "quick and powerful, sharper than a two-edged sword, piercing even to the dividing asunder of the soul and the spirit, the joints and the marrow." The scenes of that evening will be remembered by not a few through eternity. Several in deep distress followed Mr. Nettleton to his lodgings. He prayed with them, and with great difficulty persuaded them to retire to their homes. Many spent the night in crying for mercy, and several found peace before morning. From

* He seems to have feared, that in such a state of mind as this lady was in, the effect of that book would be to make her believe that she was believing in spite of the absence of all appearance of regeneration.

this time the work became very powerful. Meetings of inquiry were held at the house of the pastor; but the place became too strait, and God provided one of greater convenience. A man who owned a large ball-room, and who had been a bitter enemy to religion, was awakened, and hopefully brought to repentance. He opened his ball-room for meetings of inquiry.

Mr. Nettleton laboured in this place a number of months, and was made instrumental, as there is reason to believe, in the conversion of many souls. The Rev. Zebulon Crocker, the pastor of the church, in a letter dated December 15, 1843, speaking of the converts in this revival, says:—

"Among the males who are members of this church, there are several who have borne the burden and heat of the day, and borne it well. They have been pillars in the temple of our God, and are so still. There are others who have gone from us and united with churches abroad, whose names appear connected with the public charities of the day, and who are known to be bright and shining lights in the world. Similar remarks apply to the female members. Several have died in the faith. As a whole, I think I have evidence on which to affirm, that they have run well, and have received a good report."

Speaking of the results of that revival, he says:—

"In the Fall of 1817, the church was in a 'cold state,' as some have expressed it. Religion, I am inclined to think, was at a low ebb. The blessed work of the Spirit which immediately succeeded, it is to me evident, changed very much the aspect of affairs for the better, as a permanent result. It gave moral courage and strength to the church. Some who had become members without piety, were hopefully converted. Faith in regard to the efficacy of the Gospel was encouraged. Christians desired a renewal of the work, and were prepared to labour and pray for another season of refreshing from the presence of the Lord. The way was prepared for the more frequent revivals with which the church has been blessed."

During this revival in Upper Middleton, a few individuals from *Rocky Hill*, an adjoining parish, attended some of Mr. Nettleton's meetings, and became anxious for their souls. The seriousness spread, and at the earnest solicitation of the pastor, the Rev. Dr. Chapin, Mr. Nettleton visited that place. He arrived on Saturday, April 4, 1818.

"When he arrived," says Dr. Chapin, "there was a meeting in the house of the pastor. At the same place, in the evening, there was another, which brother Nettleton attended. His acquaintance with the state of the public mind among us began that evening. From that time, during the greater part of several months, he was indefatigable, labouring in season and out of season, to the full extent of his health and strength. In connexion with impressions and experience realized in 1818, eighty-four persons became members of Christ's visible Church. How many of them were brought to this performance of external duty by brother Nettleton's labours, we shall know hereafter. How many of their names, or whether all, will be found written in the Lamb's Book of Life, we shall see at the opening of that perfect book. During the almost twenty-six years that have fled since the delightful and interesting events above mentioned, it appears that twenty-five of the eighty-four have gone the way of all the earth. Their departure was either while resident here, or in some distant location. Fifteen, also, of the same fourscore and four, have removed from us, and, so far as we know, are yet living. So far as man can judge, those eighty-four have adorned the doctrine of God our Saviour, in a manner equal, at least, to the fruits of those other revivals which Christ has permitted us to enjoy.

"In an important sense, brother Nettleton's talent was *one*. In the cultivation and improvement of that *one*, he was unwearied. By the concentration of study, always directed to the most useful point, which is practical piety, that talent had risen to the first order. Hence the depth and exactness of his knowledge in true experience of the things which are essential to salvation. Hence, too, the quickness of discernment relative to the specific instruction, and the manner of imparting instruction, that every mind needed with which he came in contact.

"He had a quick and precise perception of the sources whence objectors and cavillers draw their difficulties. In replies, shewing the true answer and the only remedy, he was ready, appropriate—generally silencing, and not rarely convincing.

"In the whole of his intercourse he was exemplary. He was remarkably cautious of appearances. He would not expose himself or his cause to reproach, by giving so much as the least occasion for the surmises of evil. If Satan's followers attempted the propagation of injurious reports, they were obliged to go far away from us for their foundation. The rumours thus procured and put in motion, if investigated, always proved to be false and infernally malicious. Even the subtile vigilance of the evil spirit could find, in his conduct here, no foundation for its eagerly coveted slanders."

In October 1818, Mr. Nettleton commenced preaching in *Ashford*, a town in the eastern part of Connecticut. His labours soon began to be crowned with success. In his journal, under date of Nov. 4, he mentions "One rejoicing."—Nov. 6, "Five or six rejoicing."—Nov. 8, "Very full. Such a Sabbath is rarely seen." The work now became powerful, and made rapid progress. Mr. Nettleton laboured in Ashford without intermission about two months, and preached there occasionally afterwards. Of the results of his labours the reader will be able to form some opinion from the following extract of a letter from the Rev. Charles Hyde, the present pastor of the church, dated May 30, 1844:—

"With respect to our departed brother's labours in this place, I know but little, except what I learn from the records of the church, and the recollections of some who were then living here. That he was remarkably wise, fervent, skilful, and successful, all bear testimony; and all, especially those who were brought into the kingdom through his labours, cherish a most affectionate and grateful remembrance of him. His influence here was permanently good; it is felt at the present day. He commenced his labours here in October 1818. The first additions to the church were in March, when fifty-six were received. In May following, there were twelve, and in July, ten, and in November, four; making in all eighty-two, of whom, I suppose, the greater part, if not all, were subjects of that revival. This is a very large number for so small a society.

"Of the character of these converts, I cannot

speak particularly, except of those who are now here. Twenty-two have died. Twenty-seven have removed from the place. Three only have been excommunicated. The remainder are, with hardly an exception, now consistent members—some of them pillars in the church. Many of those who have left us, I am informed, continue to adorn their profession. Upon the whole, I think it must be admitted that the revival here under Dr. Nettleton's labours, was a remarkably pure one; and happy is the church that receives such a blessing. Its influence goes down to succeeding generations."

In the month of December 1818, Mr. Nettleton commenced his labours in *Eastford*. Here was a small church, destitute of a pastor, and in a very depressed condition. The influence of their last minister, who became a Universalist, was very disastrous to the cause of religion. He had been dismissed about four years when Mr. Nettleton visited the place.

"During this interval," says their present pastor, the Rev. Francis Williams, "they were supplied some part of the time by such preachers as they could obtain; some part of the time the deacons conducted meetings on the Sabbath; and a considerable portion of the time they had no public worship.

"During this state of things, the interests of religion greatly declined, and the light of the church was well-nigh extinguished. According to the most correct information which I can obtain, there were but about twenty members in the church, and only six male members. Most of these were persons advanced in life. At this critical period Mr. Nettleton came among the people. A powerful work of grace immediately commenced, such as neither they nor their fathers had seen. He preached the distinguishing doctrines of grace so pointedly, that persons have often informed me they felt themselves in the hands, and at the disposal of God. They felt that if they were ever saved from their dreadful depravity and wretchedness, it must be by sovereign grace. He made practical application of these doctrines* to the heart and conscience in such a plain and forcible manner, that they felt, that if they were lost they should be without excuse.

"The work was characterized by such stillness and power, that every one felt that the finger of God was in it. To repeat a remark made by an observer at the time: 'It was so evidently the work of God, that not a dog dared move his tongue.' I am not able to ascertain the number who indulged hope. I find by the church records that forty-eight united with the church by profession, March 28, 1819; and in June following, eleven more,—making, in all, fifty-nine by profession. Several were also added by letter. This,

* Dr. Green, of Princeton, (see Appendix to *Sprague on Revivals*,) remarks: "I say briefly, that in a time of revival, so far am I from thinking that the preaching employed should be merely hortatory, or principally addressed to the feelings, that I am persuaded it ought to be eminently doctrinal. Lively, and tender, and close, and full of application, it certainly should be; but the great and fundamental doctrines of the Gospel should be brought out clearly, be lucidly explained, and be much insisted on Of what may be denominated, by way of eminence, *Gospel preaching, there ought to be no lack;* that is, the all-sufficiency of the Lord Jesus Christ to save even the chief of sinners; and His readiness to receive them when they come, to cleanse them in His atoning blood, to clothe them with His perfect righteousness, to justify them freely, to sanctify them by His Spirit, to adopt them into His family, and to crown them with eternal glory, should be set forth in the most clear and persuasive manner. The true nature of regeneration, of evangelical faith, genuine repentance, and new obedience, should be carefully explained and illustrated. The danger of grieving away the Spirit of Grace, by those with whom He is striving, and the danger of all *delay in accepting the* Gospel offer, should be often brought into view."

in the then existing state of the church, was life from the dead. The church was soon after supplied with a faithful pastor, who laboured here for more than twenty years; and the church has been, on the whole, prosperous. Of those admitted to the church as fruits of this revival, fifteen have left this world, while the rest continue unto this present. Most of them have given pleasing evidence of piety. No one acquainted with the facts can doubt that the cause of Christ was greatly promoted by the labours of Mr. Nettleton. And perhaps so few evils seldom follow a great revival in any place.

"You ask: How is Mr. Nettleton regarded by the good people in Eastford? They look up to him with the most ardent affection as a spiritual father. This may be ascertained by any one who will mention his name in their hearing. He will see indisputable proof of affectionate regard."

In the month of April 1819, Mr. Nettleton went to *Bolton*, where he remained two or three months, labouring with his friend, the Rev. Mr. Parmele. It appears from an account published by Mr. Parmele in the *Religious Intelligencer* for November 1820, that some time previous to Mr. Nettleton's arrival, there had been an unusual spirit of prayer among the people of God. But God saw fit to try their faith.

"While," says Mr. Parmele, "Christians were thus daily wrestling in prayer for the salvation of sinners, and were committing the cause of religion into the hands of God, their faith and patience were brought to the test. Satan, as though aware that his kingdom was soon to receive an attack, rallied his forces, and marshalled his bands to make resistance. Iniquity rushed in like a flood. The youth who we expected would be awakened, if our prayers were answered, were generally never more dissolute. Their minds were supremely occupied with scenes of mirth and parties of pleasure. If they received any impressions on the Sabbath, or at a religious meeting during the week, these were soon banished through the influence of worldly companions and vain amusements.

"To counteract the influence of these things, in the month of April, (about the time Mr. Nettleton commenced his labours in Bolton,) meetings were appointed for religious conversation with the youth, which were generally well attended, and soon became interesting. At one of these meetings eight or ten of the youth were alarmed with a sense of their sins. Their convictions deepened, until they became overwhelming; and within a few days they were brought to rejoice in hope. This spread conviction like an electric shock through the society of young people, until it was evident that the Lord had appeared in His glory to build up Zion. The volatile youth could no longer resist the influences of the Holy Spirit; but in deep solemnity were daily inquiring what they should do to be saved. Vain amusements were entirely suspended, scenes of pleasure were forsaken, and the trifles of time were lost in the awful concerns of eternity. No object could divert the anxious mind from inquiring the way to life.

"The convictions of the subjects of this work were deep, increased rapidly, and were of short continuance. Unconditional submission was urged as the only ground of acceptance with God. And as soon as this was exercised, in most instances, the sinner was filled with joy. One expressed herself thus: 'I attempted to pray for mercy while in my sins; but my conscience flashed conviction in my face. What! will such a sinner as you attempt to pray? You are so vile, your prayers will not be heard. I then felt the reasonableness of my condemnation so forcibly, that I took up the side of justice, and pleaded the cause of God against myself. In this condition I soon found relief.'

"May and June with us were interesting months. Most of the subjects of this revival became reconciled to God during this period. On the first Sabbath in July, thirty-five united with the church, nine of whom received the ordinance of baptism. This was a day so interesting, that the solemn scenes which transpired can never be forgotten. The youth, the middle aged, and the aged, composed this number. On the first Sabbath in September, twenty-one united with the church, and two have been added since,—making, in the whole, fifty-nine. Five living in families not connected with my society have united with the Baptist Church. The subjects of this revival are of all ages, from twelve years old to upwards of sixty; but by far the greater portion are youth.

"We would express our gratitude to those brethren in the ministry, who occasionally preached for us during this revival; and especially to Mr. Nettleton, whose labours were signally blessed. We trust the Lord will reward them for their labours of love. But we desire to look beyond all instruments to the great first Cause, and, as a church and people, to express our unfeigned gratitude to the Father of all mercies for this work of His grace. *This is the Lord's work, and it is marvellous in our eyes;* and to His great name be ascribed the *kingdom, the power, and the glory, for ever.*"

CHAPTER VI.

THE BLESSING ON HIS LABOURS IN SARATOGA COUNTY AND NASSAU.—EXTRACTS FROM HIS LETTERS.

In July 1819, being very much exhausted by his labours in Connecticut, Mr. Nettleton repaired to *Saratoga Springs* for rest. He did not expect to preach in that region, as his sole object was to recruit his strength. After he had been there a short time, the Rev. Mr. Tucker, of Stillwater, (now the Rev. Dr. Tucker, of Providence, Rhode Island,) called to see him. In the course of their conversation something was said respecting waste places. This led Mr. Tucker to give him some account of *Malta*, a town in that vicinity, which had long been a waste place, and in which there was no Presbyterian or Congregational church. This account awakened in Mr. Nettleton a desire to visit that place. Mr. Tucker kindly offered to accompany him, and introduce him to a Mr. Hunter, a professor of religion, and a very respectable and worthy man. They spent a night at his house, and attended a prayer meeting with a few neighbours who were invited in. Mr. Nettleton agreed to come again and pass a Sabbath with them; and accordingly, on the 1st day of August 1819, he preached in their meeting-house to a congregation of about fifty souls.

On Monday he returned to *Saratoga*, and at the request of the Rev. Mr. Griswold, attended the monthly concert in the evening. He shortly after attended some other meetings, when it became apparent that the Spirit of God was operating upon the minds of the people. Mr. Nettleton confined his labours principally to Saratoga, occasionally preaching at *Malta*, till November. He then laboured most of the time in Malta, occasionally preaching in the neighbouring towns, until the beginning of March, when he went to Schenectady, where he continued till near the close of April. The revival which began at Saratoga spread into Malta, and thence into all the surrounding region, and into *Union College*.

While Mr. Nettleton was at Schenectady, he wrote to a friend in Connecticut:—

"I can at present give you nothing more than the outlines of what the Lord is doing for this section of His Church. This region, and especially the county of Saratoga, has heretofore been as destitute of revivals of religion as any part of this State. The commencement of this work was at Saratoga Springs last summer. At that place, about forty have made a profession of religion. These include some of the most respectable characters in the village. Directly south is the town of Malta. For a number of years there has been no Presbyterian church in that place. But the year past, there has been a very interesting revival among that people. Our meetings have been crowded, and solemn as the house of death. A church has been recently organized, which now consists of one hundred and five members. You can hardly imagine the interest which this revival excited in the surrounding region. Although the inhabitants are scattered over a large extent, yet, I verily believe, I have seen more than fourteen hundred people assembled at once to hear the Gospel. On the east of Malta is the town of *Stillwater*. Here, also, there has been a very powerful revival. Although there has been some excitement as to serious things in this place in years past, yet this revival exceeds any they have ever before witnessed. On the 27th of February last, one hundred and three publicly presented themselves a living sacrifice unto the Lord; and about one hundred more are rejoicing in hope, and expect soon to follow their example. The work is still advancing; numbers are under conviction. In *Ballston*, adjoining Malta on the west, the work has been very powerful. At their two last communions, they admitted one hundred and eighteen as the fruit of this revival, and the work is yet increasing. Directly north is the town of *Milton*. I visited that people Sabbath before last, and preached three times to a crowded and solemn assembly. In this place a revival has just commenced. Twelve are rejoicing in hope, and a number more are anxious for their souls. Eight miles to the north-west, adjoining Milton, is the town of *Galway*. Here the work is overwhelming. In less than two months past, more than one hundred and fifty have been brought to rejoice in hope. Dr. Nott, from this college, visited them last Sabbath, and admitted ninety-five to the church; and the work is still progressing. On the south of this is *Amsterdam*. Here fifty have recently been led to rejoice in hope. Adjoining this is a place called *Tripe's Hill*. Here thirty are rejoicing; and the work in both these places is increasing.

South from Malta, about twelve miles, is the city of *Schenectady*, and Union College, where I now reside with Dr. M'Auley. He takes a lively interest in this good work. I first became acquainted with him last summer at the Springs, and more particularly at Malta, where he frequently visited us, and preached, and conversed, and attended the meetings appointed for those anxious for their souls. On a Sabbath, when a number were to be admitted to the church in Malta, he brought with him a number of students from the college. Some of them became anxious. About this time, one of the students was called into the eternal world. He was laid out in Dr. M'Auley's study. The Doctor was anxious to improve this solemn providence to the best advantage. He assembled the students around the lifeless remains of their departed friend, and conversed and prayed with them in the most solemn manner. A number of them engaged to attend to the subject of religion in earnest. From that time, many of the students became deeply impressed with a sense of their lost condition. For them were appointed meetings of inquiry; and in this very room, where they lately beheld the breathless corpse of their young companion, and where I am now writing, was witnessed a scene of deep and awful distress. About thirty of the students are brought to rejoice in hope. The revival is now very powerful in the city. Such a scene they never before witnessed. More than one hundred have been brought to rejoice in hope. Besides these, we had more than two hundred in our meeting of inquiry, anxious for their souls. We met in a large upper room, called the Masonic Hall. The room was so crowded, that we were obliged to request all who had recently found relief to retire below, and spend their time in prayer for those above. This evening will never be forgotten. The scene is beyond description. Did you ever witness two hundred sinners, with one accord, in one place, weeping for their sins? Until you have seen this, you can have no adequate conceptions of the solemn scene. I felt as though I was standing on the verge of the eternal world; while the floor under my feet was shaken by the trembling of anxious souls in view of a judgment to come. The solemnity was still heightened, when every knee was bent at the throne of grace; and the intervening silence of the voice of prayer was interrupted only by the sighs and sobs of anxious souls. I have no time to relate interesting particulars. I only add, that some of the most stout, hard-hearted, Heaven-daring rebels, have been in the most awful distress. Within a circle whose diameter would be twenty-four miles, not less than eight hundred souls have been hopefully born into the kingdom of Christ since last September. The same glorious work is fast spreading into other towns and congregations. '*This is that which was spoken by the prophet Joel.*'"

The above letter was dated Union College, April 28, 1820.

A letter from a student in Union College, dated March 6, 1820, gives a very similar account of this revival, except that it had made greater progress at the date of Mr. Nettleton's letter.* After having given some account of the revival at Saratoga Springs, the writer says: "It commenced then in Malta, about

* Both letters appeared in the fourth volume of the *Religious Intelligencer*.

ten miles from this place, under the labours of a Mr. Nettleton, a missionary from Connecticut. It commenced, I said, in Malta; and with such displays of the power of God's Spirit in crushing the opposition of the natural heart to everything holy, as are very seldom seen. The *Deist* and *Universalist*, the *Drunkard*, the *Gambler*, and the *Swearer*, were alike made the subjects of this heart-breaking work. Four months ago, Christ had no church there. It was a place of great spiritual dearth; and, like the top of Gilboa, had never been wet by rain or dew. But the Lord has now converted that wilderness into a fruitful field. They have an organized church of eighty-five members; and the work of conviction is going on."

This revival, which commenced at Saratoga Springs, and spread into the surrounding region, resulted in the hopeful conversion of not less than two thousand souls.

In the month of April 1820, Mr. Nettleton commenced his labours in *Nassau*, a village a few miles east of Albany. Among his papers has been found the following sketch of the revival in this place. Had he kept a similar journal of his labours in all the places in which he preached, it would have contained a vast amount of interesting intelligence. But this is the only thing of the kind to be found among his papers. It is here given as presenting a specimen of the revivals which occurred under his preaching:—

"A sketch of a revival of religion in Nassau, which commenced April 1820.

"The state of religion in this village and its vicinity, has, for years, been deplorable. The village contains a house for public worship, held, in common, by two denominations,—the Dutch Reformed, and the Presbyterians. The former, during the winter past, have had one sermon every alternate Sabbath; and the latter have had no settled minister, and no regular preaching for years. Indeed, their little church had become nearly extinct. The revival of religion in this place commenced as follows:—

"In the month of February, a number of persons from this village visited Malta, during the revival there. One of this number was left at Malta, became a hopeful subject of divine grace, and, shortly after, returned to this village. The sacred flame began to kindle in the hearts of a few old professors. The news of distant revivals began to excite inquiry; and some few sinners became more solemn. One, after a season of distress, became joyful. For a moment, hope was cherished that a glorious day had dawned; but the surrounding darkness prevailed, and hope at length expired. For a few weeks I had been absent from Malta. On my return, I received repeated and pressing invitations to visit Nassau. Prompted by this state of things, instead of returning to Schenectady, as was expected, I concluded to defer it for one week, and visit Nassau.

"April 19.—Arrived at Nassau. Attended a meeting in the schoolhouse. About fifty assembled, and nothing particular occurred.

"April 20.—This evening attended a meeting in a large dining-hall in a public-house. The room was crowded. A number stood around the doors and windows, and listened with respectful silence and much solemnity. It afterwards appeared, that not less than twelve or fifteen dated their first serious impressions from that meeting. A Mr. P—— subsequently observed: 'I went to that meeting full of prejudice. You began to tell me the feelings of my heart; and I began to be vexed and angry at one or two of my neighbours for informing you what I had said. I thought you were a man of great brass. On returning from meeting, I asked Mrs. P—— how she liked it? She burst into tears, and we both wept.'

"Another whose mind was impressed at this meeting, was a young woman who had passed through a revival in the town of Salisbury, Conn., five years before. She had been somewhat anxious, and lost her concern, and, as I have since learned, had made light of the subject. She entered the room this evening in company with others, without suspecting that the preacher was a man whom she had ever seen before. She remarked afterwards: 'As soon as I saw the preacher, I felt distressed. I observed it was the same man that preached in Salisbury. I was expecting a revival.' From this time her former feelings returned; and, in addition, she was overwhelmed with a sense of her guilt in having dropped the subject.

"April 21.—This evening met those that were anxious at Dr. M——'s. About thirty were present. As I commenced speaking to them in general, all were very still and solemn. Suddenly a youth, sitting near the window, as if pricked in the heart, cried out in distress. This produced no diversion of attention, but increased the solemnity; for the cause was perfectly understood. After conversing with each one, we bowed the knee together at the throne of grace, and then, in solemn stillness, retired at an early hour. A number of these anxious souls belonged to one family. They reached home weeping. The father of the family had retired to rest. As the carriage came up to the door, he heard the cry of distress, and started from his bed to learn the cause. His daughter-in-law, on entering the house, threw her arms around his neck, and exclaimed: 'My father, what shall I do?—what shall I do?' She continued for some time in great distress; but, before morning, was rejoicing in hope.

"April 22, Saturday.—Was in some doubt what course to pursue, as the meeting-house on the next Sabbath was engaged. Rode to Greenbush, and negotiated an exchange with the Rev. Mr. Marselus of the Dutch Reformed Church.

"April 23, Sabbath.—Mr. Marselus preached at Nassau with power and effect; and at the close of the services, at my request, read a letter from Dr. M'Auley, containing an account of the revival in Union College and Schenectady. This increased the solemnity. I preached at Greenbush in the forenoon; and at 3 o'clock, P.M., preached again in a ball-room, at a public-house on the road, about two miles from this village. When I arrived, I found the ball-room crowded to overflowing. At the close of the services a number assembled around me. Some from curiosity, but many in deep distress, weeping aloud. I requested them to suppress their cries, and be as still as possible. At this meeting a number were awakened. This evening preached in the meeting-house in this village for the first time, to a crowded and solemn audience.

"April 24.—This evening met about sixty in a meeting for anxious inquirers. Among them were many in deep distress. This, I expected, would be my last meeting in this place. But I found so many in distress for their souls, and the number increasing, that I announced the appointment of one public meeting more in the meeting-house, on the following evening.

"April 25.—Met in the meeting-house. More crowded than ever, and solemn as eternity. Preached on the *nature* and *reasonableness* of Gospel repentance; and urged the duty of immediate compliance, and the danger of delay. Never more expecting to meet my anxious hearers in this world, I urged them, by all the solemnities of the judgment, not to pass the threshold of the meeting-house that night with impenitent hearts. They seemed to hear as for their lives. In the midst of the discourse one found relief from deep distress, and lifted up a joyful countenance. No sooner had I closed and stepped from the stage, than she came near; and, taking her husband by the hand, urged him to come to Christ. It was like a two-edged sword. It pierced him to the heart. At this moment the anxious ones assembled around me, and took me, some by the hand, some by the arm, and some by the coat, exclaiming: 'Don't leave us! What shall I do? —what shall I do?' Nearly the whole congregation tarried. Those who could not come near stood, some on the seats, and some on the sides of the pews, to hear and see. From the midst of this scene of distress, I addressed the whole congregation for about five minutes. Among other things, I said:

"My hearers, I now no longer hesitate to tell you, what I have hitherto been afraid to speak, that a revival of religion is begun in Nassau. Yes, from what I have seen, I can no longer doubt the fact. I believe you are about to witness a solemn and trying time in this place; and now you must prepare either to be taken or to be left. I then told them I would meet them in the morning at sunrise, in the school-house, and pray with them before I left, if they choose. I advised them to depart as still as possible, and to be retired through the night.

"April 26.—Met them in the morning before sun-rise. Two of those who went away in distress last night, came to me rejoicing this morning. They found relief before they slept. I prayed and conversed with them a few moments, and started for Schenectady before breakfast. Heard of one more rejoicing this morning. I called and found it so, and found others in distress. The distress in one house led me to another, and that to another, until I visited nine families before I left the place. It was truly affecting to witness these strangers crying for mercy. In this state I left them, and went to Schenectady. During my absence, I felt a deep interest for those in Nassau. The scenes that I had there witnessed were continually before me. It rained, and I tarried two nights.

"April 28.—Started from Schenectady for Nassau. Arrived at Mr. B——'s, within three miles of the village, late in the evening. In this house, some whom I had left in great distress met me with joyful countenances. Here I was informed, that the Baptists had a meeting at the meeting-house this evening. Wishing to embrace the opportunity to make an appointment, I drove on to the meeting-house, and found the house nearly full. All were standing, and about to retire, as the meeting had just closed. I made my way through the crowd, as I suppose, unobserved, stepped upon the stage, and announced an appointment for the next Sabbath. The effect of this little circumstance was almost incredible. I could hardly say which was most prominent, the burst of joy or of grief. A number came to me with joyful countenances, while others were borne down with grief. It is this night just one week since the first instance of hopeful conversion occurred, and now about thirty appear to be subjects of grace. Many of these, it was afterwards found, obtained relief on the day I left them, and some a few moments after. This was a memorable day; for when they afterwards came together to give a relation of their Christian experience, we found that some on that day retired into the groves and fields, and some into their chambers and closets, to cry for mercy. I have since thought that the effect of my leaving them as I did —*in the advanced stages of their conviction*—was evidently beneficial. It drove them from all human dependence. Distressing as it is, and cruel as it may seem, it is necessary for them to feel that no arm but God's can help them. Similar effects from like circumstances have heretofore been witnessed.

"April 30, Sabbath.—The congregation was crowded and solemn. This day an event took place, unknown to me at the time, which was designed by the enemy to check and put a stop to the work; but which, in the hand of God, was made subservient to its advancement.

"May 1.—Met about eighty-five in the meeting of inquiry.

"May 2.—This evening, held a meeting in the meeting-house, and took up the *common sayings of*

Christians,* which are calculated to check a revival by lessening the sinner's sense of obligation, and quieting him in his sins.

"May 4.—At this date, we find about forty rejoicing in hope. From this date to the 14th, preached nine times, and held one meeting for inquirers.

"May 15.—This evening, attended a meeting of inquiry, and found the number and distress of anxious souls rapidly increasing. The distress of W—— is greatly augmented. This is the person who had been a little anxious during the revival in Salisbury, and whose attention had again been excited, on entering our meeting the second evening in this village. From this time, her distress continued about three days and nights. Providentially she was in a family, a number of whom were thoughtless and far from religion. This was loud preaching. So great was her distress, that she was unable to attend meetings, and was confined to the house. Many called to witness her distress. She had concluded that the day of grace was over; and she was now past the fear of mortals. She continued crying: '*Lord, have mercy on my soul! I am lost! Oh! for ever lost!*' In this situation she sent for me to call and see her, that she might beg my pardon for what she had said, before she died. I called, and such was her agitation, that it was difficult to keep her in one position. Sometimes sitting, and then kneeling, in a piteous tone she would cry out: '*Young people, take warning from me! Young people, take warning from me!*' The house was constantly visited by curious spectators, often till late at night. Many thought that she could not live long. One physician

* A specimen of this is given in a future chapter.

asked my opinion, whether I thought she would die? From past facts, I have noticed that this *extreme* distress does not generally continue long, especially in seasons of revival; sometimes but a few moments; *commonly* a few hours; and rarely over three days. And when this extreme distress exceeds this time, I begin to fear that it may subside (as it has sometimes done) without a change of heart. On the third day she was rejoicing in hope.

"The question is often asked, Why is it that the convictions of some sinners are so much greater than those of others? I answer, I do not know. The sinner's distress does not always appear to be in exact proportion to his crimes. But one thing I have learned from observation, and that is, that when persons of a particular description have been brought under conviction, they have been exercised with severe distress. Those who have once been anxious for their souls, and have been laughed out of it, and returned to the thoughtless world, if again awakened, are more distressed than ever. Those who once made it a business to retire and pray, and have long since dropped the subject, are usually, if their attention is again excited, greatly distressed. Those who have laboured hard to stifle and throw off their convictions, or those who have formerly resisted the strivings of God's Spirit, are usually the subjects of keen distress, if convinced of sin a second time. Those who have scoffed at the subject of religion, and have mocked the messengers of Christ, and ridiculed the worship of God, are usually filled with great consternation and agony, when brought to a just sense of their character and state. Those who have made light of revivals of religion, by calling them enthusiasm, fanaticism, and the work of the devil—especially those who have taken an active part in ridiculing the conviction and conversion of sinners in the season of a revival—those who have called revivals by the hardest names, who have expressed the greatest contempt of them, and who have done the most to bring them into disrepute—persons of this description have been the most frightful monuments of distress that I have ever witnessed. They despair of ever becoming the subjects of that work which they have treated with so much contempt. We have sometimes heard the champion of infidelity expressing his horror from fear of having committed the unpardonable sin. I am acquainted with the names of persons who have become perfectly deranged, in consequence of *their own opposition* to the progress of revivals. Conscience, without any other accuser, has driven the enemy of revivals out of his reason into a state of settled delirium. The confession and fate of Judas shew the power of conscience, and stand recorded as a warning to the opposers of religion to beware.

"May 17.—This evening we met in the school-house. The room was crowded, and the meeting was exceedingly joyful. Every word that was spoken seemed to find a place in some heart. Such a season of rejoicing is rarely witnessed. '*Old things are passed away, and all things are become new.*' It is not yet quite one month since the work commenced, and about sixty are supposed to be the subjects of grace.

"May 19.—This evening we met in a private house; and, at the close of the exercises, one of the young converts spoke to a stout-hearted sinner who had been struggling against his conscience, and he dropped upon his knees in distress of soul. Another followed me nearly home, inquiring *what he must do to be saved?* In this situation I left him; but before we retired to rest, he came in with a new song in his mouth. The other went home in great distress; but found relief before morning.

"May 20.—This was a solemn day throughout this village. Mr. L——, a young lawyer, who had been anxious for a few days, and who had retired to rest in my chamber, came to my bedside early this morning in distress. He sat down to breakfast with us, and while at the table heard the tidings that another of his mates had found the Saviour the last night. He instantly left the table, and retired to my chamber. Some time after, I entered the chamber, and found him prostrate on the floor, crying for mercy. While he thus continued, waxing worse and worse, a number came up to see him; but he seemed to take no notice of them, and continued pleading for mercy. About ten o'clock, A.M., (whether with a new heart, I cannot say, I only record the fact,) he came down stairs expressing his joy that he had found the Saviour. At the same time, his fellow-student, M——, in a house a few rods distant, lay prostrate in his chamber. I called and found a number assembled around him, while he lay crying for mercy. The burden of his prayer was, that God would pardon his self-righteousness. The fact was this: A few days previous, he and his brother lawyer had shut themselves in a chamber, seeking, and striving, and praying together for a long time, thinking, without doubt, they should ere long succeed in becoming Christians. Here they continued, until both had become exceedingly self-righteous. They could see it in each other; and each was alarmed at it, and asked my opinion if they had not better separate. 'By all means,' I told them. This sight of his heart was, doubtless, what most distressed him. About three o'clock, P.M., he arose, in like manner, rejoicing that he had found the Saviour.

"May 21, Sabbath.—Held a meeting at a public-house, (Mr. B——'s,) four or five miles from this village. When I arrived the rooms were filled—doors and windows thronged. Those who seemed the most anxious had placed themselves near the seat of the speaker. When I named the Psalm, all was silence, except the sighs and sobs of anxious souls. The moment I began to speak, I felt that God was there. I addressed them from Gen. vii. 1: '*Come thou, and all thy house, into the ark.*' I felt unusual freedom and satisfaction in speaking. The solemnity of the scene will long be remembered. When I had pronounced the benediction, I know not that a foot moved. All were standing, and still anxious to hear. I gave them an account of what I had witnessed up in the village the week past. Many had assembled from the surrounding regions of desolation, doubtless from motives of curiosity, having heard something of the wonderful movement in the village. While giving a relation of these wonderful things every ear was attentive. Some were sighing, and some were gazing in wild amazement. The language of every look seemed to be, *We never heard such things before!* In one large room, which was crowded entirely full, nearly all were in deep distress, besides many crowding round the doors and windows, all apparently equally anxious, except here and there a joyful convert. They were crowded so closely together, that I could not pass among them to converse; so I spoke to one and another, here and there, at a distance, as I could catch their eyes as they lifted them streaming with tears. All were utter strangers whom I addressed, and not a name could I call. My only method of designation was by pointing, and saying, 'I mean you, and you,' or 'this sinner, and that sinner.' Never did I feel a deeper compassion for sinners than for these poor strangers. A number (I know not how many) were awakened this day.

"Preached in the village in the afternoon and evening. At this time we concluded that the crisis of solemnity was past in the village.

"May 22.—This evening attended the meeting for inquirers; and, all things considered, it was the most distressing and painful scene hitherto witnessed in this revival. Unexpectedly, a number who had never before attended, came from the region of solemnity above described. Some came four or five miles, and crowded the meeting, and threw it into a scene of awful distress. The distress was so great, and the suppressed sighs and sobs became so loud, that I could scarcely hear my own voice. One or two found relief on the spot; and some lost their strength, so that we were obliged to help them out of the chamber. It was with the utmost difficulty that I could prevail on them to separate. Some would start to retire, but the cry of distress would call them back again; and in this state we were long detained. After leaving the chamber, the distress was so great, it was almost impossible to prevail on them to retire. At length all retired but one, who, in great agony, tarried through the night: but many who came from a distance remained over night in the neighbourhood.

"May 24.—This evening attended a meeting at Mr. G——'s. A number sobbed and wept.

"May 25.—This evening met again at the same place. One who formerly thought he had obtained a hope, but lost it, was again awakened, and at the close of the meeting cried aloud. He professes to have found relief, but I think without any good evidence of a change of heart. I fear he has again deceived himself.

"May 26.—This evening met the young converts in a social meeting, and began to hear a relation of their Christian experience.

"May 27.—This afternoon held a general meeting of the young converts, and of all others who chose to attend; the object of which was, to address the subjects of this work on the nature of a public profession of religion. Spoke of the duty; the qualifications requisite; and stated and answered objections. The duty: 1. To God. 2. To yourself. 3. To the Church. 4. To the world, &c.

"May 28, Sabbath.—Preached thrice to a crowded, attentive, solemn, and yet joyful audience.

"May 29.—This evening met nearly 200 in a meeting for inquirers. This meeting was anticipated by many with secret dread. Some Christians (doubtless, among the rest, those who were present and witnessed the scene of distress at the last inquiry meeting) were heard to say, that they dreaded to attend this evening; they could hardly endure the thought of passing through such a scene of distress a second time. And I can truly say, that, for the first time, I felt the same reluctance. But, to the astonishment of all, instead of an anxious, we had a joyful meeting. Most of those in such distress at our last meeting for inquirers, had found relief, and were exceeding joyful. What an astonishing change in one week! I felt that it could hardly be possible. We had lost our anxiety, and had little else to do but to render united thanks to God for what He had done. But before we parted, I went round and collected into a circle a number who were without hope, conversed with each one, addressed the whole, and prayed with and for them, as those professing no hope. This was evidently the means of deepening their impressions.

"May 30.—This evening met in the schoolhouse. The room was crowded, and the audience were still, solemn, animated, and joyful. The same was the general character of our meetings after this date.

"From this time we spent a number of half days and evenings in hearing a relation of their Christian experience, preparatory to a public profession. These were interesting and animating seasons, affording the best opportunity of learning the human heart in all its foldings of depravity and opposition; and the astonishing change wrought by the power of God's grace.

"June 25, Sabbath.—This day sixty-eight made a public profession of religion, thirty-two of whom were baptized. At this time, more than a hundred had, to appearance, become the subjects of divine grace. A number more have since publicly professed Christ; and of these, five young men are preparing for the Gospel ministry."

This sketch was drawn up by Mr. Nettleton, a few months after he left Nassau, from brief memoranda which he kept at the time. It is, on the whole, a good specimen of the revivals which occurred under his preaching. In not less than forty or fifty places there were revivals in connexion with his labours, quite as interesting as this; and in some of them, the hopeful converts were twice or thrice as numerous.

When he first went to Nassau, he expected to remain there but a short time. This circumstance induced him to hold meetings more frequently than he did in ordinary cases; and as he was obliged to close his labours there in about two months from the time the revival began, and as the church was destitute of a pastor, he admitted some of the converts to the church sooner than he was wont to do. With these slight exceptions, the foregoing sketch will give the reader a very good view of his ordinary course of proceeding, and of the effects which accompanied his labours.

CHAPTER VII.

OTHER SIX CONGREGATIONS VISITED — LETTERS TO YOUNG CONVERTS—TESTIMONY OF EYE-WITNESSES.

In the summer of 1820, there was some unusual seriousness in *New Haven* and in *Yale College;* and at the earnest solicitation of the pastors, Mr. Nettleton again visited that city. He arrived August 5, and, as appears from his journal, continued his labours there, with some occasional absences, until the December following.

The *Religious Intelligencer* of September 2, contains the following notice of the state of religious feeling in New Haven at that date :—

" Reports have doubtless gone abroad, that a revival of religion has commenced in this city. We have felt desirous to communicate this good news to our readers, that they might rejoice with us; but believing that ill effects are sometimes produced by a premature disclosure, when a revival has but partially commenced in the hearts of individuals, or in a community, we have heretofore observed a silence on this subject, waiting to see what the Lord was about to do for us. A revival of religion has been felt in the hearts of some Christians in this place for some time past; and they have had a holy confidence, that a shower of divine grace was about to be poured out, in answer to their prayers, on this dry and thirsty place. We have seen the cloud like a man's hand, and we now hear the sound of abundance of rain; verily the Lord is among us, convincing of sin, of righteousness, and of judgment—many are pricked in the heart, some are rejoicing in the Lord, and convictions and conversions are daily multiplying. The power and the mercy of God are extensively felt in College; and many of the dear youth have been brought to submit to the sceptre of Immanuel, and many others are bowed down under a sense of sin, and are anxiously inquiring what they must do to be saved. We cannot be more particular at present. Christians, pray for us. Forget not that there are nearly three hundred young men of talents in this college, and their hearts are in the hands of that God who hears your prayers, if you are Christians. May we be humble, and rejoice in the Lord, and wait for His salvation!"

The following letter to the young converts at Nassau, was written by Mr. Nettleton five days after the above statement was published:—

"NEW HAVEN, *September* 7, 1820.

"MY DEAR FRIENDS,—The moment I take my pen to address you, I imagine myself seated in the midst of that same dear circle. Every name and every countenance appears familiar. The inquiry meeting, the crowded assembly, the heaving sigh, the solemn stillness, and the joyful countenances, awaken all the tender sensibilities of my heart. My dear friends, no friendship, no attachment in this world, is equal to that created in a revival of religion.

"'The fellowship of kindred minds
Is like to that above.'

"What is felt at such a season is an anticipation of the joys of the heavenly world. I doubt not your hearts retain the sweet recollection of what Paul hints to the Ephesian converts: 'Who hath raised us up together, and made us sit together in heavenly places in Christ Jesus.' But, my dear friends, after all, *the milk and the honey lie beyond this wilderness world.* A voice from heaven is heard: 'Arise ye, and depart, for this is not your rest.'

"By this time some of you begin to learn, that you are on the field of battle. The world, the flesh, and the devil, are potent enemies. You will have need to buckle on the whole armour of God. But whatever may betide, never, *no never*, think of dropping the subject. True, the conflict may be sharp, and the pathway to heaven steep and difficult; but, brethren, *the time is short.* The conflict will soon be over. Think not so much about present enjoyment, as about present duty.

"I must give you a short account of the revival in this place. Meetings are held every evening in the week—crowded, still, and solemn as eternity. Every Monday evening we meet the anxious ones in a large ball-room. We have had from sixty to about three hundred assembled at these meetings, all solemn, and many in deep distress of soul. The cloud of divine influence has gone rapidly over our heads, and covered us with awful solemnity. And there is the sound of abundance of rain. The fields have whitened everywhere, and we are in danger of losing much of the harvest, because we cannot reap everywhere at once.

"We visit by appointment, and make a number of visits in a day at a given hour. We sometimes meet ten or fifteen, and sometimes thirty at once. We converse a little with each one, speak a word to all in general, pray, and pass on to another circle; and so we spend our time. Our visits are generally short, except one which will never be forgotten. This was August 25, at two o'clock, P.M., at the house of Mr. B——. We entered the house at the time appointed, and found about twenty persons sitting around the room in pensive silence. All had been more or less anxious for a number of days, and one was in awful distress. This one I addressed more particularly, and urged the duty of immediate repentance,—not without some hope that relief would be obtained on the spot; for I felt sure that this state of feeling could not long be sustained. While pressing the conscience of this sinner, I found that this distress had spread nearly throughout the circle. I detained them the usual time, and advised them all to retire home to their closets. Some started and went out of the door, and others sat still with heavy hearts. Very soon Emily returned, exclaiming: 'Oh! I cannot go home, I dare not go. I shall lose my concern. What shall I do?'—and threw herself down in a chair, and her head on the table, in the deepest agony. All at once she became silent, and gently raised her head with a placid countenance, and was heard to say in a mild tone of voice: 'Oh! I can submit, I can love Christ. How easy it is! Why did I not do it before?' We sat in silent amazement. Every word sunk deep into our hearts. We felt the conviction that God was there. She seized her next companion by the hand, and with all the tenderness becoming a fellow-sinner, began to press those very truths which had so distressed her own heart,—the duty of immediate repentance and submission to God. Every word became an arrow. I felt that the work was taken out of my hands, for I perceived that God had made her the most powerful preacher. All at once A—— became silent, and lifted her head with a countenance beaming with joy. 'The Saviour has come, oh! how happy!' This sent fresh alarm through every heart. And now A—— and E—— unite heart and hand, and begin with H——, who had been in deep distress for some time. They urge, with all the tenderness and firm decision of those who had felt the conviction, the necessity and reasonableness of immediate repentance and submission to God. The subject pressed harder and harder, and harder still, when all at once H—— was brought out of darkness into marvellous light. These three now unite heart and hand, and with one voice bear testimony to the same heart-rending truth, that God is right, and the sinner wrong. The time would fail me to finish the story of this visit. We met at two o'clock, P.M., and were detained more than three hours. Suffice it to say, I never saw or heard of such an afternoon visit before, for the one half has not been told. At the close, we began to look about us to see and inquire, *What hath God wrought?* We brought them into one circle. I said: Is it possible? This is too much! Had I not seen it, I could not have believed it. For nine of those who entered the room in deep distress were now rejoicing in hope. The anxious ones had retired, and we were left in a circle of young converts, if they are not deceived.

Not a hint had been given that one soul had experienced religion, or had any reason to hope. This was the feeling: 'It is right I should love and serve God; and this I intend to do, whether saved or lost.' Oh! it was a delightful circle,—humble, tender, affectionate, and joyful. They appeared like children of the same great family.

"About eighty have been brought to rejoice in hope in this city during five weeks past. Besides these, about twenty-five students in Yale College have become hopeful subjects of divine grace. But we much fear the bustle of commencement. It would be nothing strange if all our prospects of a future harvest should be blighted before another week shall end. Pray for us. My love to all my dear friends in Nassau, and tell them how I long to see them. *Live near to God. Live in peace, and the God of love and peace shall be with you.* In short, '*Only let your conversation be as it becometh the Gospel of Christ, that whether I come and see you, or else be absent, I may hear of your affairs, that ye stand fast in one spirit, with one mind, striving together for the faith of the Gospel.*'—Yours, as ever."

The reader will observe, that in describing the scene of thrilling interest which occurred at the house of Mr. B——, Mr. Nettleton says: "*Not a hint had been given that one soul had experienced religion, or had any reason to hope.*" This accords with his uniform practice. He never told persons that they had reason to hope. He would set before them, with great plainness, the distinguishing evidences of regeneration, and enjoin it upon them to be faithful and honest in the application of these evidences to themselves.

The reader may be curious to know what became of these nine individuals, who were thus suddenly, and almost simultaneously, brought to rejoice in hope; and the suspicion may perhaps have crossed his mind, that with most of them the change was the effect of sympathy, and would be only temporary. This, however, appears not to have been the case. There is evidence that they all gave very satisfactory evidence of piety. Five of them have departed this life; all of whom died peacefully, and some of them very triumphantly. Those who survive, it is believed, continue to adorn their Christian profession. Of two that are dead,—viz., Susan B. Marble, and Adeline Marble, interesting memoirs were published. Susan B. Marble was the youngest of the nine, being in the fourteenth year of her age. She died February 4, 1821, the day on which she, with one hundred other individuals, was to have been received into the church. She appears to have been a youth of remarkably amiable disposition. Her biographer, speaking of her state of mind while under conviction, says: "It was peculiarly interesting to converse with her at this time. A person ignorant of the natural character of man, as delineated in the Scriptures, would think that one so young and amiable could need nothing new; yet, according to the estimate of the Saviour of sinners, she still lacked one thing. This she felt and deplored. What chiefly distressed her was the sinfulness and hardness of her heart, and its opposition to God.

I quote this remark for the purpose of turning the attention of the reader to the fact, that those who were converted under Mr. Nettleton's preaching, however young, and however amiable, were brought to see *the sinfulness and hardness of their hearts, and their opposition to God.*

In a letter from Mr. Nettleton to Mrs. Parmele, of Bolton, dated May 15, 1822, there is a touching allusion to the scenes above described.

"You recollect reading an account of the death of Susan B. Marble, in New Haven. She was one of the nine who were brought out rejoicing in an afternoon's visit. When I was in New Haven last, Betsey Bishop, another of that number, died. She was an interesting youth. I had then so far recovered my health, that I went to the conference-room, and addressed the people on the subject of her death, and alluded to that interesting afternoon. A number of that same circle called to see me one evening, and to talk over the interesting event. They used to meet frequently by themselves, and converse and pray together. It was a little band of love. Adeline Marble, Susan's sister, was one of this happy number. She was present at that evening visit—still clad in mourning. Last evening, I saw from the paper that she, too, has *gone to her long home.* I retired, and could not but weep—'Child of mortality.' Thus, three of these blooming youth have found an early grave. Had you seen them as I have, you too would weep as well as rejoice."

The *Religious Intelligencer* for October 7, contained the following statement in relation to the progress of this revival:—

"We mentioned not long since, that a revival had commenced in this city. Since that time, God has done great things for us, which has given joy on earth, and, we believe, great joy in heaven. Since the commencement of this glorious work of grace, there have been, within the bounds of charity, about two hundred souls, belonging to the two Congregational societies, including about thirty in College before its recess, who have been called out of darkness into marvellous light. This, when compared with the five preceding years of dearth, will be considered as the *commencement*, at least, of a glorious harvest. And we still hope for greater things than these. Truly, this is the Lord's doing, and it is marvellous in our eyes. He works like himself, and none can hinder. The blindest infidel must see and acknowledge that it is the work of God; and could he witness our assemblies, where three or four hundred are convened for the purpose of inquiry, and behold the solemnity and the distress for sin, we think he would feel that the Lord was there; and could he behold the same company of convicted, trembling sinners, in smiling crowds, rejoicing in the mercy of God in Christ Jesus, he would be equally convinced that the same Holy Spirit who convinced them of sin, is, when the sinner has submitted, the blessed Comforter which Christ promised to send.

"The work is still in progress. It is the still small voice that convinces of sin. 'The wind bloweth where it listeth; we hear the sound thereof; but cannot tell whence it cometh or whither it goeth.' We have no new Gospel, no other terms of salvation than those that have always been held out for acceptance. The sinner has been taught invariably that he must not look for comfort without submission. And such has been the faithfulness of our spiritual teachers, that, in most cases, those who have been slain by the law, and brought to despair of climbing up some other way, have been led directly to the Saviour, who is the Way, the Truth, and the Life; and who has always been ready and willing to receive them."

This revival continued for many months, and spread into all the surrounding region. In the *Religious Intelligencer* for June 9, 1821, was the following statement:—

"On the last Sabbath, twenty-six were added to the church under the pastoral care of the Rev. Mr. Merwin,—making, in all, about three hundred added to the Congregational churches in this city, as fruits of the revival. We trust a goodly number more will still come over from the ranks of the enemy, and publicly avow their friendship for Him who has said: 'Whosoever shall confess me before men, him will I confess also before my Father which is in heaven.'

"Since the revival commenced in this city, it has extended to most of our neighbouring towns. Out of thirty-one congregations in the county of New Haven, at least twenty-five have been visited, during the past winter and spring, with the special presence of the Lord; and it is estimated, that within these limits between fifteen hundred and two thousand souls have been called, by His grace, out of nature's darkness into marvellous light."

Mr. Nettleton confined his labours to *New Haven* and *Yale College* until the 18th of September, when he repaired to North Killingworth, his native place. He returned to New Haven, October 10, and continued there about a week, preaching several times. He laboured there also for a season in the month of December.

His labours were greatly blessed in *North Killing-*

worth. He went there from New Haven, September 18. He mentions in his journal, that on the 25th of that month he attended an inquiry meeting, at which sixty-two were present. From this time the work became very powerful and rapid in its progress. On the 29th, thirty were rejoicing in hope; and on the 23d of October, there were ninety rejoicing.

The Rev. Asa King, who was at that time pastor of the church in North Killingworth, in a letter dated July 16, 1844, says: "That ever-to-be-remembered revival commenced about the last of August, in a Bible class, which, for some months, I had weekly attended; and it had been in pleasing progress for some time before brother Nettleton's arrival, when, under his labours, it received a fresh impulse, and went forward with unusual power. As he used occasionally to visit his native place, to rest awhile from the exhausting labours of a revival, I had the privilege of gathering many useful hints from his communications; and I am free to say, that to him, under God, I am very much indebted for the measures I adopted, and for the course which, with a good degree of success, I pursued, before he came to my assistance. After spending several weeks at North Killingworth, he was called to New Haven, and then to Wethersfield, and visited us only occasionally.

"The hopeful converts were one hundred and sixty-two,—one hundred and seven of whom united with the church at the communion season in January, and soon after twenty-five more,—making, in all, one hundred and thirty-two. So far as I have known, with very few exceptions, they have been careful to maintain good works.

"The influence of that revival upon the church was very happy. It produced unanimity of sentiment on doctrinal points about which they had long contended, and cordiality of feeling where there had been prejudices of long standing. Though brother Nettleton was a 'prophet in his own country,' yet I doubt whether in any place his labours were more highly appreciated than they were by those who had known him from his childhood."

In the months of October and November he preached a few times in *North Madison*, where was a very interesting revival of religion, which was greatly promoted by his labours.

At the earnest solicitation of the Rev. Dr. Tenney, on the 23d of December 1820, he came from New Haven to *Wethersfield*, where a work of grace had already commenced. He laboured here with great success for three or four months, occasionally visiting other places in the vicinity.

The *Religious Intelligencer* for April 13, 1822, contains an account of this revival, written by Dr. Tenney, from which the following is an extract:—

"Previous to the revival, our church consisted of about two hundred and sixty members. As its fruits, precisely two hundred more have been added. Of this addition seventy-nine are heads of families. Sixty-two are males, and thirty-two are young unmarried men, who, with ten previously in the church, make forty-two. A number of others have indulged hope who have not professed religion. Generally, the subjects of the work still appear well. Some instances of conversion have been strongly marked. The awakening of some has been sudden and powerful, and has soon issued in triumphant peace. In others it has been as the still small voice. One individual, who had been a total disbeliever in Revelation, began and continued to examine the subject of religion with all the coolness of a mathematician, until, in the course of a few weeks, the great truths of Scripture bore upon his conscience with insupportable power, and had almost that 'keen vibration' through his soul which makes hell; and his heart yielded to God. One aged man said: 'If I have ever been born of God, it was on the day I was seventy-six years old.' Another said respecting himself: 'It was the day when I was sixty-eight.' In one family, a mother of eleven children, who had long gone to the table of Christ, mourning that of her great family there was not one to accompany her, now hopes that eight of her children, and two children-in-law, are the children of God. In another family, consisting of parents and seven children, all have indulged hope, excepting one son who was absent at sea. Two of these are united to a different denomination. A widow, the mother of seven children, some of them pious years ago, now has hope of all the others: the whole family belong to the church. Nearly at the very time that a woman experienced religion at home, her husband experienced it at sea. Of the nature and joy of their next meeting let Christians judge.

"Greatly are we indebted to a number of neighbouring ministers, whose labours here were of great use. Peculiar are our obligations to the Rev. Asahel Nettleton, who was much with us, and whose labours were blessed eminently and extensively. To us and the churches in this region he has been of as great use as were to ancient Israel their chariots and horsemen. Though in this work there has been the strongest coincidence between the means used and the success, and between the prayerfulness of Christians and the conviction and conversion of sinners, yet God has displayed His glorious sovereignty as well as faithfulness. Here, and in this section of the country, God has illustriously displayed His perfections in the work which is emphatically His. To Him all the glory is due. To Him let it be given now and evermore."

While in Wethersfield, Mr. Nettleton laboured a part of the time in *Newington*, a parish in the town of Wethersfield, under the pastoral care of the Rev. Joab Brace. Here, as in other places, his labours were accompanied by the outpouring of the Spirit of God. There is an account of the revival in this place, published by Mr. Brace, in the *Religious Intelligencer* for May 11, 1822. The following is an extract from this account:—

"In the summer of 1820, an uncommon emotion was felt. There was *a sound in the top of the mulberry trees;* and although the indication was not distinctly understood at the time, yet the result has proved that God had then actually gone forth. A number of serious persons were under distressing apprehension of ruin as coming on this place, and they cried unto the Lord for help. Several women of the church privately instituted a weekly concert in the closet, to implore the outpouring of the Holy Spirit. A few sinners were uneasy, and yet without very definite impressions; and there was no awakening of a decisive character until three or four months after this period.

"This religious concern may be traced to Wethersfield, and thence to New Haven, where the present series of revivals appear to have commenced in the summer of 1820. In Wethersfield the work appeared with some distinctness in October, and in November it began to be spoken of abroad; but there was no visible effect in this place. I thought it would be a local work, as revivals in this vicinity had generally been in former times, and did not suppose that any measures were to be taken for extending it among our people; but it is of great benefit that neighbouring ministers and people visit frequently a place favoured with the energy of the Spirit of God. The people heard with awe of what God was doing in the first parish in this town; some persons went over to their meetings, and were distressed at the thought of this place being still passed by. Above all other means, what raised the general attention, was the coming of the Rev. Asahel Nettleton, on the last of December, 1820, as unexpectedly as a messenger from heaven, apparently commissioned from the Almighty Head of the Church, and accompanied by the Holy Spirit. Next morning he preached on 'Being ashamed of Christ.' This fixed a listening ear. In the afternoon he dwelt upon the causes of alarm to awakened sinners. In the evening the assembly was crowded, and the attention profound. His text was, *Behold, I stand at the door and knock.** The discourse was closed with surprising effect by repeating the hymn, 'Behold, a stranger at the door.' When prayer was ended, while the people were standing, he made a very close application of the subject to their hearts in a short address, which was very silently and solemnly heard. He requested them to retire without making a noise.

* Notes of this discourse are given in a subsequent chapter.

'I love to talk to you, you are so still. It looks as though the Spirit of God were here. Go away as still as possible. Do not talk by the way, lest you forget your own hearts. Do not ask how you like the preacher; but retire to your closets, bow before God, and give yourselves to Him this night.' After the benediction, he inquired of many persons individually: 'Have you made your peace with God? Do you calculate to attend to this subject?' Many promised that they would try to make their peace with God immediately—that they would repent that night; and a permanent impression was made. From this the flame spread over the parish—the current of feeling was turned—the people gathered around their minister with peculiar attachment—meetings were crowded and solemn—the things of eternity filled the people with awe. The work of God seemed to be in almost every house. Mr. Nettleton continued his visits from the last of December to the first of April with a beneficial influence, which, it is hoped, will be felt in the world of glory.

"Friday, January 26, 1821, was observed by the church as a special fast, in which they were joined by almost the whole congregation. It was a solemn season, and, as we hope, a day of new life to some souls. In the evening, at sunset, a meeting for inquirers was held at my house, under the direction and management of Mr. Nettleton, while I met the church at another house for prayer. In the meantime, a great congregation had assembled at the meeting-house, many from the neighbouring parishes; and there Mr. Nettleton discoursed with great effect upon the story of the woman that washed the Saviour's feet with her tears,—Luke viii. 37 to the end of the chapter. At this time experimental religion had become the great theme of reflection and conversation, and it seemed as though all my people were pressing into the kingdom of heaven; numbers were every week embracing the hope that they had passed from death unto life. . . The characteristics of the work may be thus stated: There were some instances of deep distress, but none of that overwhelming kind in which subjects faint or fall to the ground, or are unable to leave their seats. In some cases convictions were long continued; in others, the heart was speedily bowed. Some, after long distress, rose almost imperceptibly to a faint hope, in others, the hope was bright and satisfying. No instances of extravagant joy occurred, though several were much elevated. In convictions the subjects were much affected with their guiltiness before God, as with fear of everlasting destruction. When the sinner was humbled, he acknowledged his great depravity, his desert of eternal condemnation, and his entire dependence on sovereign grace in the sight of God, and was pleased with the idea of unconditional submission to the will and glory of God. One prominent feature in the converts was a fear of deception. Much was said on the danger of false hopes, which probably had an influence to check flights of joy; for they were much and anxiously inquiring how far the adversary might possibly beguile. . . . .

On the whole it has been a serious and delightful season. Many souls, we hope, have been truly brought home to Christ; but also many, we fear, have quenched the Holy Spirit, and taken up their portion in this world; still, prayer is made without ceasing for them.

During Mr. Nettleton's stay with us, this place was a common centre of divine entertainment, in comparison with which all the pleasures of this world are faint and feeble. The multitudes who flocked in from the neighbouring congregations appeared to feel themselves richly repaid for their pains; and some of them carried home the spirit, where it spread and operated powerfully, until the region appeared like the garden of God."

February 18, 1821, Mr. Nettleton commenced his labours in *Farmington*. The results which ensued may be learned from the following account, written by the Rev. Dr. Porter, pastor of the church in that place, and published in the appendix to Dr. Sprague's *Lectures on Revivals*:—

"The year 1821 was eminently, in Connecticut, a year of revivals. Between eighty and a hundred congregations were signally blessed. From the commencement of the year a new state of feeling began to appear in this town. On the first Sabbath in February, I stated to the assembly the tokens of the gracious presence of God in several places of the vicinity, and urged the duties peculiarly incumbent on us at such a season. This I had often done before, but not with the same effect. Professors of religion now began evidently to awake. They had an anxiety for themselves and for the people that would allow them no rest. In their communications with each other and with the world, they were led spontaneously to confess their unfaithfulness; and a few without the church, about the same time, were pungently convicted. In this state of things Rev. Mr. Nettleton made us his first visit. His preaching, on the evening of a Lord's day in this month, from Acts ii. 37, was sent home by the power of the Spirit upon the hearts of many.* His discourse on the Wednesday evening following, from Gen. vi. 3, was blessed to the conviction of a still greater number. As many as fifty persons, it was afterwards ascertained, dated their first decided purpose of immediately seeking their salvation from that evening; and it is worthy of remark, that the same sermon was preached on the following week to two other large and solemn assemblies in the adjoining parishes, with no special effect that could afterwards be traced. The fact probably was, that here it convinced numbers whom the Spirit was already striving with them, and that then was their day. 'A word spoken in due season, how good is it!' At a meeting of the anxious on the evening of Feb-

* The following is a fragment of the close of the discourse here referred to:—

"And here permit me to ask, Are there any who are listening to my voice who begin to feel that they are condemned, and that not one of their sins is pardoned? If out of Christ, let me tell you, your fears are not without foundation. You are condemned, and, oh! that thou might realize it more and more! Again; Do any of you begin to fear that you are exposed to eternal punishment? If out of Christ, your fears are not without foundation. It is even so; and, oh! that you might realize it more and more! Again; Do any of you begin to realize the uncertainty of life? Do you tremble lest you should be suddenly cut down by the stroke of death, and hurried into a miserable eternity? If out of Christ, your fears are not without foundation. You are in just such danger. You know not what a day may bring forth. And, oh! that you might realize it more and more! Again; Do any of you begin to fear that you never shall be pardoned Let me tell you, your fears are not without foundation. It is yet an awful uncertainty whether your sins will ever be pardoned. And, oh! that you might realize it more and more!

"Again; Do any of you fear that the Spirit of God may cease to strive with you? Your fears are not without foundation. There is great danger that the Spirit will cease to strive. Many who were as anxious as you are, have gone back to stupidity, and have lost their souls. Do any of you begin to realize that you shall never do anything to better your condition short of repentance? It is a correct conclusion. You never will. If you have anything to do before you repent, I beg that you will make haste and do it soon; for, after all, you must repent or perish.

"Do any of you begin to realize that you are altogether without excuse

ruary 26, there were present about a hundred and seventy. Here were persons of almost every age and class—some who, a few weeks before, had put the subject of serious piety at a scornful distance, and others who had drowned every thought of religion in giddy mirth, now bending their knees together in supplication, or waiting in silent reflection for a minister of the Gospel to pass along, and tell them individually what they must do. Twelve were found to have lately become peaceful in hope, and a great number to be powerfully convicted of sin. From this time so rapid was the progress of the work, that at the next similar meeting, March 12, there were present a hundred and eighty, (the room would hold no more,) of whom, fifty supposed that since the commencement of the revival

for not repenting now? It is even so. Hardness and impenitency of heart are awful sins in the sight of God. Do any of you begin to feel that if you do not repent now, you never shall? This, in all probability, is a correct conclusion. If you now resist the Spirit, and turn back to stupidity, there is the greatest reason to fear that you will slumber on in impenitence till you perish.

"I perceive that all my hearers are going to be under conviction of sin. It may not be to-day or to-morrow Perhaps it will not be in this life. Oh! that it might be! How much better to be awakened now, while pardon is offered, than when the day of grace is past!

"But those who are not convinced of sin now, will be hereafter They will be convinced of all their sins; and it will be conviction that will be succeeded by no conversion, but will last for ever. 'Behold! the Lord cometh with ten thousand of His saints, to execute judgment upon all, and to *convince* all that are ungodly among them of all their ungodly deeds which they have ungodly committed, and of all their hard speeches which ungodly sinners have spoken against Him'

"'Sinners, awake betimes; ye fools, be wise;
Awake before this dreadful morning rise;
Change your vain thoughts, your crooked works amend,
Fly to the Saviour, make the judge your friend;
Lest, like a lion His last vengeance tear
Your trembling souls, and no deliverer near.'"

The sketch of the other discourse, on Gen. vi. 3, is also preserved in his *Remains;* but is so meagre as to give no idea whatever of what it must have been when spoken they had become reconciled to God; and a week afterwards I had the names of more than ninety who indulged the same persuasion concerning themselves.

"The state of feeling which at this time pervaded the town was interesting beyond description. There was no commotion, but a stillness in our very streets, a serenity in the aspect of the pious, and a solemnity apparent in almost all, which forcibly impressed us with the conviction that, in very deed, *God was in this place.* Public meetings, however, were not very frequent. They were so appointed, as to afford opportunity for the same individual to hear preaching twice a-week, beside on the Sabbath. Occasionally there were also meetings of an hour in the morning or at noon, at private dwellings, at which the serious in the neighbourhood were convened, on short notice, for prayer and conference. The members of the church also met weekly, in convenient sections, for prayer, and commonly on the evenings selected for the meetings of the anxious. From these various meetings the people were accustomed to retire directly, and with little communication together, to their respective homes. They were disposed to be much alone, and were spontaneously led to take the Word of God for their guide. The Bible was preferred to all other books, and was searched daily with eager inquiry.

"Mr. Nettleton continued with us, except during a few short intervals, till about the middle of April. To his labours, so far as human instrumentality was directly concerned, the progress of the revival must be chiefly ascribed. The topics on which he principally dwelt were the unchangeable obligations of the divine law; the deceitful and entirely depraved character of the natural heart; the free, indiscriminate offers of the Gospel; the reasonableness and necessity of immediate repentance; the vanity of those excuses to which awakened sinners are accustomed to resort; and the manner, guilt, and danger of slighting, resisting, and opposing the operations of the Holy Spirit. His addresses were not formal discussions, first of one, and then of another of these subjects; but a free declaration of the truth of God concerning them all, just as they lie in the course of spiritual experience, and would best subserve the particular end which he was labouring at the time to gain. They were too plain to be misunderstood, too fervent to be unheeded, and too searching and convincing to be treated with indifference.

"It was a favourable circumstance that, among the first subjects of the work, there was a large proportion of the more wealthy and intelligent class. A considerable number of youths, belonging chiefly to this class, had just finished a course of Biblical instruction, for which I had met them weekly for more than a year. These, with scarcely an exception, at the very commencement of the revival, embraced the Gospel which they had learned, and, by their experience of its power, commended it to the families where they belonged. Within about three months, I suppose, there were about two hundred and fifty members of the congregation who supposed that they had passed from death unto life. On the first Sabbath in June, a hundred and fifteen were added to the church, and, at subsequent periods, a hundred and twenty besides. Of these a few have since been rejected, and others have declined from their first love. But I have not perceived that a greater proportion of hopeful conversions in this revival than in others, previous or subsequent to it, have proved unsound. Many have died, and many have removed from our immediate connexion; but those who remain now constitute the chief strength of the church."

This account was written in 1832, eleven years after the revival.

The *Religious Intelligencer* for 1st September, 1821, gave an extract of a letter, dated 16th July of the same year, in which is the following brief notice of this revival:—

"Of all the revivals that I have ever witnessed, none have so deeply interested my heart—none appear so strikingly to manifest the power of God, or the excellence of the Christian character, as that with which Farmington has been blessed. Oh! I have often thought, while residing among this people, what glorious work a revival of religion would make in this town! The blessed effect of such a work I have now witnessed; and it is beyond anything I could have had faith to pray for. The change in the moral aspect of things is astonishing. Many who have been very far from God and righteousness, have, as we humbly hope, recently been brought nigh by the blood of His Son. Some, whose moral condition once appeared hopeless, are now in their right minds at the feet of Jesus. Many of the professed devotees of Mammon have recently parted with all for Christ. A large class of this community have been eagerly engaged in the pursuit of riches; and their clashing interests, combined with these feelings of selfishness and pride which avarice fosters, have produced, as might be expected, quarrels among neighbours, and much hostility of feeling. The quelling of this hostile spirit was among the first visible effects of the Spirit of God. Of many who have formerly been not even on speaking terms, it may now be said, as it was of the early disciples: 'See how these Christians love one another!' Let any person witness the glorious effects which this work of grace has produced in Farmington, and still disapprove of a revival of religion, and it would not be difficult, I think, to decide to whose kingdom that person belongs."

CHAPTER VIII.

ABOVE TWENTY CONGREGATIONS BLESSED—TESTIMONIES TO THE WORK.

In the year 1820, there was a revival of religion in *Pittsfield, Mass.* The Rev. Dr. Humphrey, late President of Amherst College, was pastor of the church in that town. The religious attention had subsided, and the revival was supposed to be at an end, when, in the spring of 1821, under the preaching of Mr. Nettleton, God again appeared in His glory to build up Zion. There is an account of this revival, from the pen of Dr. Humphrey, in the sixth volume of the *Religious Intelligencer*, of which the following is part:—

"Early in the month of May, the Rev. Asahel Nettleton, whose name is so familiar both to the friends and enemies of revivals, came to this town to 'rest awhile,' and to await the future calls of Providence. But he was not to remain long inactive; and the three or four weeks which he thought of spending in retirement here, were prolonged through as many months of unceasing labour. By the middle of May there was some excitement; but whether it was the effect of mere curiosity, or of the Spirit beginning to move on the hearts of the people, it was at first impossible to determine. For a fortnight or more, nothing very decisive took place. Which way the scale would turn, was to us altogether uncertain. Everything appeared to be hushed into silent and anxious expectation. It was the stillness that precedes an earthquake, though the subsequent shock was neither sudden nor violent.

"In the latter part of May, we ventured, though with considerable solicitude, to appoint a meeting for the inquiring, if there should be any such in the congregation. Nearly twenty attended, and some of them were found to be under very serious impressions. No professor of religion was invited or expected to attend. It was a meeting exclusively for those who were beginning to realize their exposure and their guilt. The next meeting was better attended; and it was found that a few were sinking in the deep waters of conviction.

"From this time the work solemnly and steadily advanced, particularly in the heart of the town, where the strong man armed had, for a long time, kept his palace. He lifted up his voice to summon the mighty to his standard; but it was in vain, for the God of Jacob was with us. So far was the enemy from making any impression upon the camp of the faithful, that his own ranks were thinned and disheartened by the desertion of many on whom he had placed great reliance, and of whose unshaken allegiance he had confidently boasted.

"During the whole month of June the revival grew more interesting and decisive every day. Many were rejoicing in hope, and more were alarmed at their own stupidity and danger. The voice of prayer

was heard, for the first time, in several of our principal families. Not less than five domestic altars were erected in one day. In this state of things, and when religion was the principal topic of conversation in all circles, whether large or small, it was natural for those who felt a new and deep interest in the subject, to wish for an appropriate celebration of the Fourth of July; and arrangements were accordingly made for a prayer meeting at sunrise, and a public religious service in the afternoon. The prayer meeting was well attended. At two o'clock our large house of worship was filled, and we had the pleasure of meeting there many of our Christian friends from different and even remote parts of the county. The audience was solemn, notwithstanding . . . . . .
But here let me draw a veil over the painful interruptions which we experienced. Charity hopeth all things, *endureth all things;* and he is but a poor soldier who can be frightened by mere powder. It is due to justice to state, that all the respectable people in the town (whatever some of them might think of the expediency of such a celebration) strongly disapproved of whatever tended to disturb us in our worship. But God meant it for good. Through the riches of His grace an impulse was that day given to the revival, which was long and happily felt, and which we shall have reason to remember, with no ordinary emotions of wonder and gratitude, for a great while to come. Instances of conviction and conversion became more frequent than they had been; and from this time the work continued, with little abatement, though never so rapid in its progress as some revivals, till the month of October.

"The third Sabbath in September will not be forgotten by the present generation in Pittsfield; for 'that Sabbath day was an high day.'

"To see more than eighty persons, and one-half of them heads of families, rising up to enter into covenant with God and His people—to look round and see who they were, and think where some of them had been—to behold them coming forward, high and low, rich and poor together, and kneeling to receive the baptismal seal—to hear their song—to witness their emotions, and to welcome them for the first time to the table of the Lord—oh! it was a scene which I shall not attempt to describe! We had our aged Simeons and Elizabeths there; and, we doubt not, there was joy in heaven. A solemn awe and stillness pervaded the great congregation; and some sinners were that day awakened by what they saw and heard in the sanctuary."

In the foregoing account there is allusion to what took place on the Fourth of July. A description of that scene was given by a person who was present, in a letter to the editor of the *Charleston* (South Carolina) *Intelligencer*. The facts were these: The opposers of religion finding that a *religious* celebration of our National Independence was agreed on, resolved to have a political celebration. They occupied the church in the morning.

"At two o'clock," says the above mentioned writer, "they who loved the Lord and respected His ordinances, began to assemble in the same place. The church was crowded. While the people were assembling, and as they passed near the rioters, crackers were repeatedly exploded in order to intimidate them.

The service began. It went calmly and sweetly forward. The Rev. Mr. Humphrey, the pastor, took his text from John viii. 36: '*If the Son, therefore, shall make you free, ye shall be free indeed.*'

"He had not proceeded far, when the word '*fire*' was given; and our ears were suddenly stunned, and the congregation startled, by the report of cannon. It was the attack of the adversary; and it was well kept up. But, unfortunately for him and his agents, every shot preached louder than ten thousand thunders. Meanwhile the drums beat, and the fifes played, and the soldiers marched back and forth before the church door, animated moreover by the music of the cannon, and the prospect of a glorious triumph over the cause of God. But, alas! they were labouring hard to defeat themselves. Some few Christians, indeed, of delicate frame and quick sensibilities, were agitated and alarmed; and others, though not intimidated, dreaded the consequences of this violent attack; but generally, there were high hopes that this tumult would be overruled for good. And so it was. So skilfully did the preacher allude to and apply his discourse to the conduct of the opposition out of doors—such advantage did he take of every blast of the cannon and every play of the drum, by some well-pointed remark, that it all went like a two-edged sword to the hearts of listening sinners. Indeed, Mr H—— afterwards informed me, that, had he shewed the heads of his sermon to his opposers previously, and earnestly requested them, when he had reached such a point in his sermon, to *fire*, and when he reached another point *fire*, they could not more effectually have subserved the purpose of his discourse than they did. Those gentlemen who had walked in the opposers' procession, hung their heads, were disgusted, and, in some instances, were convicted deeply of sin. One gentleman, who had been previously somewhat serious, declared to me, that every shot of the cannon pierced his soul, filled him with a kind of indescribable horror, and brought him, through the blessing of God, to such a hatred and detestation of sin in himself and others, as constrained him quickly to fly to Christ.

"I confess I trembled for the ark of God. Indeed, I was so uneasy, that after the sermon was concluded, I went and expostulated with the ringleader, whose companion in wickedness I once had been, and over whom I thought I might have some influence. But I had reason to believe, that in general the spirits of the children of God were perfectly unruffled. I sat near the Rev. Mr. Nettleton, and so delighted was he with the discourse, and so accurately *prescient*, too, was he of the result, that whenever an apt allusion dropped from the lips of the preacher, he would turn round with a holy smile, and whenever a shot from the cannon pierced our ears, he would say—it would involuntarily escape from him: '*That is good—that is good.*' Speaking afterwards of the events of this day, he observed to me: '*Did you not feel calm? I thought there was a deep and majestic calmness overspreading the minds of Christians.*' I found that very many did indeed feel so. Nothing could be more appropriate, or more naturally arise out of his text, than Mr. H——'s description of the miserable bondage in which those out of doors were faithfully serving their master.

"The ministers looked forward with an alternation

of hope and fear to the *meeting of inquiry*, as that meeting was generally esteemed a kind of spiritual thermometer, by which the degree of warmth and feeling in the society could be measured. This was held for an hour previously to the evening service. The time arrived. It was crowded—never so full before. The daring and outrageous attack in the day had driven many to the place in which he that appeared was always supposed to be asking: '*What must I do to be saved?*' This question was emphatically asked in the meeting. It was found that a most powerful impulse had been given to the revival. Nor was this impulse at all weakened by the evening service.

"The house was overflowing. You were there. You marked the progress of things. Mr. Nettleton that evening put forth his mightiest efforts. His discourse was one continued flash of conviction. He spoke from that part of Genesis xix. which treats of the destruction of Sodom. '*Up, get ye out of this place,*' was closely and powerfully applied; and when he had given a full account of the nature and circumstances of Lot's expostulations with his sons-in-law, he came to speak of the awful stillness which remained over Sodom while Lot was taking his leave. Oh! then, when all his warnings were despised, and they would not believe a word he said, then—then when Lot was safely out of Sodom—what a terrible storm of fire ensued! You remember he turned the heads of the audience completely towards the windows. They involuntarily looked round to see the conflagration—to see Sodom in flames. It was quite overpowering.

"This was an eventful and glorious day for Pittsfield. From that time forward Emmanuel spread His trophies among great and small. They who thought to crush the work of God were bitterly disappointed, and retired with shame. The fruits of this revival are *one hundred and forty converts.* Praise the Lord!"

While Mr. Nettleton was labouring in Pittsfield, he preached frequently in *Lenox.* With what success will appear from the following statement of the Rev. Dr. Shepard, pastor of the church in that place:—

"In the spring of 1821, Dr. Nettleton came to Pittsfield, in consequence of an invitation from Dr. Humphrey. Dr. Nettleton was in poor health; and Dr. Humphrey invited him to his house, with the hope that, by being relieved from pressing calls, he might recover his health. When Dr. Nettleton first came to Pittsfield, he took no part, I believe, in religious meetings. After awhile, he preached once or twice in the course of a week. His preaching was soon attended with a divine blessing, and was undoubtedly instrumental of a revival of religion in Pittsfield and several other towns in the vicinity. When I was from home on a journey, Dr. Nettleton preached in *Lenox* on the Sabbath, and two or three times in the course of the week after; and, on my return, I found a revival begun, and progressing in the town. Many were awakened, and some were rejoicing in hope. He afterwards preached occasionally in my parish, as his engagements elsewhere permitted. The number of hopeful converts who were received into the church, as the fruits of that revival, was ninety-one. Almost all of them continued to adorn the doctrine of God their Saviour, by the virtues of a sober, righteous, and godly life. '*These,*' as I find stated in my church record, '*These are the fruits of a revival of religion in this town last summer. Rev. Asahel Nettleton was apparently instrumental of great good in that season of refreshing from the presence of the Lord. May the Lord reward him for his labours of love; and may we, as a church, be more humble and prayerful; and may God, in His sovereign mercy, continue to shed down His divine influence here!*'

"You ask: 'What were the characteristics of his preaching, and in what did its chief excellencies consist?' I answer: He held no protracted meetings; nor did he adopt any new measures apparently for *effect.* His labours consisted principally in preaching the *Word.* He sometimes appointed what was called an Inquiry Meeting. At such meetings he manifested an almost instinctive discernment of character; and his remarks, in accordance with it, were sometimes attended with a powerful effect. In his preaching, his humility was apparent to all. He was, I believe, eminently a man of *prayer.* That he entered the pulpit or the inquiring meeting directly from the 'mount of communion' with his Maker, no one would readily doubt who was witness of the holy calm, the indescribable, the almost unearthly solemnity and earnestness of his manner. His countenance was peculiarly expressive, his demeanour was dignified, and his voice was at times very melodious. The joy with which his heart seemed to be filled by a contemplation of the love of Jesus, in giving His life a ransom for sinners, marked his preaching, and imparted an unction and uncommon energy to his eloquence. When he spake of the glories of heaven, it was, *almost,* as if he had been there himself. When he made his appeals to the sinner, he made them with a directness which placed before him, as in a mirror, his utterly lost state. It seemed, at times, as if he was about to uncover the bottomless pit, and to invite the ungodly to come and listen to the groans of the damned; and then, drinking deeply of the spirit of his Master when He wept over Jerusalem, to urge them to flee from the wrath to come, with an expression of countenance which it is not in my power to describe. Many who came with a sceptical and cavilling spirit to hear him, had their attention arrested at once to the great truths communicated by him, and, at the close of the meeting, were anxiously inquiring what they should do to be saved. The success attending his preaching seemed, in short, to be a plain and clear illustration of all the distinguishing doctrines of the Gospel by a humble, devout, praying, unpretending man, constrained to his duty by the love of Christ.

"The influence of the revival upon the interests of the Church in this and other places, was very happy, and is plainly to be seen, especially in regard to the faith once delivered to the saints, up to this time. The tendency of Dr. Nettleton's preaching, and, indeed, of all his labours here and elsewhere, as far as I have learned in regard to them, has been to establish the churches in the faith and order of the Gospel, and to strengthen the hands of every clergyman with whom he laboured. I never heard that any minister, among whose people Dr. Nettleton laboured, ever expressed any regret that he had been with them. On the contrary, when I at any time meet with a minister who formerly had assistance from Dr. Nettleton, especially in a season of revival, he never fails to express great respect for him, and unfeigned gratitude for the benefit derived to *him* and *his people* from his labours."

In the month of August he spent a few days in *Lee*. In the letter of Dr. Hyde, published in the Appendix to Dr. Sprague's *Lectures on Revivals*, there is a brief notice of his labours in that town. Dr. Hyde says: "In the summer of 1821, there was an evident increase of solemnity in the church and congregation, and some individuals were known to be anxious for their souls. This appearance continued for several weeks, under the same means of grace which the people had long enjoyed; but none were found who rejoiced in hope. The church often assembled for prayer; and in the month of August, we observed a day of fasting and prayer. The meeting-house was well filled, and a deep solemnity pervaded the congregation. The hearts of many seemed to 'burn within them,' and there were increasing indications in the rising cloud, 'of abundance of rain.' We began to hear from one and another a new language—the language of submission to God.

"At this interesting crisis, the Rev. Asahel Nettleton spent a few days with us. He preached five sermons to overflowing assemblies; and his labours were remarkably blessed. The Spirit of God came down upon us 'like a rushing mighty wind.' Conversions were frequent, sometimes several in a day; and the change in the views and feelings of the subjects was wonderful. At the suggestion of Mr. Nettleton, I now instituted what are called *inquiry meetings*. More than a hundred persons attended the first. These meetings, as I found them to be convenient, were continued through this revival; and I have ever since made use of them, as occasion required,—sometimes weekly for many months in succession."*

Mr. Nettleton continued his labours in Berkshire county, making Pittsfield the principal theatre of his operations, until about the middle of August, when he returned to Farmington, where he spent a few days in delightful intercourse with his Christian friends; and then, in the early part of September, repaired to Litchfield. He had laboured much in *Litchfield* at different times previously, in connexion with the Rev. Dr. Beecher. His labours at these different periods were highly appreciated, both by Dr. Beecher and his people, and were evidently blessed to the salvation of many souls. In the autumn of 1821, Dr. Beecher was obliged to suspend his labours, and travel for his health. At this time, Mr. Nettleton supplied his pulpit from the beginning of September till the middle of January 1822. When he commenced his labours, he found things in a very unpromising state. A bad state of feeling existed in the church, and great spiritual apathy pervaded the congregation. But it was not long before things began to assume a new aspect. The church seemed to awake out of sleep, and to mourn over their backslidings. A spirit of prayer

* Dr. Hyde makes a further statement worth quoting, in order to shew that in all these revivals the truth taught was the plain, well-known Gospel:—"The ruined and helpless state of sinners, the exceeding wickedness of their hearts, and the awful consequences of neglecting the great salvation, have been explicitly stated on these occasions, and pressed on the minds of the inquirers. They have not been directed to take any steps *preparatory* to their accepting of Christ: but, being acquainted with the nature and terms of the Gospel, repentance towards God and faith in Him who came to seek and to save that which was lost, have been enjoined upon them as their *immediate duty, and only safe course.*"

was poured out upon the people of God; and sinners began to inquire what they must do to be saved.

Soon after the revival commenced, some events occurred which he feared would divert the attention of the people from the great concerns of the soul. One was a cattle show, and another a military review But this unhappy result was prevented by the blessing of God on his prudent management. He particularly feared the effect of the military review on certain young men who were military officers, and whose minds were seriously impressed. He requested those individuals to meet him on the morning of that day at the early dawn. They came. He told them that he was convinced that the Spirit of God was striving with them, but he feared that their impressions might be dissipated by the bustle of that day. He warned them to be on their guard—to refrain from all vain and trifling conversation—and especially to avoid tasting a drop of ardent spirits. He then affectionately and earnestly commended them to God in prayer. This timely warning had the desired effect.

The following extract of a letter of his, dated Litchfield, October 15, 1821, shews the state of the revival at that date:—

"I have attended many meetings of late, and some of them crowded and awfully solemn. More attend meetings than can crowd into the lower part of the meeting-house—more, it is said, than usually meet on the Sabbath. I think I may say, there is great solemnity throughout this place. A number are in deep distress of soul—some of them men of influence. About fourteen are rejoicing in hope. I have ventured to appoint one meeting of inquiry. About one hundred attended; but they were not all under conviction. We are truly in an interesting state, trembling between hope and fear. I wish I had time to tell you a number of anecdotes about us in Litchfield."

In another letter written by him at New Haven, in March 1822, he thus speaks of the revival at *Litchfield*:—

"The number of hopeful converts is about seventy, of whom thirty-eight have made a profession of religion. There is much Christian feeling in that place, and the work is gradually advancing, as a joint letter from a number of the young converts has recently informed me."

In January 17, 1822, Mr. Nettleton again visited *New Haven*, and laboured with great success in the city and college, between two and three months. The following is an extract of a letter written by him at New Haven, March 20, 1822:—

"After more than a year's absence, I have come again to New Haven. In the first place, I made an appointment exclusively for young converts in a spacious ball-room, where we used to hold meetings of inquiry. Though the evening was dark and muddy, about three hundred assembled. Here we called to mind the sighs, and sobs, and songs, and *joys that are past*—scenes never to be forgotten. And when I spoke of three of their number who used to mingle their tears and joys with theirs on that floor, but whose faces we should see no more, for they had gone triumphantly to rest, it was truly melting. We knelt, and wept, and prayed together.

"I did not intend to tarry long in this place; but I

have preached more than twenty times, and attended a number of inquiry meetings; at one, one hundred and sixty attended. There are seventeen recently rejoicing in hope, and five of them are students in college."

On May 12, 1822, Mr. Nettleton commenced his labours in *Somers*. He laboured in this town and South Wilbraham alternately, occasionally preaching in Tolland and some other towns in the vicinity, until the following October, when his labours were suddenly arrested by a dangerous sickness. A powerful revival of religion commenced under his preaching at Somers, which spread into the surrounding region. The Rev. William L. Strong was pastor of the church in Somers. In a letter to the editor of the *Religious Intelligencer*, dated August 1, 1822, he gives the following account of the state of things among his people, and the people of *South Wilbraham*, an adjoining town:—

"DEAR SIR,—I am prompted by my own feelings, and by a knowledge of your solicitude to communicate to the public such information as relates to the enlargement of Christ's kingdom, to announce the fact, that God is in the midst of us displaying the wonders of His grace. About eight weeks since, it began to be manifest that the Spirit was moving upon the hearts of God's people, and that sinners were no longer indifferent to the momentous question of the trembling jailer. Soon the voice of distress was heard; and soon, too, it was mingled with that of rejoicing and praise. The work has been still and powerful. Between ninety and a hundred are rejoicing in hope. At our last meeting of anxious inquiry, about one hundred and seventy were present, including sixty who hope that they have recently passed from death unto life. The work is still spreading, and has, perhaps, never been more interesting than at the present moment.

"In South Wilbraham, adjoining this place on the north, God is also doing a great work. Nearly forty have, within a few weeks, taken up hopes; and the revival is extending itself with singular power. These are the Lord's doings, and they are marvellous in our eyes. To Him be all the glory.—Yours very respectfully,

WM. L. STRONG."

The following is an extract from a detailed account of the revival in South Wilbraham, published in the seventh volume of the *Religious Intelligencer*:—

"In the early part of May last, the Rev. A. Nettleton (who, under the providence of God, has been the great instrument in this work) retired from New Haven to Somers—the town adjoining this on the south—for the purpose of recovering his strength, which was much impaired by sickness. A few weeks after he arrived, a report reached this people, that there was some religious excitement at Somers, and that a Mr. Nettleton was there attending one or two evening meetings during the week. Indeed, it was shortly announced, that there were several persons anxious for their souls. Awakened by principles of curiosity, some of the young people of this place concluded to go down and test the verity of these reports. The evening fixed upon was Friday, June 21; and a number, at an early hour, repaired to the house of worship in Somers. To their astonishment, they found a crowded audience, and awful solemnity pervading it. The subject of humble submission to Christ was effectually enforced. To some of these visitors it proved to be a word in season. One young person was in such deep anxiety as to be unable to return, and therefore tarried in one of the families in the neighbourhood. The next day she expressed a hope of having passed from death to life. This, together with other circumstances, awakened with Mr. Nettleton an interest in the people of South Wilbraham, which, I may safely add, was by many heartily reciprocated. Express invitations were, at this time, as well as previously, forwarded by the minister and individuals of this people, urging Mr. Nettleton to visit South Wilbraham.

"Tuesday, 25.—Mr. Nettleton, this afternoon, for the first time, consented to have an appointment made for him in the village hall at South Wilbraham, at sunset. This appointment, though of few hours' previous notice, like an electric shock, reached every extremity of the society. At the set time, the hall was literally crowded, and multitudes yet assembling. Mr. Nettleton took his station, from which, in the hall, little else was to be seen than a dense surface of expressive countenances; and, at the same time, from the windows might be seen trees and roofs of adjacent buildings occupied by anxious hearers. Subject—*Ground of alarm to awakened sinners.* Many were awakened to anxiety this evening. During this and several succeeding weeks he laboured alternately in South Wilbraham and Somers.

"July 9.—At the close of public services this evening, several of our most interesting youth were deeply affected with a sense of their situation as sinners. One young female, who had sacrificed many of the evenings of the winter past in the ball-room, and who highly valued her excellency in that amusement, was this evening overwhelmed with a sense of her guilt. As she dwelt some distance from the village, she was invited by one of her companions residing near to spend the night with her. At the midnight hour a request was sent to Mr. Nettleton to repair to this house. It was thronged with spectators of the scene of distress there exhibited. He found this young female sustained in the arms of her friends, and in a piteous and doleful tone repeatedly exclaiming: 'Lord Jesus, have mercy on my soul!' The next day, while in a circle of young persons with whom Mr. Nettleton was conversing, she, with one or two others, expressed joy and peace in believing.

"Thursday, 11.—This afternoon Mr. Nettleton met sixty or eighty in an anxious meeting—an awful scene of distress. From this we repaired to the church, where he addressed us on the danger of grieving the Spirit of God. It was indeed a heart-searching subject. The sighs and sobs of anxious sinners were to be heard from every part of the house. When the speaker dismissed his audience, a large number rushed toward him, as if expecting assistance from an arm of flesh. In this situation Mr. Nettleton addressed them about five minutes, and requested them to retire as silently as possible. Some individuals were so overwhelmed with a sense of eternal realities, that it became necessary to urge, and even assist them home.

"The whole number expressing hope at this time

is about one hundred.* Sixty-five are propounded as candidates for admission to the church on the first Sabbath of October next.

"This revival has extended its influence to many of the adjacent towns. In Somers and Tolland there are two hundred and fifty subjects hopefully."

At the close of the foregoing account mention is made of *Tolland.* Here Mr. Nettleton laboured considerably, and with great success, in the months of August and September.

The following extract of a letter written by him, November 27, 1823, shews that this revival became very extensive in the eastern part of Connecticut:—

"The revival of religion in the eastern part of the State of Connecticut has, perhaps, never been more interesting than within a few weeks past. I propose to give you the outlines of this work from the commencement down to the present. It has heretofore been a common remark among Christians, that revivals have been much less frequent and less powerful in the eastern than in the western part of this state. Most of these churches, in years past, have been favoured with seasons more or less reviving, but never with such a general and powerful refreshing from the presence of the Lord. This work commenced in Somers, June 1822, and has continued increasing and spreading like fire, from house to house, and from heart to heart, with more or less power and rapidity, until the present moment. The following towns are contiguous, and have shared in one extensive revival.

"In Somers, one hundred and fifty have hopefully been made the subjects of divine grace. In South

* This account is dated September 25, 1822.

Wilbraham, one hundred. In Tolland, one hundred and thirty. In *North Coventy*, one hundred and twenty. In *South Coventy*, *North Mansfield*, and *South Mansfield*, about one hundred in each. In *Columbia*, forty. In *Lebanon*, ninety. In *Goshen*, thirty. In *Bozrah*, between sixty and seventy. In *Montville*, ninety. In *Chaplin*, fifty. The work has recently commenced, and is advancing with power in *Hampton*, and within a few weeks, fifty or more are rejoicing in hope. Within a few weeks past, the Spirit of God has descended with overwhelming power in *Millington* and *Colchester*. In the former place about seventy, and in the latter, sixty are already rejoicing in hope. They have never before witnessed the like in rapidity, power, and extent. In the above cluster of towns, all contiguous, more than thirteen hundred souls have hopefully experienced a saving change, in the Congregational churches, since the commencement of this revival; and of these more than eight hundred have already made a profession of religion.

"In *Chatham*, also, the work is interesting; about seventy are rejoicing in hope, and fifty or more have made a public profession. In *Hampton*, *Colchester*, and *Millington*, many are now anxious for their souls, and inquiring, *What must we do to be saved?*

"New instances of conviction and of hopeful conversion are daily occurring in these towns. The prospect of the continuance and spread of this work is as favourable now as at any period, if not more so. The Lord hath done great things for Zion, whereof we are glad, and let all her friends humbly 'rejoice and thank His name together.'"

CHAPTER IX.

SPECIMENS OF DR. NETTLETON'S PREACHING.

HERE we may rest awhile in our survey of the amazing labours of this evangelist, and give a few specimens of his preaching, *so far as that can be done;* for the truth is, that while he thought much, felt deeply, and digested thoroughly all he spoke, he committed little to writing. His biographer adds, that to write became, in the end, to him an irksome employment. Outlines of many sermons were found among his manuscripts, but almost none fully written out. And then, we are told, there was that in his manner of delivery which gave astonishing interest and efficacy to his words; but of which nothing can be learned by reading his discourses, even if we had them accurately taken down.

None can convey to others the tone and spirit with which a man speaks to his fellow-sinners, when enabled to "preach the Gospel *with the Holy Ghost sent down from heaven*," (1 Pet. i. 12.) Old men in the west of Scotland who heard *Whitfield* preach, have told how he brought tears to their eyes by the manner in which he uttered, "O Glasgow, Glasgow!" as if enabled to enter into his Master's feeling, when he cried: "O Jerusalem, Jerusalem!" And it is recorded of that old divine, Perkins of Cambridge, by his hearers, that when he uttered in their ears the word "*Damned!*" they went away with the echo of it in their hearts for many a day. There was something of this in *Nettleton* also. There seems to have been subduing solemnity in his ministrations. The awe of God fell upon the people. It was as if they were filled first with *Bethel-like* fear: "How dreadful is this place!"—and then brought to *Bethel-like* holy joy: "This is none other than the gate of heaven!"

But though we cannot exhibit the peculiar secret of this evangelist's power, it is useful to give some specimens of his style, and of the truth he preached. One thing will strike every reader,—namely, that there is not one single peculiarity of language. He uses not one uncommon word, nor ever seeks for any but the most natural figures. The fervour of his kindled soul arranges his ideas, and expresses them in plain and obvious words; but the thoughts themselves are great, and heaped up like masses of dark clouds. And when he reasons, or answers objections, every one feels that he wields the Word as "*a hammer* that breaketh the rock in pieces."

We select, then, a variety of extracts, fitted to give some idea of the substance and style of his discourses. They are all taken from Dr. Bennet Tyler's volume of "*Remains.*" In reading these, we have sometimes felt the wish, that Dr. Nettleton had more frequently brought forward the person and work of the Saviour when rousing sinners to flee, as well as shut them up to the necessity of going to Him alone.

Here is a sketch of a sermon on JOHN iv. 29.

The words are: "*Come, see a man which told me all things that ever I did;*" and are thus laid out:—

"1. The duty of preachers. It is to tell sinners their hearts. '*He told me.*'

2. Preaching which discloses the hearts of sinners, is likely to be remembered. It will be remembered and conversed upon, while other preaching and other things are forgotten. '*She saith to the men of the city, He told me all things.*'

3. The preacher who tells sinners their hearts, is not likely to want for hearers. The invitation will be given: '*Come, see the man which told me.*'.

4. The conversion of one sinner is likely to be followed by the conversion of others. The invitation '*Come,*' &c., was complied with, and a great spiritual harvest followed."

LECTURE ON LUKE xvi. 19-31.

Here is the close of what we would call "A Lecture on the Rich Man and Lazarus." Having given a general exposition of the whole, he draws the following truths out of it:—

"1. *Those who die Christians go immediately to heaven.*

2. *Those who die sinners go immediately to hell.*

3. *We learn from this subject that all sinners will pray sooner or later.*

4. *Those who lose their souls will remember what took place on earth.*

(The following heads we give at length:—)

5. We see what the damned would say were they to come back to this world.

They could not state what they have seen and felt, better than in the language of the Bible. They could not describe the torments of the lost in better language than they are described in the text. They would call upon their companions to repent, lest they come to the place of torment. This, we know, is the substance of what they would say.

6. We learn that sinners in hell are not yet entirely convinced of the awful depravity of the human heart. The rich man thought that moral suasion, if increased to a certain amount, would be sufficient to bring sinners to repentance. 'If one went unto them from the dead, they will repent.' But he laboured under a mistake.

7. Finally. We learn from this subject that our Saviour was a very plain preacher. 'Never man spake like this man.' Some think they should like to hear Christ preach. But while it is true that He spoke in the most melting strains to the penitent, it is also true that none ever preached so much terror to the wicked. Who is it that says: 'Wide is the gate, and broad is the way which leadeth to destruction, and many there be who go in thereat?' Who is it that says: 'Because strait is the gate, and narrow is the way which leadeth unto life, and few there be that find it?' Who is it that says: 'Ye serpents, ye generation of vipers, how can ye escape the damnation of hell?' Who is it that speaks of the worm that shall never die, and of the fire that shall never be quenched? Who is it that describes, in language inimitable, the solemnities of the last judgment: 'Then shall the King say to them on His left hand, Depart from me, ye cursed, into everlasting fire, prepared for the devil and his angels?' The discourse before us, of the rich man and Lazarus, is also a specimen. How solemn it

would be if a departed soul should come back from the invisible world, and enter this congregation! Do you wish to hear what such a soul would say? You shall be gratified. The Saviour holds him up, and makes him now speak to sinners in this congregation. He knows all the feelings of every damned soul in hell, and can tell us just what he would say. He holds him up to your view, and permits you to hear him speak. You hear him plead for one drop of water. You hear him beg that Lazarus, or some glorified saint, may be sent to warn you. Oh! with what importunity does he press upon you the duty of immediate repentance! 'Nay, father Abraham, but if one went unto them from the dead, they will repent.'

And now you hear a voice from heaven proclaim —and let it sound in every ear—let it ring in every conscience: '*If they hear not Moses and the prophets, neither will they be persuaded though one rose from the dead.*'"

In a Lecture on LUKE xv. 3-7, after a continuous series of remarks on the words, he comes to the lessons, and they are:—

"1. Sinners are lost. If they were not lost, Christ would not have come to seek and save them. 'For the Son of Man is come to seek and to save that which was lost.' And since He has come from heaven to earth and shed His precious blood to save them, they 'will not come to Him that they might have life.' They are out of His fold, having no part or lot in His kingdom. 'He that believeth on the Son hath everlasting life; and he that believeth not the Son shall not see life; but *the wrath of God abideth on him.*' They lie in the open field, exposed to the storm of divine wrath which is coming upon the world of the ungodly. They are wandering farther and farther from God, and every moment liable to fall into the pit of destruction. They are lost, and yet totally insensible of their condition.

2. Christ knows His own sheep before they are brought into His fold. The good Shepherd knows just the number that are missing. If one of them be gone astray, He knows it. Indeed, He would not go after it, did He not know it was gone, and would not, of itself, return. He says: 'Other sheep I have, which are not of this fold; them also I must bring, and they shall hear my voice; and there shall be one fold, and one shepherd.' He knows who they are, and what are their names. 'He calleth His own sheep *by name*, and leadeth them out.' He knows how far they have wandered in the paths of sin and folly. His eye is ever upon them, and follows them in all their wanderings. Is there one more lost sinner in this place to be saved? Where is he? What is his name? Christ knows. Yes; 'The foundation of God standeth sure, having this seal, The Lord knoweth them that are His.'

3. Christ finds the sinner. He finds him in his sins—careless about his soul—casting off fear and restraining prayer—wandering farther and farther from God, from happiness, and from heaven. He often comes upon him by surprise in the midst of his wickedness, and awakens him to a sense of his guilt. He trembles and is alarmed; but he is unwilling to

return, and would fain flee out of the Saviour's hand. No sinner will ever awaken himself. Left to himself, not another sinner in this house will ever begin in earnest to seek the salvation of his soul. 'The wicked, through the pride of his countenance, will not seek after God.' 'There is none that understandeth, there is none that seeketh after God.' Every Christian knows this to be true in relation to himself. He knows that, after he was awakened, if the Spirit of God had left him, he should have returned to his sinful courses. All who have found the Saviour will acknowledge that the Saviour first found them. 'Since we have known God, or *rather, are known of God*,' is the language which they are ready to adopt.

This parable may serve to correct a very common mistake among sinners, and, I may add, among some professors of religion. They often think they are seeking Christ, and wonder why they fail of success, when they are actuated only by the fear of hell. They think they are following hard after Christ, and that He is departing from them. They flatter themselves, that if they hold on their way they shall soon overtake Him. They take it for granted that they are *ready* and *willing;* and they are now labouring hard to make Christ willing. But the very reverse is true, as we are taught in this parable. Sinners are departing from Christ; and in order to find Him, they must not hold on their way, but stop, and turn. They are all as sheep going astray; and the great Shepherd and Bishop of souls is calling upon them to return, saying: 'Turn ye, turn ye, for why will ye die?' When He finds them, He finds them wandering farther and farther from Him. And when they hear His voice, it is *behind them*, saying: 'This is the way, walk ye in it.'

4. How great must be the joy occasioned by the repentance of one sinner! It is contrasted with that over just and holy beings who need no repentance. Joy so great was never occasioned by any other created being as that occasioned by a repenting and returning sinner. Joy so great was never occasioned by an angel of light. Gabriel, who stands in the presence of God, never occasioned so much joy in heaven. We may number ninety and nine holy angels, and then say: 'There is joy in heaven over one sinner that repenteth, more than over these ninety and nine just persons.' The creation of the world was a joyful event, when 'the morning stars sang together, and all the sons of God shouted for joy.' But this is not to be compared with the joy over one sinner that repenteth. The earth itself was created to subserve God's purpose of saving sinners—as a stage on which to display the wonders of redeeming love to an admiring universe. 'To the intent that now, unto principalities and powers in heavenly places, might be known by the Church the manifold wisdom of God.' If it be asked: Why did the Son of God become incarnate? In the repentance of a lost sinner you have the answer. 'He came to seek and to save that which was lost.' 'He came not to call the righteous, but sinners to repentance.' Why did the angels announce to the shepherds the news of His birth, and sing: 'Glory to God in the highest?' In the repentance of a lost sinner you have the answer.

Nor is this joy confined to angels. The Lord himself rejoices. Why did the Son of God leave the bosom of His Father—condescend to be born in a manger—and to suffer and die on the cross? In the repentance of a lost sinner you see the glorious object which He had in view accomplished. For this He bled and died. Here He sees of the travail of His soul, and is satisfied. This is the fruit of His toil, His shame, His sufferings, and His death. 'Who for the *joy* that was set before Him, endured the cross, despising the shame.' Every Christian, in his turn, has occasioned this joy in heaven.

5. The repentance of every sinner, when first discovered, is the cause of new joy. The joy of angels is most sensibly felt every time one more is added to the company of the redeemed. The ninety and nine already redeemed seem to be forgotten, when, with wonder and joy, they behold their new companion, with whom they expect to dwell for ever. Could we know, as well as angels do, the reality of a sinner's repentance, we should know better how to rejoice. The tidings of his repentance must be received by Christians on earth with mingled emotions. They 'rejoice with trembling.' While they delight in each other, the news that a soul is converted to God excites in them peculiar joy. For a time they seem to forget themselves and each other. They cannot forbear to assemble and rejoice together on the occasion. And well they may, for Christ himself rejoices; and He says unto His disciples: 'Rejoice with me, for I have found my sheep which was lost.'

6. What must have been the hearts of the Scribes and Pharisees who stood murmuring, while publicans and sinners drew near to Christ to hear the

gracious words which proceeded out of His mouth! While angels in heaven were rejoicing over these sinners there they stood *murmuring*. What a contrast! Angels, and the Saviour himself, and all holy beings, were rejoicing over the repentance of these sinners; but they stood murmuring and finding fault, and saying: 'This man receiveth sinners, and eateth with them.' How must their conduct have appeared to angels and to God!

My hearers, had you been present on this occasion, what part would you have acted? Would you have rejoiced at the sight of sinners flocking to the Saviour, and weeping for their sins? Or would you have joined with those that murmured? Bring the subject home to your hearts. How would you like to see sinners flocking to Christ in this place? Are your hearts prepared to welcome a scene like this? Scenes similar to this may now be in the recollection of many present. At least you must have heard of the conviction and conversion of sinners—some of them perhaps of your own acquaintance. And how did the news affect your hearts? Did you hear the news with angelic joy, or with sullen sadness? I would put the question to the consciences of all my hearers. How does the subject of the conviction and conversion of sinners affect your hearts? It is a subject in which God, and Christ, and the Holy Spirit, and saints, and angels, are all interested. All heaven is moved at the repentance of one sinner. And, my hearers, if your hearts are not deeply interested in this subject, it is because you have no claims to the Christian character. Beware of deceiving yourselves in a matter of such infinite moment. If you cannot rejoice in the repentance of sinners, you have none of the spirit of Christ. If you cannot rejoice at the repentance of other sinners, you have never yet repented of your own sins. Your hearts are not right in the sight of God. For those who die with such hearts there is no happiness and no heaven hereafter. If such tidings vex the heart, and grate on the ear now, and if you would fain fly from such a scene, whither can you go at the solemn hour of exchanging worlds? Can you enter heaven and be happy there? Heaven is filled with this joyful theme. There the tidings of the conversion of every penitent on earth will be told. And every saint, and every angel that sings in glory, will proclaim it in loud hosannas around the throne of God and the Lamb. There, too, the story of your own repentance must be told, ere you leave this world, or *you* can never join the company of angels and the spirits of just men made perfect.

To all my impenitent hearers in this assembly let me say: You have seen what a lively interest angels take in the repentance of *one sinner*. Will there ever be joy in heaven over *your* repentance? Wherever the Gospel is preached with the Holy Ghost sent down from heaven, there angels are hovering round to witness the effects. 'Which things the angels desire to look into.' Yes, angels attend on our worshipping assemblies to witness the effect of a preached Gospel.

> 'Invisible to mortal eyes they go,
> And mark our conduct, good or bad, below.'

Sinners, these heavenly messengers are now waiting to carry back the tidings of your repentance to the courts above. And shall they stoop, and gaze, and wait in vain? Have you no tears to shed for your sins?

'O ye angels! hovering round us,
Waiting spirits, speed your way,
Hasten to the court of heaven,
Tidings bear without delay;
Rebel sinners
Glad the message will obey.'"

One full-length discourse may be desirable, and such is the following, so far as it has been preserved:—

"SOME WHO ARE LIVING, GREATER SINNERS THAN SOME WHO ARE IN HELL.

LUKE xiii. 1–5.—'There were present, at that season, some that told Him of the Galileans, whose blood Pilate mingled with their sacrifices. And Jesus answering, said unto them, Suppose ye that these Galileans were sinners above all the Galileans because they suffered such things? I tell you, Nay; but except ye repent, ye shall all likewise perish. Or those eighteen, upon whom the tower in Siloam fell, and slew them; think ye that they were sinners above all men that dwelt in Jerusalem? I tell you, Nay; but except ye repent, ye shall all likewise perish.'

It is extremely natural for mankind to talk and complain of the sins of others. This we have all had occasion to witness. The same propensity existed in the days of our Saviour. 'There were present, at that season, some that told Him of the Galileans, whose blood Pilate had mingled with their sacrifices.' The fact to which they alluded was this:—A number of Galileans refused subjection to the Roman government. And on a certain occasion, while they were assembled for religious worship, Pilate sent a company of armed soldiers, who slew them, and mingled their blood with their sacrifices. The persons who related this fact to our Saviour did it, doubtless, with feelings of self-complacency. This led Him to address them in the language of the text, which suggests the following thoughts :—

I. Some sinners have already perished.

II. They perished through their own fault.

III. The greatness of their sufferings is proof of the greatness of their criminality. But,

IV. The greatness of their sufferings is no evidence that they were greater sinners than those who are spared.

I. Some have already perished. Of this the text is sufficient proof. 'Except ye repent, ye shall all *likewise* perish.' What a vast multitude perished in the time of the general deluge! And they were not only drowned, but they were damned. They are now spirits in prison. The inhabitants of Sodom perished. And they were not only destroyed from off the earth, but were cast into hell, and are now 'set forth for an example, suffering the vengeance of eternal fire.' That some have perished, is evident from the story of the rich man and Lazarus. This was intended to give us a correct view of the invisible world. 'The rich man died and was buried, and in hell he lifted up his eyes, being in torment.' 'Are there few that be saved?' 'Strive to enter in at the strait gate, for many, I say unto you, shall seek to enter in and shall not be able.' Compare the character and conduct of multitudes who have died, with the declarations of Scripture, and we shall be compelled to admit the truth of the proposition we are considering. The fact, indeed, is acknowledged by all who believe the Bible, that some sinners have already perished.

. . . . . .

II. They perished through their own fault.

God never inflicts undeserved punishment. 'Shall not the Judge of all the earth do right?' The very fact that they suffer, is proof that they were sinners, and deserved to die. 'Who ever perished being innocent?' The fact that all are sinners, shews that all deserve death. But this is not all. Even after they had sinned and deserved death, they might have been saved if they would. That they were not, was peculiarly their own fault. They had the offer of pardon. They were invited, entreated, and warned. The inhabitants of the old world were warned by the preaching of Noah, and by the strivings of the Spirit. The inhabitants of Sodom were warned by Lot. But they perished through their own neglect. *They did not repent.* The sinner sometimes says: What have I done that I should deserve death? It is not merely for *doing*, but for *not doing*, that the sinner must die. It is on the ground of neglect that Gospel sinners perish. They did not repent. 'Except ye repent, ye shall all likewise perish.' 'He that believeth not shall be damned.' 'If any man love not our Lord Jesus Christ, let him be Anathema Maranatha.' The Bible does not say: How shall we escape if we lie, and swear, and cheat, and steal? but, 'How shall we escape if we *neglect* so great salvation?' It places the sinner's condemnation on the ground of neglect.

Nor can the sinner plead that he would repent if he could. He is as really criminal for not repenting, as for his overt acts of wickedness. 'Then began He to upbraid the cities wherein most of His mighty works were done, because they repented not.'

. . . .

III. The greatness of their sufferings is proof of the greatness of their criminality.

They suffer only for their crimes. In this world, God often, and indeed always, inflicts punishment for less than the sinner's real desert. But in inflicting punishment, either in this world or the world to come, He never exceeds the measure of the sinner's desert.

God has selected and set forth some sinners of the human race, as 'examples to those who should thereafter live ungodly.' The old world and Sodom are specimens. Their punishment was awful. But awful as it was, it did not exceed the greatness of their iniquity. In the greatness of their punishment we may read the greatness of their guilt. . . .

. . . .

IV. The greatness of their sufferings is no evidence that they were greater sinners than those that are spared.

When God inflicts heavy judgments upon a people, we are apt to conclude that it is because they are greater sinners than others; and some seem to suppose, that if any are sent to hell, it must be only sinners of the worst kind—such as all would pronounce monsters in wickedness. This was the opinion of those whom our Lord addressed in the text. They supposed that the Galileans, on whom God permitted Pilate to inflict such signal vengeance, must have been greater sinners than others who escaped these sufferings. But this conclusion was erroneous. 'Suppose ye,' said our Lord, 'that these Galileans were sinners above all the Galileans because they suffered such things? I tell you, Nay.' There were sinners then living in Galilee whose crimes were as great as the crimes of those who had suffered the wrath of Heaven. Sinners who had gone to hell from Galilee were no worse than sinners then living there.

The same was true of the inhabitants of Jerusalem. 'Or those eighteen, on whom the tower in Siloam fell, and slew them, think ye that they were sinners above all men that dwelt in Jerusalem? I tell you, Nay; but except ye repent, ye shall all likewise perish.' Sinners who had gone to hell from Jerusalem were no worse than some who were then living in that city.

Again; sinners to whom our Saviour preached in Chorazin, Bethsaida, and Capernaum, were as great sinners as some who were then in hell. This our Lord explicitly told them. 'But I say unto you, it shall be more tolerable for the land of Sodom in the day of judgment, than for you.' This sentiment was then true in our Saviour's day. Sinners of other countries and of other times, who had gone to hell before them, were no worse sinners than many of the Jews then living. Indeed, our Saviour gave them to understand, that a more fearful doom awaited them than that which had overtaken the inhabitants of Sodom, although they 'are set forth for an example, suffering the vengeance of eternal fire.'

Let us bring the warning home to this congregation. Suppose ye that sinners who have died and gone to hell from other places, were sinners above all the sinners dwelling in this place? 'I tell you, Nay; but except ye repent, ye shall all likewise perish.'

To all of you who have not yet repented, this subject speaks a solemn warning. What think ye of sinners now in hell? Suppose ye that they were greater sinners than yourselves? They, no doubt, were great sinners, and deserved to perish. But for what crimes are they punished? Will it be said that their hearts were totally depraved? This is true. 'God saw that the wickedness of man was great in the earth, and that every imagination of the thoughts of his heart was only evil continually.' But the same is true of sinners now living. The eye of God is on every sinner's heart. He takes cognizance of every thought and every imagination. These are all evil, only evil continually. Thousands of thoughts and imaginations which persons think little of, may be awfully wicked in the sight of God.

Sinners who are now in hell had no love to God, and no love to the duties of religion. The same is true of all impenitent sinners now living.

Will it be said that they resisted the strivings of the Spirit? And may not the same be said of you, my impenitent hearers? When the Spirit of God has moved upon your heart, and conscience has begun to awake, have you not laboured to silence your fears?

. . . .

Will it be said that they lived long in sin? The same may be said of many now living. How many years of your probation have gone out? Thousands and millions have died younger than some of you. There are those here whose day of salvation has been prolonged beyond that of most of the human race. Many in this house are doubtless older, and have lived longer in sin, than many who are now in hell.

Will it be said that they sinned against great light? The same may be said of sinners now living. Sinners in this house have enjoyed far greater light than many sinners now in hell. The inhabitants of the old world and of Sodom never enjoyed such light as sinners now living under the Gospel. They never enjoyed such privileges as are enjoyed by sinners of this assembly. Their light, when compared with yours, was like that of a taper compared with the noon-day sun. The guilt and punishment of sinners are to be measured by the light rejected. 'He that knew his Lord's will, and did it not, shall be beaten with many stripes.' Many in this house have known their Lord's will for years, and have not yet done it.

Were they stupid and thoughtless? So are you. Were they warned of God, and did they slight these warnings? Did they put far off the evil day, and vainly presume that there is time enough yet to secure their immortal interests? The same is true of you. Suppose ye that they were greater sinners than yourselves? 'I tell you, Nay; but except ye repent, ye shall all likewise perish.'

Inferences.

1. Sinners often talk and complain of the sins of others when they have not repented of their own sins, and when they are greater sinners than those of whom they complain, and are every moment in danger of perishing for ever.

. . . .

2. God does exercise sovereign mercy. When our Saviour delivered this discourse, there were some of His hearers who were greater sinners than some in

hell. These very persons were indebted to sovereign mercy. Nothing but sovereign mercy kept them from the world of woe.

. . . .

3. There may be redeemed sinners in heaven, who were greater sinners than some who are now in hell.

. . . .

4. The chief of sinners may be saved if they will repent.

. . . .

5. The least of sinners will be lost except they repent.

. . . .

6. There may be sinners now in this house who are more guilty than some who are in the world of despair."

. . . .

In a sermon on HEBREWS ii. 2, he closes thus:—

"How will you escape? Who will be able to stand? Do you expect to be overlooked in the transactions of the judgment-day? Will you be unobserved in the vast assembly? But how can you escape the omniscient and all-searching heart of Jehovah?

Will you resist? Have you an arm like God? Will you raise your feeble arm against omnipotence? How shall you escape?

Now the righteous Judge descends. The long-neglected Saviour comes. Every eye thall see Him. Mercy turns to wrath. Sleeping vengeance now awakes. Rebels, once deaf to His call, now shall hear His voice.

'See the Judge's hand arising,
Filled with vengeance on His foes.'

Jesus, whose charming and inviting voice once sounded in the Gospel, shall now pronounce their final doom—*Depart!* And how will you escape the dreadful sentence? Horror and despair shall seize their guilty souls. And how will you escape the everlasting fire prepared for the devil and his angels? Now they that are filthy will be filthy still. When ages on ages have rolled away, how will you escape the wrath to come? How will filthy and horrid blasphemers pay the still increasing debt, or pass the fixed gulf, or enter the pure and spotless regions of immortal life?

Once more, I entreat you, cast your thoughts forward into a boundless eternity, before you take the tremendous leap into the bottomless pit; and remember, that the great salvation is still within your reach. What must be the reflection of that sinner who has lost his soul?—'Once I enjoyed a day of salvation—once I heard the offer of pardon; but, wretch that I am, I rejected it.'

. . . .

He suffers on, millions of ages, and then reflects again: 'Once I enjoyed a day of salvation; once, millions of ages back—I remember well the time—it was near the commencement of my being—I was for a moment on trial for eternity. I heard of heaven, and I heard of hell. I was warned to flee from the wrath to come; but I neglected the great salvation.'

. . . .

Again, he suffers on millions and millions of ages, and then reflects again: 'Oh! what a precious season I once enjoyed! but, alas! it is gone for ever. Oh!

that I could once more hear the voice of the Saviour, and the sound of the Gospel; but—

> 'In that lone land of deep despair
> No Sabbath's heavenly light shall rise,
> No God regard your bitter prayer,
> Nor Saviour call you to the skies.
> No wonders to the dead are shewn,
> The wonders of redeeming love:
> No voice His glorious truth make known,
> Nor sings the bliss of climes above.'

I look forward to blackness of darkness for ever —Eternity!—It is an ocean without a shore. Oh! eternity, eternity! But stop, my hearers; here you are out of hell. This is the time which thousands will lament for their neglect of salvation, through a long eternity. Awake, sinner! 'Behold, now is the accepted time!—behold, now is the day of salvation! Now heaven, with all its glories, is brought within your reach.

> 'Salvation, oh! the joyful sound.'

Yet a little while, my hearers, and time with you will be no more.

> 'Seize the kind promise while it waits,
> And march to Zion's heavenly gates;
> Believe, and take the promised rest;
> Obey, and be for ever blest'"

On ROMANS xiii. 2, he thus pointedly addresses languid believers:—

"Brethren! are heaven and hell fables? If so, let us treat them as such. Or are they eternal realities? Whence, then, this seeming indifference to the interests of the soul? Do you verily believe that, within a few days, you shall be in heaven, singing the song of redeeming love, or in hell with the devil and his angels? Have you seen your own danger, and fled for refuge from the wrath to come; and do you feel no concern for the souls of others? Or are there no sinners in this place? Have they all become righteous? Do all profess to know the Lord, from the least to the greatest? Is there no prayerless family in this place, on which God has said: He *will pour out His fury?*—No prayerless youth, to whom God hath said: I will cast thee off for ever? My brethren, if there is one impenitent sinner here who is in danger of going into that place of eternal torment, *can you sleep?* One sinner in this house!—one inhabitant of hell! Solemn thought! One soul in this house that will be for ever lost! Who can it be? Could you bear to hear the name? 'Who among us shall dwell with devouring fire? Who among us shall dwell with everlasting burnings?' Have you not reason to believe that many are now living without hope, and without God in the world? 'Wide is the gate, and broad is the way which leadeth unto death, and many there be which go in thereat. Because strait is the gate, and narrow is the way, which leadeth unto life, and few there be that find it.'

Wherever God pours out His Spirit, and calls up the attention of sinners to divine things, He will be inquired of by His children to do it for them. This He has taught us in His Word, and often in the language of His providence. This He has taught you in days that are past. It is high time for you to awake out of sleep, for others are awake. Sinners at a distance are alarmed, and hundreds are flocking to

Christ. And can you sleep? Are there not souls here to be saved or lost for ever? And are not these souls as precious as others? And is not God a prayer-hearing God? Hath He forgotten to be gracious? Is His mercy clean gone for ever; and will He be favourable no more? No, my brethren, 'the Lord's hand is not shortened that it cannot save; neither is His ear heavy that He cannot hear.' Come, then, 'ye that make mention of the Lord keep not silence, and give Him no rest, till He establish, and till He make Jerusalem a praise in the earth.' 'For Zion's sake hold not your peace, and for Jerusalem's sake do not rest.' 'It is time to seek the Lord till He come and rain righteousness upon you.' And to your prayers, my brethren, fail not to add a friendly warning to the sinner.

You who know by experience the awful condition of a sinner out of Christ—who know that he must be lost, unless excited to inquire: 'What must I do to be saved?'—have you not sorrow enough in your hearts for your brethren, your kindred according to the flesh, to take them by the hand, and say: Friends, I fear that all is not well with your souls—ye must be born again: prepare to meet your God? Have you not courage? Dare you not act a part so friendly to the souls of men? How many, think ye, may be lost through your neglect? If we do not warn sinners, my brethren, God has warned us. He will make inquisition for blood. To every watchman on the walls of Zion, God saith: 'If thou speak not to warn the wicked; the same wicked man shall die in his iniquity; but his blood will I require at thine hand.'

What is your zeal, brethren, for the salvation of

souls, compared with that of the Son of God? 'He beheld the city and wept over it.' 'O Jerusalem, Jerusalem!'

> 'Did Christ o'er sinners weep,
> And shall our tears be dry?'

What is your zeal when compared with that of Paul? 'I have great heaviness and continual sorrow in my heart for my brethren, my kindred according to the flesh.' 'Many walk, of whom I have told you often, and now tell you even weeping, that they are the enemies of the cross of Christ.' There is a dreadful storm of divine wrath coming upon the world of the ungodly. It is high time, then, to awake out of sleep, for 'their damnation slumbereth not.'

Again, consider how long you have slept, and you will see that it is high time to awake.

How many months, and of some may we not ask, how many years, have ye slept in God's vineyard? And still you continue to sleep away the day of salvation. Let me tell you, that your sleep is awfully dangerous. If not shortly awaked, God, in anger, will say: 'Let their eyes be darkened that they may not see.'

Again, consider what time of day it is with you, and you will see that it is high time to awake.

How long has your sun been up? Your best season is already gone. With some, I perceive, the sun has already passed the meridian. Yes; it is now hastening its rapid descent. Aged fathers! your sun is now casting its last beams upon the mountains. 'Yet a little while is the light with you.' 'Work while it is day; the night cometh when no man can work.' If, then, you have any work to do—if you have any word to leave for your brethren, or for your children, they are now waiting to hear it. Delay not, for while I am speaking, the night is coming on. 'Whatsoever thy hand findeth to do, do it with thy might; for there is no work, nor device, nor wisdom, nor knowledge in the grave, whither thou goest.'"

He preached the doctrines of Calvinism fully and cordially, because he felt them, as well as believed them. But thus he addressed those who alleged their *original sin* as a *palliation of guilt*, in a sermon on—

PROVERBS xxviii. 13.—'He that covereth his sins shall not prosper.'

"Does the sinner plead that he did not make his own heart? What an excuse is this! Suppose your neighbour should injure you, and should plead, in his justification, that he did not make his own heart,—would you be satisfied with such an excuse? Are you the only being who did not make his own heart?

The principle involved in this excuse, if true, will exculpate every sinner in the universe. All the fallen angels may plead that they did not make their own hearts.

Suppose a number of men in a boat. By some means one of them gets overboard. He exclaims: How came I here? No matter, says one of his friends, let us help you into the boat. No, says he, there is an important question first to be settled: how came I here? We cannot tell, says his friend. There are different ways in which you may have got where you are. You may have jumped overboard—or you may have been thrown overboard—or you may have fallen overboard in your sleep. But take hold of this rope. No, he replies, if you will not tell me how I came here, I am determined to drown."

A full outline of a sermon on the *Divine Decrees* is preserved.

PSALM xcvii. 1.—'The Lord reigneth, let the earth rejoice.'

"The simple truth contained in these words is, that it is a matter of rejoicing that God governs the universe. I shall not spend time at present in shewing what is implied in the government of God. I shall barely state, that He exercises absolute control over both the natural and moral world—that He 'worketh all things after the counsel of His own will'—and that no event, great or small, ever takes place which is not included in His eternal purpose, and which is not made to subserve His ultimate designs.

My present object is to shew, that it is a matter of rejoicing that the Lord thus reigns.

I am aware that it is not thus regarded by wicked men. There is no doctrine to which the natural heart is more bitterly opposed than that of the absolute sovereignty of Jehovah.

Wicked men are willing that God should govern the natural world—that he should regulate the motions of the planets, order the vicissitudes of day and night—of summer and winter—of seed time and harvest, and perform His pleasure in the animal, vegetable, and mineral kingdoms. They do not object to the doctrine of God's decrees so far as it relates to the natural world merely. But when we speak of the government of God over the moral world, the enmity of the heart is roused. 'What! does God reign over moral agents?'

All the objections which I have ever heard against the doctrine of decrees or election, may be reduced to this one: If God operates on the hearts of men, and determines their actions, how can they be free? Though the objection is stated in different forms, yet the whole difficulty is resolved into this. My hearers, am I bound to obviate this difficulty? Does it lie against none but those who hold the doctrine of God's decrees? We will drop the doctrine of decrees—how is it then? Does God operate on the hearts of men, or does He not? If not, then we must not pray that He would do it. . . . . . .

No person can pray for himself without admitting that God can operate on his heart, and yet he be free. '*Turn thou me, and I shall be turned*'—'*Turn us, O God of our salvation*'—'*Draw us and we will run after thee*'—'*Create in me a clean heart, O God, and renew a right spirit within me.*' These prayers are found in the Bible. But persons ought not to have prayed in this manner if God could not answer their prayers without destroying their free agency. Ought we to pray that God would destroy our freedom?—that He would make us machines? This no one will pretend. How, then, can we pray that God would work in us that which is well-pleasing in His sight, if, as the objection supposes, He cannot operate on our hearts without destroying our freedom? I would ask the objector: How he can pray for himself consistently with the views which he maintains? Can he deem it right to pray that God would do what he believes God has no power to do?

No person can pray for others, without admitting that God may operate on their hearts, and yet they be free.

It is a doctrine clearly taught in the Scriptures, that a change of heart is absolutely necessary to prepare sinners for heaven. 'Except a man be born again he cannot see the kingdom of God.' We are also taught that God is the author of this change. 'Born, not of blood, nor of the will of the flesh, nor of the will of man, but of God.' But if God cannot operate on the hearts of men without destroying their freedom, then we ought not to pray that God would renew the hearts of sinners. Surely we ought not to pray that God would convert men into machines. However wicked mankind may be, we cannot pray that God would stop them in their career of sin, because He cannot do it without destroying their freedom. When sinners have proud, stubborn, and rebellious hearts, we cannot pray that God would make them humble, submissive, and obedient; because He cannot do it without converting them into machines.

When sinners are invited to Christ, they all, with one consent, begin to make excuse. And Christ declared: 'Ye will not come to me that ye might have life.' Sinners, then, are in awful condition. They will not come to Christ, and God cannot make them willing without destroying their freedom. What shall be done? It will be of no use to pray for them. Nor is it proper to pray for them; for surely we ought not to pray that God would do what He is unable to do.

We have dropped the doctrine of decrees, and the

same difficulty still remains. The grand objection which is urged against the decrees of God, lies with equal force against the duty of prayer. If it be true, that those who hold the doctrine of decrees, make men machines, it is equally true of those who pray. 'Therefore thou art inexcusable, O man, whosoever thou art that judgest; for wherein thou judgest another, thou condemnest thyself; for thou that judgest, dost the same thing.'

Now, whether we can see *how* God operates upon the hearts of free agents or not, it makes no difference. We know but very little of the *mode* of divine operation. The question is: Does God govern 'all His creatures and all their actions?' Does He govern the actions of wicked men and devils?

No, says one; He cannot do it without destroying their freedom.

No, says another; He cannot do it without becoming the author of sin.

My present object is *not to prove* the doctrine that God does reign over all His creatures; but to shew that it is a desirable thing; and that if He *can* and *does* thus reign, it is matter of rejoicing; and that if He does not thus reign, it is matter of mourning and lamentation.

If indeed God cannot govern human beings without destroying their freedom, or becoming the author of sin, and if He must resign His dominion over them, or let them alone, the universe is truly in a melancholy condition. Let us for a moment contemplate the condition we are in. Cast your eyes abroad, and see how the wickedness of men prevails. The adversary of souls goeth about as a roaring lion, seeking whom he may devour. What, then, shall be done? God cannot govern these things, it is said, without becoming the author of sin. The Church of Christ is truly in a lamentable condition. What will become of the Church we know not, for the devil has come down with great wrath. He will do all he can to destroy the kingdom of Christ on earth. He will do all he can to destroy heaven itself. What shall be done? We live under a government which can afford us no protection. Wicked men and devils are let loose upon us. They have entered the dominions of Jehovah, and are fast subverting His kingdom. Nothing can be done. The work of desolation must go on through eternity, for God cannot control the actions of His creatures without destroying their freedom, or becoming the author of sin. Thus, my hearers, you see the condition we are in. It is gloomy and awful beyond description. And is it so? Must God for ever look with regret and grief upon His creation, because He cannot stay the work of ruin carried on by His rebellious creatures?

That wicked men and devils very much need a governor—one who can control them at pleasure—you must, I think, be convinced. And why, then, do you object to the absolute supremacy of Jehovah? Is not God qualified to reign?

He is infinitely wise. He knows perfectly what is for the best. There can be no objection to His government on this ground.

He is infinitely good. He is disposed to do everything in the best possible manner. In this respect He is qualified to reign.

The only question relates to His power. But His

power is as infinite as His wisdom and goodness. All things are possible with Him. All His creatures are the workmanship of His hands. And has He made creatures whom He cannot govern? No, my hearers, the Lord reigneth. 'He sits on no precarious throne.' 'He doeth according to His will in the army of heaven, and among the inhabitants of the earth; and none can stay His hand, or say unto Him: What doest thou?'

> 'Rejoice, the Lord is King,
> Your God and King adore;
> Mortals, give thanks and sing,
> And triumph evermore.
> Lift up the heart,
> Lift up the voice;
> Rejoice aloud,
> Ye saints, rejoice.'"

The perseverance of the saints is thus defended in a sermon on PHILIPPIANS i. 6:—

"1. It is said: That if Christians believe that their salvation is certainly secured, they will feel that it is no matter how they live.

This objection involves the grossest absurdity. It may be thus expressed: If we believe we shall certainly persevere, it is no matter how we live; because we shall certainly persevere, whether we persevere or not. If the righteous shall hold on his way, it is no matter if he stops, or even goes back. Nor is the supposition, that the belief of this doctrine tends to make the Christian careless, less absurd. It is true, that the formal professor, the self-righteous, the hypocrite, and all who esteem the service of God a weariness, and who are building their hopes of heaven on the sand, may think to find some relief in this doctrine. But the person who can thus pervert this doctrine has no evidence that he is a child of God. The objection involves this plain absurdity: I have evidence that I love God and the duties of religion; and now, since I shall certainly continue to love God and the duties of religion, I care nothing about the honour of God and the duties of religion.

This objection, if made sincerely, is likely to prove that the objector has no religion, and that he would be glad to give up all attention to the duties of religion as an intolerable burden. No one who feels disposed to make this objection can possibly have good evidence that a work of grace has been begun in his soul. On the contrary, this disposition itself is positive evidence against him. Besides, there are many zealous Christians who firmly believe this doctrine. I adduce Paul as an example. He says: 'I am persuaded that neither life nor death *shall be able to separate us from the love of God.*' And yet Paul was not a careless Christian.

2. The following passage of Scripture has been supposed to militate against the doctrine of the saints' perseverance:—'*For it is impossible for those who were once enlightened, and have tasted of the heavenly gift, and were made partakers of the Holy Ghost, and have tasted of the good word of God, and the powers of the world to come, if they shall fall away, to renew them again to repentance.*'—Heb. vi. 4-6.

It may admit of a question, whether this passage was intended to describe the experience of real Christians? There is nothing said respecting their love to God, their faith in Christ, and their repentance for sin, which are the common evidences of regeneration.

If the text was intended to describe the condition of those only who have been greatly enlightened and outwardly reformed, it proves nothing against the doctrine we are considering. But if it was intended to describe the experience of real Christians, it is only hypothetical. It does not affirm that any such ever did, or ever will, fall away. It barely states what the consequence would be if they should fall away.

But, it may be said, if Paul was not fearful that those Christians to whom he wrote would fall away—if he was persuaded that they would persevere—why did he speak in this manner? I answer: Paul was persuaded that they would persevere, and yet he did speak in this manner. Anticipating this very objection, he adds: 'But, beloved, we are persuaded better things of you, and things that accompany salvation, *though we thus speak.*' This passage, therefore, taken in connexion with the context, goes to establish the doctrine which we are considering. For Paul here declares his full persuasion, that his Hebrew brethren had experienced something which was infallibly connected with their final salvation.

3. It is said the Scriptures mention cases of total and final apostacy, such as Hymeneus, Philetus, Alexander, Demas, Saul, Judas, and others.

In reply to this objection, I would say, that the lives of these persons clearly proved that they never were true saints. Their case is described by the apostle: 'They went out from us, but they were not of us; for if they had been of us, they would, no doubt, have continued with us,' (1 John ii. 19.) It seems that, in the opinion of the inspired apostle, *there could be no doubt of the perseverance of true believers.*

Besides, when the wicked shall all be assembled on the left hand of Christ at the day of judgment, there will not be found among them one whom Christ ever did acknowledge as His disciple. Although it is now maintained that Saul, and Judas, and others, were once real saints, and although they may stand up at the last day and plead for themselves, saying: 'Lord, Lord, have we not prophesied in thy name, and in thy name cast out devils, and in thy name done many wonderful works?'—He will profess unto them: 'I *never* knew you; depart from me, ye that work iniquity.'

I shall dismiss the objections with a short contrast.

On the one hand it is said: 'He that believeth and is baptized shall be saved.'

On the other hand it is said: He may be lost.

On the one hand: 'Verily, verily, I say unto you, He that believeth on the Son of God hath everlasting life, and shall not come into condemnation.'

On the other: He may be condemned.

On the one hand: 'There is, therefore, no condemnation to them that are in Christ Jesus.'

On the other: They may be condemned.

On the one hand: 'The Gospel is the power of God unto salvation to every one that believeth.'

On the other: Some who believe will be lost.

On the one hand: 'Whosoever liveth and believeth in me shall never die. Believest thou this?'

On the other: No, we do not believe it!

Inferences.

1. We see a reason why angels rejoice at the repentance of *one sinner*. If angels did not believe this doctrine, they could have no ground on which

to rejoice. They must wait till the sinner gets to heaven.*

The true penitent will certainly arrive safe at the mansions of the blessed. A firm belief of this doctrine lays the only foundation for joy in heaven over his repentance. If angels did not believe this doctrine, their joy would be unfounded. Their language would be: That sinner has truly repented. He is now a child of God—an heir of heaven. But whether he will ever reach this happy place—whether he will ever sing with us in glory, is a matter of great uncertainty. He may yet become a child of the devil, and an heir of hell. Could we *know* that he would certainly arrive safe at heaven, we might now tune our harps, and sing: *Glory to God in the highest.* But since we have already been disappointed, and devils and damned spirits are now triumphing over some at whose repentance we once rejoiced, it is best to wait and see how he holds out. Hear them triumph in the regions of despair: 'Ye angels,' say they, 'ye may suspend your songs, and hang up your harps. Let your joy be turned into mourning. Victory is ours.'

What think ye, my hearers? Has there been joy in heaven over some who are now in hell? If they so rejoiced at the news of the sinner's repentance, what messenger shall carry back the mournful tidings that he is lost?"

* A short conversation on this subject, of the following import, was mentioned by Dr. N in another sermon:—

"A person who denied this doctrine was expressing his joy in believing He was interrogated on this subject: 'Why do you rejoice, my friend? Do you think there is any certain connexion between your believing now, and your final salvation?' He perceived that, if he answered in the affirmative, he must admit the doctrine; and so he replied in the negative. The question was then put to him: 'If there is no certain con-

He often vindicated and enforced the sovereignty of divine grace, electing wheresoever and whomsoever the Lord pleaseth. The following is a specimen of his mode of address on such occasions:—

LUKE xiv. 18.—'And they all with one consent began to make excuse.'

"Much as unrenewed men may differ in other respects, there is one thing in which they are all agreed. When invited to come to Christ, they all with *one consent* begin to make excuse. They do not say, in plain terms, that they will not come. But they plead some reason to justify themselves in refusing to come.

nexion between your present belief, and your final salvation, why do you rejoice?' He replied: 'Because my sins are forgiven.' 'But why rejoice because your sins are forgiven? You say you have no evidence that you are not to suffer in hell for your sins after all. Why rejoice because your sins are forgiven?' 'Why, if I am faithful, if I persevere to the end, I shall be saved.' 'Very true; unless you persevere you cannot be saved. But what reason have you to conclude that you shall persevere? What makes you so confident that you shall be saved? Shew us the ground of your confidence Do you trust in your own resolutions?'—'No.' 'Well, what then? Do you trust in the stability of your own will? Do you feel superior to the power of temptation? Do you think you are a person of such decision, such stability and firmness, that, when you undertake the work, you shall certainly go through with it? Is this the reason you have to think that you shall persevere and be saved?'—'No.' 'Well, what then? What reason have you to think you should be faithful—that you shall persevere and be saved? If God is not first faithful to you, you will not be faithful to Him.' And, my hearers, he could see no reason why he should rejoice He could find no rest for the sole of his foot, until he was driven back on the ground of our text.—'*Being confident of this very thing, that He which hath begun a good work in you will perform it until the day of Jesus Christ.*' And, my hearers, what evidence have you that you shall persevere? Do you trust in yourselves? You lean on a broken reed; you build on the sand There is depravity enough in your hearts to sink you to hell if left to yourselves If you have never seen and felt this awful truth, you have never yet seen your own hearts, nor been thoroughly awakened. If you have not felt this awful truth, you have not yet been driven out of yourselves—not yet left the stronghold of self-righteous deception—not yet *fled for refuge to lay hold on the hope set before you.*"

That we may view this matter in a clear point of light, let us look at the parable of which the text is a part.

'*A certain man made a great supper, and bade many: and sent his servant at supper-time, to say to them that were bidden, Come, for all things are now ready.*'

The servant, faithful to his orders, delivered his message to one. He said to the servant: '*I have bought a piece of ground, and must needs go and see it.*' You know it is our duty to take care of our worldly interests. This I am bound to do; and this, I trust, is a sufficient reason for declining the invitation. '*I pray thee have me excused.*'

The servant goes to another, and receives a similar answer: '*I have bought five yoke of oxen, and I go to prove them. I pray thee have me excused.*' He goes to a third; he pleads a different excuse: '*I have married a wife; and therefore I cannot come.*'

At length the servant begins to expostulate with them. He speaks of the expensive entertainment which his master has made. He tells them that there is sufficient for all who will come, and that everything is prepared in the best possible manner. '*All things are now ready.*' My master is liberal: the invitation is free. Whosoever will, may come and take without money and without price. Thus he attempts to allure them.

Finding no success, he tries a different method. He attempts to alarm their fears, by pointing them to the consequences of a refusal. He informs them that his master will be displeased, and that fearful consequences will follow. This also proves ineffectual. Perceiving that no considerations which he can present to their minds have any influence to persuade them, the servant at length speaks in plain terms: You are all so opposed to my master, that not one of you ever will come, unless my master comes and brings you. On hearing this, one of the persons invited becomes angry, and begins to dispute with the servant. Did you not tell us, says he, that we are freely invited, and that whosoever will may come?

I did, replies the servant; and so it is. You are all freely invited. Nay, you are commanded to come, and threatened with a fearful punishment if you do not come. But since my master has made such large provision, he is determined that it shall not be lost. And as all my arguments prove ineffectual, and I cannot persuade one of you to come, he has determined to exert his own power on a certain number, and make them willing.

Then your master is partial, and does not give us all an equal opportunity to come to the feast.

The servant replies: You just now acknowledged that all were freely invited, and that whosoever will may come. Have you any reason to find fault because you are left to your own choice? Will you find fault even if my master has not determined to make you willing to come?

The other replies: I do not believe your master has determined to make any willing. I believe that all are left to their own choice.

Why, then, replies the servant, do you not come? If no special power is necessary to make you willing, why do you stand making excuses? Why do you not come now? I tell you again, you are so opposed, that you never will come, unless my master exerts his power to make you willing. And there is but one way for you to prove my declaration false; and that is, to come. Now, contradict what I say by coming of your own accord. I call upon you to do it; and again I repeat the assertion, that you never will do it unless my master makes you willing.

But instead of coming to the feast, he stands disputing with the servant: How discouragingly you talk. You tell us, if your master has not determined to make us willing, we never shall be willing. Is not this a discouraging doctrine?

If it is discouraging, the servant replies, to hear that my master has determined to make some willing, and to leave others to their own choice, let us suppose that he has not determined to make any willing, but to leave all to their own choice. Is this more encouraging?

He now pleads another excuse. He says: If your master has not determined to make me willing to come to the feast, I cannot come. How can I?

This, replies the servant, is giving up the point. If you cannot come, unless my master makes you willing, then what I said is true—that you never will come unless he makes you willing. And remember, your opposition is all that hinders. You labour under no other inability.

But, says the other, if your master has not determined that I shall come, I cannot, and I am not to blame.

It is your duty to come, says the servant, whether he has determined to make you willing or not. Thousands who have been invited, have never come, nor has my master made them willing, and he has punished them for not coming. And thus he will deal with you; and I leave you to settle the matter with him."

He preached from ACTS xviii. 10.—'I have much people in this city.' In this sermon he undertakes to shew, that "The doctrine of Election furnishes the only ground of encouragement to the use of means." This position he establishes by shewing the utter inefficacy of all means when not accompanied by the blessing of God. The following is the close of the sermon:—

"From this subject we may infer the mistake of those who consider the doctrine of Election a discouraging doctrine. Are there not many present who are still without God and without hope in the world? They have spent the best of their days in sin. All means have hitherto proved ineffectual. So many years of their probation have gone, and they are still enemies of God. They have heard the Gospel, and have rejected it. Permit me to summon these individuals to the bar of their own consciences.

I would ask you: What reason have you to believe that the Gospel which you have heard in vain for so many years, will take effect when your hearts are still more hard? I would that you might feel the difficulty. We have no more powerful means than those which have already been used. Now, if you deny the doctrine of election, where is your hope? We will suppose that the doctrine is not true—that God will leave you to do as you have done, and leave the means to operate as they have done. Is this encouraging? Deny the doctrine of election, and there is not a sinner in this assembly who has the least reason to conclude that he shall ever be saved.

Perhaps some of my hearers are displeased with this doctrine, and hope that it is not true. Then let me address you on your own ground. Whether this doctrine be true or false, it is an eternal truth, acknowledged by all, that '*Except ye repent, ye shall all likewise perish.*' Strike out the doctrine of election, yet the doctrine of regeneration is true. '*Verily, verily, I say unto you, Except a man be born again, he cannot see the kingdom of God.*' Strike out the doctrine of election, and let the means operate just as they have done, yet the doctrine of faith is true. '*He that believeth not shall be damned.*' Here is a given character, which all the heirs of salvation must possess. Now, you are at liberty to become Christians on the easiest plan you can. If you will repent and believe, and be born again, you shall be saved, whatever may become of the doctrine of election.

But why have you not repented and believed, and become Christians already? Why do you stand disputing about this doctrine, when you know that you must repent and believe, and be born again, or be lost? What will your disputing about this doctrine accomplish? If it be true, disputing will not alter it. Is it necessary for you to prove the doctrine to be false before you can repent? If you will repent, the doctrine of election will not hurt you if it be true. But if it be not true, then you have got to repent, and believe, and be born again, without it; and it is high time that you were in earnest on the subject.

If you say you cannot repent unless God grant you repentance; that is the same as to say, you cannot repent unless the doctrine of election is true. For, if the doctrine of election is not true, it is certain that God has not determined to grant repentance to one of the human race. If this doctrine is not true, it is certain that God has not determined to grant you repentance.

Instead of troubling yourselves about the doctrine of election, I will shew you a more excellent way. Begin to trouble yourselves about your own wicked hearts. The day of salvation is drawing to a close; and what have you done? and where are you now? Hitherto you have rejected all the melting invitations of a bleeding Saviour; and where are you now? Hitherto you have resisted the Holy Ghost; and where are you now?

In spite of the offers of Heaven—the calls of a bleeding Saviour—the invitations, commands, and threatenings of Almighty God, you have hitherto resisted; and will you continue to force your way down to hell? There is but a gleam of hope. 'Turn ye, turn ye, why will ye die?'

Come, O thou Spirit of the Lord, and breathe upon these slain, that they may live."

The apparent inconsistency of pressing home *duty*, while preaching *special grace*, is thus repelled (in a sermon on Jer. xxxi. 19: 'Surely after I was turned, I repented') by the example of our glorious Master.

"Permit me here to remark, I have not asserted that the sinner is not under obligation to repent previous to regeneration. It is unquestionably the duty of every sinner immediately to repent. We are not considering now what is duty, but what is fact. It is the duty of sinners to do many things which they never have done, and which some of them never will do. It is their duty to stop sinning, and to love God with all the heart, soul, mind, and strength. So it is their duty to repent without delay. But they have not done it, and some of them never will.

By this time some of my hearers will perceive a great difficulty in this subject. It is this: 'If sinners do not repent previous to regeneration, then you call on them to do what it requires almighty power to influence them to do.' This difficulty is not peculiar to this subject. It runs through the whole system of evangelical truth.

There are many who think they see a great inconsistency in the preaching of ministers. 'Ministers,' they say, 'contradict themselves—they say and unsay—they tell us to do, and then tell us we cannot do—they call upon sinners to believe and repent, and then tell them that faith and repentance are the gift of God—they call on them to come to Christ, and then tell them that they cannot come.'

That some do preach in this manner, cannot be denied. I well recollect an instance. A celebrated preacher, in one of His discourses used this language: '*Come unto me*, all ye that labour and are heavy laden, and I will give you rest.' In another discourse, this same preacher said: 'No man *can come unto me* except the Father which hath sent me draw him.' Now, what think you, my hearers, of such preaching, and of such a preacher? What would you have said had you been present and heard Him? Would you have charged Him with contradicting himself? This preacher, you will remember, was *none other than the*

Lord Jesus Christ! And, I have no doubt, that many ministers have followed His example, and been guilty of the same self-contradiction, if you call it such.

Now, my hearers, what will you say? Will you say that the difficulty, so far as it relates to Christ's preaching, can be easily explained? If it can, it can also be explained in reference to the preaching of others; and there is no cause of complaint. Or will you boldly assert that Christ contradicted himself? If you take this ground, you turn infidels at once. Or, will you say that you believe Christ to be consistent with himself, whether you can explain the difficulty or not? If so, why not say the same in regard to the preaching of His ministers, who preach in the same manner? I wish you to remember, that the difficulty complained of existed in our Saviour's preaching."

But now, hear how he preached an unfettered Gospel, welcome to all returning sinners, from a sermon on Luke xv. 11-25 :—

"The father was affected with what he saw. He said nothing, but ran. Mercy is swift. But what did he see? And why did he run? Yonder, at a distance you may see him. Come, anxious sinners—come, careless sinners, all assemble round, and behold this sight. Yonder is something worthy of your notice. Borne down with distress, he has long been a wretched wanderer from his father's house — has squandered his substance—is worn down with hard labour in the service of the vilest of masters—has left all his sinful companions—is coming directly from the field, and from the mean employment of feeding swine—is famished, and just ready to perish with hunger, and has not a friend to help him. Borne down under a sense of his sins, he moves slowly along, while his father hastens to meet him. Ashamed and confounded you see him coming home, just as he is, in all his poverty and rags. In this situation, 'his father met him, *fell on his neck, and kissed him.*' What a meeting this! Is it possible? Yes; for it is the compassion of God. Not a frown is seen on the father's face—not an angry word drops from his lips.

With what kind reception does the poor broken-hearted sinner meet who goes home to God *just as he is!* But a little while since, you saw him arise to go to his Father, that he might make his acknowledgment. But before he has time to carry his resolution fully into effect, he is graciously received. But does he keep back his confession? Listen—what do you hear? '*Father, I have sinned against Heaven and in thy sight, and am no more worthy to be called thy son.*' But why this confession, since he is already received to favour? Because a sense of pardon, so far from lessening, tends only to increase the sorrow of the penitent. He esteems it a privilege to confess his sins. This confession of the prodigal is a striking example of genuine repentance. You will perceive that it was not prompted by a slavish fear of punishment; for his father had already kindly received him. Thus it is with every true penitent. If there were no future punishment, he would still confess his sins with godly sorrow. Though forgiven of God, he will feel that he can never forgive himself. When the prodigal first adopted his resolution, he intended, after confessing his sins, to petition for a low place among his father's hired servants. But before he had time to offer his petition, he was interrupted by his father."

He urges Christ's call to every sinner in a sermon on REVELATION iii. 20:—

"The sinner sometimes says: I am willing to receive Christ, but He is not willing to receive me. But what says the text? 'Behold, I stand at the door, and knock.' Does not this imply His readiness and willingness to come in? Nor is this all. He calls: 'Open unto me—open unto me.' Nor is this all. He says: 'If any man hear my voice and open the door, I will come in.' He positively declares that He is willing. Nor is this all. You may say: I am such a great sinner—I have rejected Him so long, that He will not receive me now. But what says the Saviour? 'If *any* man hear my voice'—vile as he may be, if he is on this side of hell—'if *any* man hear *my* voice and open the door, I will come in to him, and sup with him, and he with me.'

If you are not now a Christian, permit me to say, that you have never yet heard His voice, nor opened the door, nor been willing to receive Him. You have never complied with the invitation in the text. The Saviour is ready and willing; but you will not come to Him, that you might have life.

Behold your danger. The Saviour *stands* at your door. He does not sit. He stands ready to enter, or ready to depart. How long would you stand at the door of your neighbour asking for admittance, if he should bar and bolt you out? And how long has Christ stood knocking? Even till His head is filled with the dew, and His locks with the drops of the night. But He will not stand long. There will be a last knock. The Saviour can do without you; but you cannot do without Him. He may say, as He once said to the Jews: 'I go my way. Ye shall seek me, and shall die in your sins.' How often '*I* would,' and '*ye* would not.' 'Behold, your house is left unto you desolate.'

I repeat, sinner, there will be a last knock at the door of your heart."

And thus he shuts up the sinner, in an appeal grounded on 2 Corinthians v. 20:—

"Are you pleased with the terms of salvation? If you are, you have doubtless complied with them. Have you repented and believed in Christ? If not, why? No reason can be assigned but the opposition of your hearts. If you were pleased with the terms of salvation, you would not remain in impenitence and unbelief another moment.

Many, I am aware, express strong desires for salvation, and sometimes say they would give all the world, if they had it, for an interest in the divine favour, while they have never found in their hearts to feel the least degree of contrition for their sins, or the least degree of love and gratitude to the God who made them, and the Saviour who died for them. Whatever value such individuals may place on a heaven of eternal happiness, they do actually prefer sin to all things else; and, in spite of the offers of eternal life, the calls of a bleeding Saviour, the invitations, commands, and threatenings of Almighty God, they are now forcing their way down to eternal perdition. What, now, is the cause of this enmity between you and God? Has

God ever injured you? Has He ever dealt unkindly with you? What have you to allege against His character, against His law, or against this treaty of peace?

Do you ask what God requires of you? The answer is plain: 'Be ye reconciled to God.' This is what God claims. And from this we cannot depart without entering on forbidden ground. He claims the heart. And from this we cannot depart without disloyalty to God. Individuals and nations may negociate a treaty of peace, though the heart be not engaged: an outward reconciliation may be effected, while the heart remains the same. But not so with God. He looketh on the heart. If that be withheld, 'To what purpose is the multitude of your sacrifices unto me, saith the Lord?' If the heart be not engaged, however sinners may treat about a reconciliation, their insolence is met with this repulsive demand: 'Who hath required this at your hand?' Without this, not a step can be taken towards settling your peace with God.

And now, all things are ready, and God is inviting and beseeching you to accept His mercy? What is the reply of your heart? Do you not like the terms of this treaty? You are required only to be *reconciled to God.* What can be more reasonable than this? Is it hard that you should be required to love God?—to feel sorrow for sin?—to confess and forsake it? Is this hard? Or is sin so lovely and so desirable that it appears hard and unreasonable that you should be required to hate and oppose it with all your heart? Why, then, will you not renounce it? Is sin so noble a thing in itself, and so desirable in its consequences, that you cannot part with it—that you will lay down your life—your eternal life for its sake? Your love of sin is all the excuse you have, or can have. Or will you plead your *inability?* What! Cannot be reconciled to God! Cannot feel sorrow for sin! Cannot cease to rebel against the King of heaven! What an acknowledgment is this! Out of thine own mouth wilt thou be condemned. If, indeed, you are so opposed to God that you cannot feel sorrow for sin, this is the very reason why you ought to be condemned. The harder it is for you to repent and love God, the more wicked you are, and the greater will be your condemnation.

God himself is beseeching you to be reconciled. And why do you not obey? Have your pride and stubbornness risen to such a pitch that you will not do the most reasonable thing, though God beseeches you?

In the name of God I come to beseech you to *be* reconciled."

He remarks, as to kindliness of tone, in his discourse on Luke xvi. 19, that even in speaking to a man in hell, no harsh words are used. "*Son, remember!*" is Abraham's address to him, though he was lost for ever. How tenderly he could preach himself, often appears in his applications. The following passage may shew it. The text is—

NUMBERS x. 29.

He shews: I. Christians are journeying. II. Christians desire others, and especially their kindred, to journey with them. III. To those whom they cannot persuade to accompany them, they must give the parting hand. And thus he appeals:—

"When our friends leave us, and remove only to a distant country, never more expecting to return, how solemn is the hour of separation! It awakens the tenderest feelings of the heart. But, my hearers, such a parting is but a faint emblem of what, in reality, is now transpiring among us. Did you never look forward with a deep concern to the separations of the last great day? Have you ever thought of different members of the same family, standing one on the right hand, and the other on the left of the Judge? And did you not feel a solemn dread, lest, perhaps, you should be found on the left hand? That awful separation which determines the eternal destiny of every soul, takes place first in our world. It is now taking place in this revival—in this assembly. That change of heart which is necessary to fit the sinner for heaven, must take place on earth, in this life, or never. And a change of heart among sinners now, will, of course, produce a change of views, and feelings, and pursuits, which will end in a separation of intimate friends. At such a season, many who feel little or no concern for their own souls, are wont to complain of being neglected by their former friends, who have become the subjects of divine grace. They imagine, that those who have embraced the Gospel, have ceased to love them.

Let me tell you, they do not love you less, but they love the Saviour more. They cannot accommodate themselves to your feelings and wishes consistently with their attachment to Him. They cannot make you their intimate associates as formerly, unless *they* change their character, or *you* change yours. With them 'old things are passed away, and all things are become new.' They have lost their relish for the pleasures of sin—the amusements and vanities of this world. They have set their affections on things above, not on things on the earth. In this sense, they 'are dead, and their life is hid with Christ in God.' They are no longer 'conformed to this world,' but 'transformed by the renewing of [their] mind.' If you will not follow them, take up the subject of religion, and become Christians in solemn earnest, they must, in this sense, forsake you. In such a case, Christ requires them to forsake father and mother, and wife and children, and all that a man hath, or he cannot be His disciple. A separation of views and feelings, of interests and pursuits, must take place, if you will not accompany them; or they must die with you in the wilderness, and never enter heaven. If you will not go with them to heaven, do you wish them to drop the subject of religion—to awaken again the terrors of a guilty conscience—to plant thorns on a dying pillow—to barter away the joys of heaven, and go to hell merely to keep you company? Will you urge the wonted affection of a brother, or a sister, or the ties of former friendship? *Will* you put them on trial of their friendship, their humanity, or their politeness, as some unfeeling wretches have done? That they love you still, their bursting hearts and streaming eyes, when they speak of you, tell. In their name, and while, as I doubt not, their prayers are solemnly offered for the success of the invitation, I now renew to every one of you the invitation: 'Come thou with us and we will do thee good; for the Lord hath spoken good concerning Israel.' 'Leave us not, we pray thee, and it shall be, if thou go with us, that what goodness the Lord shall do unto us, the same He will do unto thee.' He will wash you in the same atoning blood, sanctify you by the same Spirit. He will grant you the same grace, the same peace of conscience, and joy in the Holy Ghost. He will meet you at the same throne of grace, will guide you by the same counsel, and, at last, receive you to the same glory.

'And thou, my son, know thou the God of thy father, and serve Him with a perfect heart, and with a willing mind; if thou seek Him, He will be found of thee; but if thou forsake Him, He will cast thee off for ever.' Ye children, for whom I travail in birth again—did you know the feelings of a parent's heart—'Come thou with us,' 'and my heart shall rejoice, even mine.' And ye parents, too—did you know the heart of a child that has left all for Christ—He *calls*, and I must go. Though I love you none the less, yet I love Him more than father or mother. Leave me not, I pray you. I need your help, your counsels, and your prayers. My father, my mother, come thou with us.

And thou, too, my bosom companion, the partner of my sorrows and my joys, 'Come thou with us.' Let us adopt the resolution together: 'As for me and my house, we will serve the Lord.' Though I love you no less than ever, yet I love my Saviour more than all. *Leave me not.*

And ye, too, the companions of my youthful days, and companions, too, in sin, I have seen my folly, and my sport is ended. Often have I invited, and you would never refuse. You, too, have invited me, and I a thousand times have cheerfully complied. One more invitation and I have done: 'Come thou with us.' The Church on earth invites; and the spirits of just men made perfect, and all the hosts of heaven invite you. 'The Spirit and the bride say, Come. And let him that heareth say, Come. And let him that is athirst come. And whosoever will, let him take the water of life freely.' If you leave us, the fault will be your own. We desire your company, and pray for your conversion, and all heaven stoops to invite you. If at last you have no part in that kingdom to which we are bound, it will be because you loved the world, and preferred the pleasures of sin for a season.

Thus, in the name of all the subjects of this revival, have I given the invitation to their friends and companions to journey with them; and, I must add, in the name of this church, and in the name of my Lord and Master. And must I leave you here? If it must be so, my hearers, then duty requires me to call even upon your nearest and dearest companions, who have commenced their heavenly journey, to stay not a moment for you.

'Cease, ye pilgrims, cease to mourn,
Press onward to the prize.'

Dry your tears, and let nothing hinder you from following the steps of your leader. Obey implicitly every command of His. Thwart all the wishes, resist all the entreaties, endure all the frowns, and renounce entirely the society of your dearest earthly companions, RATHER *than neglect the least command of Christ.* To Him you are bound by obligations infinitely greater, and ties of affection infinitely dearer, than you can be to them. They never died to save your souls from hell. And His unalterable decision is: 'He that loveth father or mother more than me, is not worthy of me. He that loveth son or daughter more than me, is not worthy of me.' 'He that seeketh to save his life shall lose it; and he that loseth his life for my sake shall find it.'

Again, I repeat it,

'Cease, ye pilgrims, cease to mourn,
Press onward to the prize;
Soon the Saviour will return,
Triumphant in the skies.
There we'll join the heavenly train,
Welcome to partake the bliss;
Fly, from sorrow and from pain,
To realms of endless peace.'

But, oh! my impenitent hearers, I cannot bear to leave you thus. If you cannot be persuadeed to accompany your friends, I must remind you that you, too, are journeying as fast as the Christian—as fast as the wheels of time can carry you. But whither. ah! whither, are you bound?

'See the short course of vain delight,
Closing in everlasting night.'

Pursue your present course a little longer, and you will soon be at a returnless distance from happiness and hope.

'To-day if ye will hear His voice,
Now is the time to make your choice;
Say, will you to Mount Zion go?
Say, will you have this Christ, or no?
Ye wandering souls, who find no rest,
Say, will you be for ever blest?
Will you be saved from sin and hell?
Will you with Christ in glory dwell?
Come now, dear youth, for ruin bound,

Obey the Gospel's joyful sound;
Come, go with us, and you shall prove
The joy of Christ's redeeming love
Once more we ask you in His name—
For yet His love is still the same—
Say, will you to Mount Zion go?
Say, will you have this Christ or no
Leave all your sports and glittering toys.
Come share with us eternal joys
Or—must we leave you bound for hell?
Then, dear young friends, a long farewell.' "

These are specimens of his preaching. After he had preached a short time, his mind was exceedingly tried on the subject of *writing* his sermons; and he seriously deliberated the question: Whether it was not his duty to remit some of his other labours, that he might devote more of his time to study, and particularly to writing? But, after having prayerfully considered the subject, and taken counsel of his brethren in the ministry, he came to the conclusion, that it was his duty to persevere in that course which God was crowning with such signal success.

His biographer has given the testimony of many to his being an *instructive* preacher, a *doctrinal* preacher, a *practical* preacher, a *wise* preacher, a *plain* preacher, a *faithful* preacher, and a *solemn* preacher. Under his ministrations an awful seriousness pervaded the assembly. No one, unless it was some bold blasphemer, presumed to trifle. Such were the manifest tokens of the presence of God, that the minds of the people were filled with awe, and the breathless silence was broken only by the occasional sighs and sobs of anxious souls.

His enunciation was distinct, and his emphasis natural; the deep bass tones of his voice was sometimes peculiarly solemn and impressive. His eloquence was not that of splendid diction or graceful delivery; it was the eloquence of sight and feeling. It was "practical reasoning animated by strong emotion." "There was nothing peculiarly captivating in his voice, in his style, or his delivery," says Dr. Humphrey; "nothing to make you admire the man, or his writing, or his speaking. His prayers were short generally, and always fervent, scriptural, and appropriate. When he rose to speak, there was a benignant solemnity in his countenance, which awed the most thoughtless into seriousness; while, at the same time, it exerted an unwonted desire to hear what he had to say. He had a voice of more than ordinary compass and power; and though there was nothing harsh or repulsive in its modulations, you sometimes regretted that he had not enjoyed better early advantages for training it. He always commenced on a low key, enunciating every word and syllable so distinctly, however, as to be heard, without difficulty, in the remotest parts of the house. So simple were his sentences, so plain and unadorned was his style, and so calm was his delivery, that, for a few moments, you might have thought him dull, and sometimes even common-place, but for the glance of his piercing eye, and an undefinable something in his whole manner, which insensibly gained and rivetted your attention. As he advanced, and his heart grew warm, and his conceptions vivid, his voice caught the inspiration; his lips seemed to be 'touched with a live coal from off the altar;' his face shone; every muscle and feature spoke; his tones were deep and awfully solemn; his gestures, though he never in his life flourished off a prettiness, were natural, and, at times, exceedingly forcible. But his eye, after all, was the master-power in his delivery. Full, and clear, and sharp, its glances, in the most animated parts of his discourses, were quick and penetrating, beyond almost anything I recollect ever to have witnessed. He seemed to look every hearer in the face, or, rather, to look into his soul, almost at one and the same moment. You felt that you was in the hands of a master, and never stopped to inquire whether he was a good or a bad pulpit-orator. Whatever the critics might say, in one thing you could not be mistaken. He arrested your attention, and made you feel, for the time, at least, that religion is indeed the one thing needful."

One who had heard him preach often remarked: "He had the art of repeating some short and striking sentence in a manner and with an effect that no other could imitate. It was like the repeated strokes of the beetle, in the hand of a giant, upon the head of the wedge, driving it into the *very heart of the knotty oak.*"

But it was not, as we have said, this man's eloquence, or high intellect, nor even his mere fervour, that produced the abundant fruit of so many souls awakened and saved. It was the Holy Ghost poured out on him and on his hearers.

In his preaching, every *Calvinistic* doctrine was brought forward in its own place. He found the Holy Ghost owned these doctrines, so far from men being thereby lulled into slumber, or repelled from salvation. The ministers whose congregations were so blessed, held these same views; nay, some, such as Dr. Hyde at Lee, (mentioned p. 164,) required of those admitted to communion full and explicit assent to every article in the *Westminster Confession of Faith.** And in all this they were owned of that God whose sovereign grace they preached. The truth is, where the *Holy Ghost is working*, these doctrines are felt, in their place, to be rays of God's glory, the Saviour himself in the midst, with the free and full Gospel, beckoning on every sinner to come at once, without money, without other qualification than his rags and unworthiness. It is only when, without seeking the special and peculiar working of the Spirit, *man is trying to work upon his fellow man, by the power of mere motives*, that these truths seem to be hindrances.

What we long for, then, is no new way of preaching, no new doctrines that seek to make the strait gate wider, nor yet mighty power of intellect or burning eloquence; but rather that anointing of the Holy Ghost which is found by close fellowship and holy walking with God; and that real, undeniable Pentecostal outpouring of the Holy Ghost, which is not of man, but of God. For these let us cry to the Lord; for these let us make request without ceasing; for these let us urge Him whose "heart is turned within Him—whose repentings are kindled together," at the sight of the perishing. Ere the Son of Man appears, let us, day and night, ask, seek, knock, cry—petitioning for these most needful, all-important blessings, from Him who stretched out His hand so gloriously in the days whose history we have before us.

* Sprague on Revivals, Appendix, Letter V.

CHAPTER X.

A THORN IN THE FLESH, AND YET ABOUT TWENTY AWAKENINGS—NEW EMPLOYMENTS.

MR. NETTLETON had now, for ten or eleven years, been labouring almost constantly in revivals of religion. During this time he preached generally three sermons on the Sabbath, and several during the week, besides spending much time in visiting from house to house, and conversing with individuals on the concerns of their souls. How he could endure such accumulated labours, was a mystery to many. Undoubtedly his constitution was so impaired by these labours as to render it impossible for him to recover from the shock of disease by which he was attacked in 1822. It pleased God in the Fall of that year to arrest his labours, and to lay him on a bed of sickness.

It appears from a memorandum among his papers, that on October 5, 1822, he visited a sick person in South Wilbraham, before breakfast, and took the typhus fever. He lay sick at Bolton at the house of his friend, Mr. Parmele. He was brought so low that his life was despaired of, both by himself and by his friends. His mind was composed and peaceful. He afterwards stated, that the scenes witnessed in the revivals in which he had been engaged, and the countenances of the young converts, were constantly before him. The hymns, also, and tunes which had greatly interested him, were running in his mind; particularly those words:—

> "Soon shall I pass the gloomy vale,
> Soon all my mortal powers must fail,
> Oh! may my last expiring breath,
> His loving-kindness sing in death."

From this sickness he never entirely recovered,—that is, he was never afterwards able to engage in arduous labour.

While in this very feeble state at Bolton, he received many letters from brethren at a distance, containing urgent requests that he would come and assist them. He experienced essential injury from these numerous and pressing requests for his assistance, so that it became necessary to intimate to friends that they would confer a favour on him, and would consult the best interests of the Church, if they would suspend their communications for the present, and suffer him to remain undisturbed in his retired situation.

Meanwhile his friend, Mr. Parmele, took the fever off him and died. Mrs. Parmele was also very sick. An interesting obituary notice of Mr. Parmele, written by Mr. Nettleton, was published in the seventh volume of the *Religious Intelligencer*.

The following letter, written early in the following year by Mr. Nettleton to a number of young converts in Wilbraham, will be read with interest:—

"BOLTON, *March* 4, 1823.

"MY VERY DEAR FRIENDS,—Some time in December last I received a very affectionate letter, signed by fourteen names, never to be forgotten. It contained a friendly invitation to me to go to Wilbraham as soon as able, and there receive the kind offices of Christian friendship. As I read the letter, and dwelt with delight on each name, the interesting scenes through which we had passed together rushed full on my view. Had it been possible, most gladly would I have accepted your invitation; and I should almost esteem it a privilege to be sick if surrounded by such a circle of friends.

"A few days since I received another token of friendship enclosed in a letter from one of the number of that same circle. You will please to accept my sincere thanks for this and all your former acts of kindness.

"I need not inform you, my dear friends, of the trying scenes through which I have been called to pass since my last visit in Wilbraham. But our mercies are greater than our afflictions. Never did I experience so much kindness from friends as during my late sickness. I have often thought that their kindness has contributed much towards my restoration. It certainly contributed much to the health of my mind by its cheering consolation. My spirits were better than they have formerly been while in usual health. I have somewhere seen an expression like this: 'The sympathy of friends in affliction charms away half the woe.' This I have found to be true by experience. But the most trying of all was my parting with our friend, Mr. Parmele. Born the same year—in the same town—anxious for his soul and having made a profession of religion, at the same time with myself, he was my nearest friend. Often have we met, and prayed, and wept, and rejoiced together in revivals of religion.

"I hope you will not forget the interesting scenes of last summer. I think I shall not. Revivals appear the most important on a sick and dying bed, and thither we are rapidly hastening. I wish I had strength to tell you my views and feelings since I read your last. During my deepest distress I was in the midst of revivals. The tune, 'Loving-Kindness,' ran sweetly through my mind again and again, thousands of times, connected with the two last verses of the 8th hymn. This I often mentioned to my friends, as also the 324th hymn.* I do not recover my health as fast as my friends have been expecting. I have not strength to answer all the kind letters I receive from my friends. It is with difficulty that I have written this. My love to all my dear friends, and tell them how much I long to see them.

"Mr. S—— is now preaching in Coventry. He calls frequently to see me; and we talk over the scenes of last summer with peculiar delight. The revival which commenced in your region last summer, is still spreading, and advancing with power in Coventry, both societies. Let us not forget to pray that it may continue. And now I entreat you all *to live near to God. Love one another. Live in peace, and the God of love and peace shall be with you.*—I am, ever yours, in the best bonds."

For two years Mr. Nettleton very rarely preached. During this period, he took a voyage to Machias, in the state of Maine, and a journey to Montreal. The following letter was written to Mrs. Parmele, soon

* He probably here refers to the Hartford Collection of Hymns.

after his return from Canada. It is dated Greenwich, Conn., August 27, 1824:—

"MY DEAR FRIEND,—Yours of the 17th instant I found at New York, on my return from my long journey. I accept of the kindness, but my *conscience will not allow me to retain the enclosed.* I have nothing special to communicate. I suppose brother King informed you of my journey to Montreal. It is more than 400 miles from New York. I went in company with Dr. M'Auley and others. On our return we came by Saratoga Springs. I was quite sick, and by the advice of friends I was persuaded to remain there a fortnight, during which time I recruited in some measure. I came to New York in the steamboat last Saturday. I am now thirty miles this side of the city, at the house of the Rev. Mr. Lewis, where I have been two nights. I may tarry here two or three days longer, and then hope to go to Hartford. I do not preach. You must pardon me for the brevity and poverty of this letter, for it still pains me to write. There is an interesting revival in Salem, Mass.; but nothing special in this region. I attended the funeral of brother Whelpley while in New York. *The time is short.* I exceedingly regret the loss of so much precious time. If your health will permit, I trust you will be diligently employed in doing good. If I were not so idle myself, I would tell you that it is good to be busily employed about something.—In haste, yours, as ever."

Before he was taken sick, Mr. Nettleton had formed the purpose of compiling a hymn-book; and had done something towards collecting the materials. As soon as he had so far recovered from his sickness as to be able to read and write a little, he entered on this work. He finished it in the early part of 1824.

The reasons which induced him to undertake this work, are thus stated in his preface:—

"With great satisfaction and pleasure have I often heard the friends of the Redeemer express their unqualified attachment to the sacred poetry of Dr. Watts. Most cordially do I unite with them in the hope, that no selection of hymns which has ever yet appeared may be suffered to take the place of his inimitable productions. Deficiencies, however, he unquestionably has. Numerous have been the attempts to supply them; but hitherto the judicious have been constrained to regret that these attempts have succeeded only in part. Whether the book here published will add something to that supply, is submitted to the decision of the religious community.

"The compiler does not overlook the valuable labours of those who have preceded him in this department; while he concurs in the opinion very generally adopted by his brethren in the ministry, that the various benevolent operations, and especially the prevalence of revivals, which are so characteristic of the present day, demand a new selection of hymns. In the year 1820, the General Association of Connecticut appointed a committee to devise measures for the prosperity of religion within their limits. I well remember that, at a meeting of that committee, the first item proposed was a new selection of hymns. Four years nearly have elapsed, and nothing has been done pursuant to their appointment.

"When, in the providence of God, I had the happiness of spending a short season, as a labourer for Christ, within the limits of the Albany Presbytery, the call for such a work in that region—and, as I learned from the most respectable sources, very extensively in the west and south—was not less imperious and pressing than in the districts where I had been more particularly conversant. In personal experience, and discoveries of this description, originated the resolution to undertake the work. The compilation here presented is the result. The task has occupied my attention much of the time for nearly two years. Especially has it cheered and comforted me during the long continued retirement to which a severe sickness subjected me.

"The book, whatever may be its defects, is now most affectionately presented

'To Zion's friends and mine.'"

The *Village Hymns* have had a very extensive circulation, and have, it is believed, been instrumental of great good. But whatever was the usefulness of these hymns to others, the compilation of them served as a recreation to his own soul. It was one of the ways in which the Master said: "Come ye yourselves apart into a desert place, and rest awhile," (Mark vi. 31.) He took great delight in poetry; Pollok's *Course of Time* was one of his favourite works. It was flowing, but solemn verse that specially gained his attention; and it did so draw him, that we find him, on one occasion, reading to a class of anxious souls some of those pieces of poetry that had stirred the devout affections of his own soul.

A twenty years' time of partial weakness was now

begun—he was never to be able to engage in active work to the extent he had formerly been permitted. This was a "thorn in the flesh" to one accustomed to such scenes as he had witnessed, and was sent to him, probably, on this very account. If Moses, after his long career of miraculous journeying—if Samson, after his victory with the ass's jaw-bone—if Jephthah, when Ammon and Ephraim were so thoroughly overthrown—if David, after Goliath fell by his hand, had not met each with a "thorn in the flesh," a trying and humbling scene, who can tell how far they might have gone in self-righteous complacency? If Paul had not been subjected to such a trial—if the Baptist, after his amazing scene of awakening, had not been left to muse in loneliness in his prison, who can tell what unsanctified self-confidence might have been the issue? But when this greatest of all prophets born of woman looked out from the grated windows of his prison, and felt himself laid aside by his God, he would pray, and meditate, and learn his own heart, and his need of Jesus, whom he had preached, in a new manner. "He must increase, but I must decrease."

Mr. Nettleton was not indeed altogether laid aside; still, he was fettered, compared with former days. Some of his letters might suggest another end in his being thus far laid aside,—namely, that he might give himself more to prayer for the places and persons who had shared in scenes of revival, and for the Church at large. The Lord still had need of him.

Mr. Nettleton, as has already been observed, was never able, after his sickness, to engage in arduous labour. For the first two years he rarely preached at all. After that, he was not able to preach constantly—

sometimes only once on the Sabbath, sometimes twice, without attending many extra meetings, or devoting much time to visiting from house to house. Still, he was able to do something for the Church; and his labours, in not a few instances, were accompanied with a divine blessing.

In the autumn of 1824, an interesting revival commenced under his preaching in *Bethlem*. He continued in this place, assisting the pastor, the Rev. Mr. Langdon, who was sick, until his strength failed, and he was obliged to suspend his labours.

In a letter to Mrs. Parmele, of Bolton, dated New York, April 18, 1825, he says: "The occasion of my first visit to Bethlem, was to see brother Langdon, who was sick, and who had not preached for six months. He was thinking about asking a dismission when I arrived, but he postponed it. I preached for him two or three months. As many as eighty persons assembled at his house occasionally, at a meeting of inquiry, of whom about forty are rejoicing in hope. The burden of anxiety on my mind became so great, that I could endure it no longer, and so I left them. Having some business which could be done in this city better than anywhere else, I accepted an invitation to spend the winter and spring here in retirement. I am so much retired, that my friends here say, I will not visit, nor be visited, and yet I have spent three-fourths of my time and strength in receiving visits."

In the spring of 1825, he preached a considerable time, and with success, in *Brooklyn*, Long Island.

In the summer of 1825, he preached in *Taunton*, Massachusetts. Here his labours were made effectual to the conviction and conversion of sinners. The parish in which he preached was at that time destitute of a pastor.

In the Fall of the same year, he commenced labouring with the Rev. Mr. Cobb, in another parish in Taunton. In a letter to a friend, dated Taunton, December 26, 1825, he says:—

"The state of things in this society has become quite interesting of late. Meetings are crowded and solemn as eternity. A number have called to see us in deep distress of soul. Some of them told us that they received their first impressions down at the green last summer. The fire was already kindled, and has recently burst into a flame in this part of the town. The number of inhabitants in this society is comparatively small; and yet, last Saturday evening we met about sixty in the meeting of inquiry. About thirty are rejoicing in hope. Of these, some are youth of the first respectability, and four or five men of influence. Old professors of religion tell us they never saw such a time before."

Mr. Cobb also bore his testimony to the work:—

"Brother Nettleton came to Taunton in the summer of 1825; and the Trinitarian church in this town being destitute, by the decease of their beloved pastor, the Rev. Chester Isham, he laboured two months and a-half in that congregation. The prospect of a general and powerful revival of religion was very fair. About thirty converts were the fruit of his labours among that people. In this state of things, a candidate for settlement was procured, who subsequently became their pastor. Brother Nettleton retired, and came to live in my family the first of October, and continued with me till the middle of January 1826.

"There had, for weeks previous, been a solemn stillness in my congregation, and many had been specially awakened, though they had kept their impressions to themselves. When brother Nettleton commenced his labours, the revival immediately became manifest, and converts were multiplied almost daily during his stay.

"His sermons were clear, sound, able, full of thought, direct, and simple, with unity of design. 'He seemed to be destined to be understood.' He enlisted the hearts and hands of all the church, and especially the aged members—our fathers who were well informed, and who had borne the burden and heat of the day. It was surprising to see what overpowering influence his kindness, devotion, and faithfulness had upon all, old and young, saints and sinners. In this state of things, there seemed to be a very bright prospect of a glorious harvest. It was manifest that brother Nettleton had ready access to every conscience. As the revival progressed, he preached more and more closely and doctrinally. 'The great truths of the Gospel' were the weapons of his warfare, and were wielded with a spirit and an energy which the people were unable to gainsay or resist. He was remarkably clear and forcible in his illustrations of the sinner's total depravity, and utter inability to procure salvation by unregenerate works, or any *desperate efforts.* He shewed the sinner that his unregenerate prayers for a new heart, his impenitent seeking, striving, and knocking, would be of no avail;* and that absolute, uncon-

* They are like the cries of blind Bartimeus; they have no merit, and God has not bound himself by any promise to answer such prayers. There is only the "Who can tell?" of the king of Nineveh in them, (Jonah ii 9,) and if depended on as more they become provoking self-righteousness—Ed.

ditional submission to a sovereign God, was the first thing to be done. To this duty the sinner was urged immediately with great power and conclusiveness of argument.

"His visits among the people were *frequent*, but *short and profitable*. He entered immediately on the subject of the salvation of the soul, and the great importance of attending to it without delay. He did not customarily propound questions and require answers, lest by this means he should turn the attention of sinners from their own wretched state, by leading them to think 'How they should reply to the minister.' He was so well acquainted with the human heart, that he seemed to have an intuitive perception of what was passing in the minds of those whom he was addressing. Thus he could so direct his conversation as to produce silence and self-condemnation, and confine their thoughts to their own lost and ruined state, sometimes remarking: '*You have no time to spend in conversation before the salvation of the soul is secured.*'

"When any indulged a hope which was not satisfactory, he would say: 'You had better give it up, and seek your salvation in earnest.' Well versed in all the doctrinal and experimental parts of the Gospel, feeling deeply in his own heart the power of divine truth, he was qualified even beyond most men to judge of the character of others' experience; and though mild and conciliatory in his manner, he was faithful in his warnings against false hopes and spurious conversions. All selfish considerations in the concerns of the soul he discarded; and he never used any art or cunning to entrap, or produce commitment on the part of sinners. In the anxious circle he was short, direct in his remarks, concluding with a short and fervent prayer—*directing his petitions solely to God*, and not displaying eloquence, or seeking to fascinate the congregation. He seemed to lose sight of man, and to be absorbed in a sense of the divine presence.

"In his intercourse with the people, he invariably produced favourable impressions on their minds in regard to their own pastor. He was not the *leader*, but only an *assistant* in the work. My people never before entertained and cherished so high and so affectionate a regard for their pastor, as in this revival; and when he left us in the midst of it, such was the effect of his course in this respect, there was scarcely a word of inquiry respecting brother Nettleton. And the work went on as though he were with us.

"In his daily habits in my family, he was constantly employed in searching the Scriptures, or in conversation on religious topics, discussing doctrinal points, and matters relating to Christian experience. He was in this way very social, and an exceedingly agreeable companion.

"In his sermons, of which I heard sixty, he was, in manner, simple. He spoke with a clear voice—rather slow and hesitating at first, but gradually rising, till, before the close, it was like a mighty torrent bearing down all before it. His eloquence was peculiar to himself, and consisted in conveying his own views and feelings to the minds of others. He never failed to impress his own ideas upon his hearers. As the revival became more interesting and powerful, he preached more doctrinally. He brought from his treasure the doctrines of total depravity, personal election, reprobation, the sovereignty of divine grace, and the universal government of God in working all things after the counsel of His own will. And these great doctrines did not *paralyze*, but greatly *promote* the good work. *Never had brother Nettleton such power over my congregation, as when he poured forth in torrents these awful truths.* And at no time were converts multiplied so rapidly, and convictions and distress so deep, as when these doctrines were pressed home to the conscience. One evening, while our house of worship was filled to overflowing, he preached on the doctrine of Election; and the people were so held by the power of truth, that when, in the midst of the sermon, an intoxicated Universalist stepped within the door, and cried out with a stentorian voice, and with a horrid oath, 'That's a lie,' scarcely an eye was turned from the speaker towards the door.

"The above remarks will serve to give a general idea of the character of this revival. The work was still; and after the lapse of nineteen years we are satisfied that the converts were, generally, truly renewed in the spirit of their minds. They appear still to believe and love the doctrines of grace, by which they were begotten to the hope of the Gospel; and they have walked in newness of life.

"The influence which that precious revival exerted upon the church and society has been good. Men who were not subjects of it have been confirmed in their belief of the truth; and their convictions that revivals may be evidently the work of God, have been deep and lasting; and they speak of that season as a day of divine power and grace."

The following letter to Mr. Cobb, written by Mr. Nettleton soon after he left Taunton, will shew how deeply his own feelings were enlisted in the work of grace above described:—

"New York, *February* 6, 1826.

"My dear Brother,—Yours of the 30th ult. was received last Friday. It was truly refreshing to me, and to many of my friends. I cannot express the joy I felt on hearing the number and the names of some who entertained hope since you wrote last. The young converts and the anxious ones have scarcely been out of my mind since I left Taunton. Your letter contains more than I had reason to expect; but my mind will not rest satisfied without possessing the names of *all* who have found the Saviour. When I left you, brother Cobb, I did feel confident the work would continue; but I did not think it would be so rapid. The family where I reside have become so interested in the state of things with you, that they occasionally mention you and your people in their prayers. I think you will do well to note facts and dates as you pass along. You will find them useful hereafter. You will prepare an account for the *Connecticut Observer*, or some other paper, ere long. My heart has been with you ever since I left, and I was really in hopes of making you a short visit, at least. But I am sorry to say, I have been very sick with a fever, and for twelve hours considered dangerous. I am surrounded with kind friends, and have everything I could wish. I feel much better to-day, or I should not be able to write. The physician says it will take some time for me to recover. I do hope you will give me some account, from week to week, of the state of things with you. I fear I shall not be able to labour anywhere during the two following months of inclement weather. If you cannot obtain help, and are unwell yourself, get together, if you only say *five words*, and pray five minutes. Meet the anxious once a-week, if you can only pray with them. Give my love to all the young converts, and to all the anxious. Tell the latter that I have not forgotten them—that they have scarcely been out of my mind since I saw them in the circle. They must never drop the subject. They will never have another such opportunity."

On the 17th of March, a little more than a month after the date of the foregoing letter, he wrote again to Mr. Cobb, as follows:—

"My dear Brother,—The lapse of time does by no means lessen the interest which I have felt in forming an acquaintance with yourself and family, and the people of your charge. Not a day or a night has passed since I parted with you, when those interesting scenes in which we mutually shared, of *sorrows and joys that are past*, have not been fresh in my mind. Brother, these are scenes never to be forgotten. Other trifles may occupy our time, and absorb the thought and feelings of our heart for a season, and be forgotten, or remembered only with regret. But, oh! the scenes through which you are now passing will follow you down through the tract of time, and are forgotten *never*. I sympathize with you in all the sorrows and joys inseparable from the duties of a faithful pastor at such a season. Now, more than ever, will be realized the weight of your responsibility.

'’Tis not a cause of small import,
The pastor's care demands;
But what might fill an angel's heart,
It fill'd a Saviour's hands.'

"I was pleased with the solemn stillness, the readiness to act, the apparent interest, and the decision of the members of your church. Were I present, I would affectionately say to them: Be humble—be thankful for what God has already done—'keep the unity of the Spirit in the bond of peace'—pray *much* and *fervently* for the continued outpouring of the Spirit—do not feel satisfied with what has already been done. Brethren, pray for us, for your pastor, that the Word of God may continue to have free course and be glorified.

"I cannot forget that interesting circle which used to meet to consult on the great concerns of the soul. Often have I fancied myself seated in the midst of that same circle,—some weeping, and some rejoicing in hope. Their countenances are all familiar to my mind. With what feelings of affection, and solemnity, and compassion, have I bowed together with you, my friends, around the throne of grace! While thus employed, often have I thought: Shall we ever meet in heaven around the throne of God and the Lamb? Shall we be companions for ever in that world of unclouded glory? The thoughts of such a meeting seem almost too much for such sinners as ourselves. But I know it is possible; and the vilest of sinners are *invited.* Some of the chief of sinners will repent, and be pardoned and saved; and why not such sinners as ourselves? Ah! none but sinners are saved; and some of the chief of sinners have already been saved. And I cannot but indulge the pleasing hope, that some—that many of your circle will meet in that world where pilgrims meet to part no more. Let all those who indulge this heavenly hope themselves, come out from the world, and, by their conduct and conversation, *declare plainly* that they seek a better country. You have yet to encounter the dangers of the wilderness, and you will need the whole armour of God. You who have long been companions in sin, will now become companions, helping one another on your way to the heavenly Zion.

> 'Invite the strangers all around
> Your pious march to join;
> And spread the sentiments you feel
> Of faith and love divine.'

"I cannot forget those anxious souls who are still out of Christ. With joy have I heard the tidings of many whom I left anxious for their souls. But I have the names of a number now before me, of whom no such tidings have been told. Where are they? Have they gone back to the world? My dear friends, if you have not already given your hearts to Christ, once more, from this far-distant region, would I lift up my voice, and warn you, by the worth of your souls, to flee from the wrath to come. I entreat you not to rest till you find rest in Christ. I have not forgotten you. I shall still remember you at the throne of grace, till the joyful tidings of your repentance have reached my ears, or the sorrowful tidings that you have dropped the subject of religion, and gone back to the world.—Ever yours, in the best of bonds."

In 1826, although in very feeble health, God made him the instrument of a great work of divine grace in *Jamaica*, Long Island. He commenced his labours in that town on the 24th of February, and continued to labour there until November. The people, when he first came among them, were very much divided; but, under his judicious management, their divisions were healed. He preached on Sabbath morning, and in the evening; omitting the usual afternoon exercise. And although he could not attend many extra meetings, or spend much time in visiting the people, yet there is reason to believe that God made him instrumental in the salvation of many souls. In his journal, under date of May 8, he speaks of fifty rejoicing in hope.

In a letter to his friend, Mr. Cobb of Taunton, dated July 13, he says: "My head, heart, and hands, are so full, and health so feeble, that I have dispensed with every business, except what was absolutely indispensable. Since you left us we have been much employed in listening to the relation of Christian experience by the young converts, preparatory to a public profession of religion. For a few weeks past we have attended to little else. Had you been present, you would have been interested, if not delighted. On the 2d of July we held our communion, and seventy-two were added by profession, and three by letter. The assembly was full, and very solemn. Eighteen were baptized. Since that day the revival has received a new impulse. Many were awakened who have since come out joyful. It has often been observed, '*that it seemed like the judgment day.*' We have had but few meetings of inquiry since you left us. At our last, including young converts, there were about one hundred and forty. The work was never more interesting than at this time. A number of strangers from other towns have visited us, and have gone home rejoicing in hope, and others are in deep distress. If I continue long in this place, I think of appropriating one evening in the week to visiting a circle of strangers.

You would be delighted with our assembly. We have long since been crowded out of our session-house: our meetings are now generally held in the church. Many professors, as well as young converts, say: We never knew what there was in religion before. 'Old things are passed away, and all things are become new.' Although a great proportion of this population are still strangers to the power of religion, yet there is little or no apparent opposition. Many who are left are struck with solemn awe, and, for their own credit, are constrained to plead the cause of God. *'Then said they among the heathen: The Lord has done great things for them.'*

"I have by no means forgotten the young disciples in Taunton, nor those I left anxious for their souls. How I do long to see you, and all my friends in Taunton once more. I can only say: *'Let your conversation be as becometh the Gospel of Christ, that whether I come and see you, or else be absent, I may hear of your affairs, that ye stand fast in one spirit, with one mind, striving together for the faith of the Gospel.'*—Yours, in the bonds of the Gospel."

The following statement has appeared in the *New York Observer*, by one who was in the midst of these scenes:—

"In perusing the life of Mr. Nettleton, I have had brought vividly to my recollection scenes and circumstances connected with the revival of religion in Jamaica in 1826, of deep interest to me; and although more than eighteen years have passed, their interest is as deep as ever, and, I think, strikingly illustrates the wisdom and the prudence of that truly wonderful man in dealing with awakened sinners.

"The first time I ever saw Mr. Nettleton was on a communion Sabbath, in the early part of the winter of 1826. Two strangers entered the church, and, walking slowly up the aisle, seated themselves in the front pew. Many eyes were fastened upon them; and after service, as is common in the country, many inquiries were made as to who they were, for they were evidently clergymen. It was some time before I learned that one of them was the 'Rev. Mr. *Nettleton*, the great revival preacher.' The church in Jamaica had been greatly divided. We were literally two bands—hostile to each other, and bitter in feeling. The apostle might have said of us: 'We were hateful, and hating one another;' and there seemed but little prospect of our ever being any better. It was but a sad spectacle on that day presented to this man of God.

"When, a few days after, I heard that Mr. Nettleton, the revival preacher, was soon going to preach for us, I never shall forget my feelings. I determined I would not hear him, and especially so when an old disciple, long since in glory, Mr. Othniel Smith, who had listened with rapture to George Whitefield seventy years before, when he preached in Jamaica, said to me: 'This Mr. Nettleton that is going to preach for us is a most wonderful man; he is said to be the greatest preacher that has been among us since the days of George Whitefield.' He said further, that, from what he had heard of him, he believed he could almost *read a man's heart*, so wonderful was his knowledge of human nature. I well remember I secretly said: 'He shall not see *my heart*, for I will not let him see me;' so bitterly did I dread anything like close experimental preaching.

"I had long been a professor of religion, having united with the Rutgers Street church in 1812, while Dr. Milledollar was the pastor; but, notwithstanding, I had always been outwardly consistent, (regularly observing secret and family prayer, constant in my attendance upon all the meetings of the church, as well the public services of the Sabbath, as the weekly lecture, and the social circle for prayer, and active in all the benevolent operations of the day,)—notwithstanding all this seeming consistency of character, there was always a fearful whisper from the faithful monitor within that all was not right. There was a secret dread of self-examination—an unwillingness to know the worst respecting my case; and the idea of coming in contact with a man who would be likely to expose my shallowness, if not hypocrisy, I could not endure. Accordingly, I resolved that something should detain me from church when Mr. Nettleton preached. But although I sought diligently for any excuse, one even the least plausible, yet I could not find one; and, contrary to my secret determination, I went to church at the appropriate time with my family.

"After the Sabbath, numbers of the church members called upon Mr. Nettleton at his lodgings to welcome him among us; and I was repeatedly requested to do so with the rest: but day after day I contrived to excuse myself, although I knew it was a civility that was expected of me. At length a brother, who had often urged me to go, called upon me to know if I would not take Mr. Nettleton a little ride in my gig, as he was in feeble health, having but just recovered from a protracted illness,—adding, that he found riding not only beneficial, but necessary; and he knew I could do it just as well as not.

"I never shall forget my feelings at this proposition. I at first refused outright, and was vexed that the proposition should have been made. I treated the brother rudely. He, however, continued to urge, and said he had gone so far as to tell Mr. Nettleton that he knew I would do it cheerfully. But it was all to no purpose. I did not do it that day, but consented to call upon him the next morning with my gig, at ten o'clock, if he would be ready. The next morning, accordingly, I called at the appointed time, and was introduced to him on the side walk; and never did culprit dread the face of his judge more than I dreaded to be brought face to face with a man who, it was said, could almost *read the heart*.

"I received him politely, and we soon entered into a pleasant conversation about almost anything and everything except personal religion. This I scrupulously avoided. I found he was in feeble health, and somewhat given to hypochondria; therefore I felt assured I could entertain him by talking about his own ailments. In less than one hour, all my unpleasant feelings had vanished; I felt as free and easy with him as if I was riding with some long tried friend; and that which I so much dreaded became to me at once a source of great pleasure and of much profit.

"The first day he rode with me about six miles; and after that, for seven months, very few pleasant days passed that we did not ride together from five to twenty-five miles. I became deeply interested in him as a man and as a preacher. Why I at first liked his preaching, I cannot exactly say; but I was unwilling to be absent from a single meeting. The class of subjects he chose as his theme of discourse was new. The distracted state of the congregation led those clergymen who supplied our pulpit to select some subject connected with Christian duty. Brotherly love, if I remember right, was the subject of discourse seven times in about three months. On the contrary, Mr. Nettleton presented *the claims of God and the duty of sinners;* and here, I remember, we had no opportunity of scrutinizing the sermon, to endeavour to ascertain on which side of the division the preacher was. This I considered a master stroke of policy.

"Thus smoothly and pleasantly, comparatively speaking, it passed along with me for about two weeks; when one evening he announced from the desk that he felt some encouragement to believe that the Lord was about to grant us a blessing. He said he had seen several individuals who were anxious for their souls, and two or three who indulged hope. How it would end with them he could not say; but he wanted the church to walk softly before the Lord, to be much in prayer, &c. I felt, then, that my own case required looking into at once, or I was lost; and I resolved soon to attend to it, and not to let the present opportunity pass. Mr. Nettleton had never yet said one word to me on the subject of experimental religion, although I had been with him a great deal.

"The next day, as usual, I called for him to ride. I was obliged to go to Flushing that day, distant about five miles. Just as we were ascending the hill, a little out of the village, and before any subject of conversation had been introduced, the horse being on a slow walk, he gently placed his hand upon my knee, and said: 'Well, my dear friend, how is it with you? I hope it is all peace within.' I could not speak for some minutes. He said no more; and there was no occasion, for an arrow had pierced my inmost soul. My emotion was overwhelming. At length, after recovering a little self-possession, I broke the silence by telling him frankly I was not happy—there was no peace within—all was war! war!! war!!! His manner was so kind, he instantly won my confidence, and I unburdened my soul to him. I told him how I had felt for years past, and how very unhappy at times I had been.

"He did not seem inclined to talk. All he said was occasionally: 'Well—well—well'—with his peculiar cadence. At length he said he did not feel very well, and he wanted to be still. This was a request he often made, and I thought nothing of it. I have rode miles and miles with him, and not a word has passed between us after such a request.

"I continued to ride with him once and twice a-day; but although I was anxious to converse, he said but little to me, except occasionally he would drop a remark calculated to make me feel worse instead of better—at times greatly deepening my distress. Some months afterwards, I spoke to him about this part of our intercourse. He said he did it intentionally, *for he had reason to believe many an awakened sinner had his convictions all talked away, and he talked into a false hope.*

"Two or three days after he first spoke to me on the subject of religion, he called at my house, and requested me to go and see a particular individual, whom he named, and who was under distress of mind, and pray with her. I told him that I could not do such a thing as that, for I was not a Christian myself. He replied: 'But you do not mean that your not being a Christian releases you from Christian obligations? If you do, you are greatly in error. Good morning!' and he left me rather abruptly. In the afternoon, when I rode with him, he did not ask me if I attended to his request; for he knew I had not. He only made the request, as he afterwards told me, to thrust deeper the arrow of conviction; and it had the desired effect. My distress became very great; and I was unfitted for my ordinary duties. I felt as if there was but little hope for such a hardened sinner as I was.

"About this time he appointed a meeting of inquiry. I told him I should be there for one. He said I must not attend on any account; it was only intended for anxious sinners. I told him I certainly should be there, unless he absolutely forbade it. 'I do,' said he, with more than ordinary earnestness. 'Then,' said I, 'you must promise me that you will appoint a meeting for anxious professors.' He made no reply. This anxious meeting was the first he appointed in Jamaica. It was to be held at the house of a dear friend of mine, and one who knew something of the state of my mind. I went there in the afternoon, and made arrangements to be concealed in an adjoining bedroom,—the door of which could not be shut, the bed being placed against it. I was on the ground an hour before the time appointed. Mr. Nettleton came soon after, to arrange the seats, about which he was very particular.* He came into the bedroom where I was concealed two or three times; he wanted the door closed, but he found it could not be without disarranging the furniture, and he gave it up. He did not know I was there until some weeks afterwards. The temptation to be present at that meeting I could not resist. Somehow I had received an impression that my salvation depended upon it. I had heard so often about persons being converted in an anxious meeting, that I thought if I could only be present at such a meeting, that was all that was necessary; and therefore I was willing not only to run the risk of offending Mr. Nettleton, but to submit to almost any humiliating circumstance to accomplish my object. I thought it was altogether a piece of cruelty in Mr. Nettleton to forbid my being present; and I determined to carry my point privately, if I could not openly.

"Situated as I was, I could hear next to nothing as to what was transpiring in the anxious room. Mr. Nettleton addressed those present individually, and in a very low tone of voice, bordering upon a whisper. As he approached the open door, I could occasionally catch a sentence, and hear a deep and anxious sob; but these words, and broken sentences, and sobs, were loud and pointed sermons to me. I wanted to get out

* He was painstaking, in no ordinary degree, in arranging such meetings. A Christian friend, who frequently had him under his roof in Glasgow, at the time of his short visit to this country, remarked, that "he seemed to do nothing, were it no more than crossing the floor of the apartment, without keeping in view how it might affect the souls of those present."

from my hiding-place, that I might give vent to my pent-up feelings; and my anxiety to be released appeared to be greater than it was to be present. At times it seemed as if I must cry out in bitterness of spirit, so agonizing were my feelings; especially so as I heard him say to one individual: 'Is it possible? Well, I am afraid you will lose your impressions; and if you should, what will become of you? If the Spirit is grieved to return no more, you *will* lose your soul.' After going around the room, and conversing with each individual, he made a few general remarks, applicable to all, respecting the danger of grieving God's Holy Spirit, and then dismissed the meeting after a short prayer.

"Instead of feeling any better after this meeting, as I expected to do, I felt worse and worse. Sleep was now taken from me, and I felt that death was better than life. Either that night or the next, (I forget which, but remember it was the 27th April,) I got out of bed about 12 o'clock, and went out into the woods. It was exceedingly dark. I fell down at the foot of a tree, and cried aloud for mercy in agony of soul. I felt that God was just in punishing me. I felt that the *longest* and the *severest* punishment He could inflict was no more than I deserved; my sins—my aggravated sins—appeared so great. I remained out of doors the most of the night. In the morning, early, before I went home, I called at Mr. Nettleton's lodgings. He sent word that he could not see me at that hour. I went away, and returned in an hour or so. He told the servant to request me to be seated, and he would be with me in a few minutes.

"Every minute now seemed an hour, and a long one too. For nearly thirty minutes he kept me in this state of horrible suspense, during which I was constantly pacing the floor with my watch in my hand. When, at length, he entered the room, I threw my arms round his neck, told him I was in perfect agony, and that I should die if he did not, in some way, comfort me. I told him it seemed as if I could not live another hour in such distress.

"'*I* can't help you, my dear friend; you must not look to me;' and he burst into a flood of tears.

"'What shall I do? what shall I do?' I repeated over and over again in a loud voice.

"'You must yield your heart to Christ, or you are lost,' said he; and then added: 'I do certainly think your situation a very alarming and dangerous one.'

"After a few minutes, he said: 'Come, let us kneel down.' This was contrary to his usual practice. He made a very short prayer, not more than a minute in length—rose from his knees—advised me to go home and remain in my room, and abruptly left me, almost overcome with emotion. Had there been any means of self-destruction within my reach, I believe I should have employed it, so agonizing were my feelings. He sent word to me by a young friend, that he did not wish to ride that day. I passed the most of the day in my room on my knees. Occasionally, I walked for a few minutes in my garden, and then returned to my room. It was the *just* and the *eternal* displeasure of an *angry* God that seemed to crush me to the earth. About the middle of the afternoon one of the elders came to see me, and expressed surprise at my distress—said there was no necessity for my feeling so bad, he knew there was not—and tried to persuade me it would all be well with me *soon*. I told him, that if he could satisfy me that it would ever be well with me, I would gladly and cheerfully endure my sufferings thousands of years. This feeling I distinctly remember. The *justice* of God, and the *eternity* of His anger, distressed me most. I sent for Mr. Nettleton; but he excused himself, and did not come.*

'Thus every refuge failed me,
And all my hopes were cross'd.'

"It was past the middle of the afternoon, and approaching sundown, and I had not yet broken my fast. After a short walk in the garden, I again entered my room, locked the door, and threw myself prostrate on my settee, as near a state of hopeless despair as I can conceive a mortal to be on this side the bottomless pit. I cried aloud: 'O my God! how long—how long? O my God! my God!' After repeating this and similar language several times, I seemed to sink away into a state of insensibility. When I came to myself, I was upon my knees, pray-

* There must evidently have been a peculiarity in this case, that called for this reserve on Dr. Nettleton's part. Every moment of this person's anguish was caused by positive *unbelief;* so that it was most undesirable to keep him in it; for to do so was to keep him resisting the Spirit, who glorifies Christ—rejecting Christ, who waited to be gracious—and making God a liar, who was testifying: "Whosoever seeth the Son, and believeth on Him, hath everlasting life." But for some special peculiarity, we should have been inclined to apply here Gambold's lines regarding our Master's manner of dealing with prodigals returning:—

"Yea, praise to Him, accessible and mild,
Who keeps no state with a returning child!

Let never narrow hearts the haste arraign
Of Jesus, to relieve a sinner's pain.
He knows what is in man: nor to His art
Are chaos and creation far apart.
There's but a word between: be that word given,
Your sinful soul shall be a saint of heaven."

ing, not for myself, but for others. I felt submission to the will of God,—willing that He should do with me as should seem good in His sight. My concern for myself seemed all lost in concern for others. *Terror* seemed all exchanged for *love*, and *despair* for *hope*. God was glorious, and Christ unspeakably precious. I was an overwhelming wonder to myself. The cry of 'Blessed Jesus! blessed Jesus!' took the place of 'Lord, have mercy!'

"After remaining in my room half-an-hour, or thereabouts, I came down stairs, and met my dear wife, who had deeply sympathized with me in my distress. I exclaimed: 'I have found Him! I have found Him! and He is a precious Saviour!' She was very much overcome. She persuaded me to take some food; but I was so happy and so anxious to go to meeting, the bell having rung, that I could eat but little. I went over to the session-house; it was crowded—benches in the aisle were filled. I obtained a seat near the door. Mr. Nettleton was reading the 211th hymn of the village collection,—

'Of all the joys we mortals know,
Jesus, thy love exceeds the rest,' &c.

I thought I never heard so sweet a hymn, nor so delightful music. I sung it at the top of my voice; of which, however, I was not aware, until I saw I had attracted the observation of all near me. My eyes were streaming with tears; while my countenance was beaming with delight, as a friend afterwards told me. I wanted to tell to all around what a Saviour I had found.

"After service, I walked home with Mr. Nettleton, and remained with him a few minutes. 'I knew this morning,' said he, 'that the turning point was not far off.' He cautioned me again and again against giving way to my feelings; urged me to keep humble and prayerful, and not say much to any one. That night I could not sleep for joy. I do not think I closed my eyes. I found myself singing several times in the night. In the morning all nature seemed in a new dress, and vocal with the praises of a God all-glorious. Everything seemed changed; and I could scarcely realize that one, only yesterday so wretched, was now so happy. I felt it perfectly reasonable, that he who had had much forgiven, should love much. I think I sincerely inquired: 'Lord, what wilt thou have me to do?' and though eighteen years have passed, God is still glorious, and Christ still precious, to my soul; and, unless I am greatly deceived, I still pray for a knowledge of my duty, and for grace to do it. I know that I still love to do good and make others happy; and of all anticipated delights which I can place before my mind, that of the enjoyment of sinless perfection in heaven is the greatest. But never was a sense of my unworthiness greater than it is at present.

'What was there in me that could merit esteem,
Or give the Creator delight?
'Twas "Even so, Father," I ever must sing,
"Because it seem'd good in Thy sight."
Then give all the glory to His holy name,
To Him all the glory belongs;
Be mine the high joy still to sound forth His fame,
And crown Him in each of my songs'

T. W. B."

In such ways as these was the arm of the Lord revealed. Mr. Nettleton left that spot in November 1826, and visited *Albany*—remaining there through most of the winter. While here, though very feeble,

God made him the instrument of the hopeful conversion of not a few souls. He speaks, in one of his letters, of eighty rejoicing in hope. In a letter to the Rev. Mr. Aikin, of Utica, extracts from which will be inserted in a future chapter, he says: "Would that I had time and strength to give you particulars on the state of religion in this region, and elsewhere. In Albany it is interesting. I have met a number of circles of different kinds. Some are rejoicing in hope, and a number are anxious for their souls."

In the spring of 1827, he repaired to *Durham*, New York. While here, his bodily weakness was so great as to lead him to apprehend that he was drawing near the close of life. The following letter, addressed to the Rev. Mr. Williston, the pastor of the church in Durham, will shew the state of his mind at that time,—a letter which, as it is found among Mr. Nettleton's own papers, may never have been delivered. It is dated Durham, April 21, 1827.

"BROTHER WILLISTON,—This day I am forty-four years old. I feel thankful that a kind Providence has led me to this place, and that I have had the satisfaction of a short acquaintance with you. I cannot express my feelings now. But, in view of the uncertainty of life, I would say that I am happy in the thought of laying my bones in your burying-ground. I cannot tell how it may be in the solemn hour of death; and a willingness to die I do not think is, in itself, any evidence of grace. But the thought of leaving the world appears rather pleasant; and, above all, the thought of never sinning. I feel it to be a *great thing* to be a Christian. Such words as these appear sweet. 'I am now ready to be offered,' &c.

'O glorious hour! O blest abode!
I shall be near and like my God;
And flesh and sin no more control
The sacred pleasures of the soul.'

"I feel a peculiar love to ministers—especially to those with whom I have laboured in seasons of revival. Remember me affectionately to them all. They will find my feelings in the twentieth chapter of Acts. I feel a peculiar interest in theological students, and I have been wishing to leave something that would be useful—something which has been learned by experience. I would say to young men, it is a good symptom when they secure the confidence of aged and experienced ministers. The younger should submit themselves to the elder, and always speak kindly of them.

"My mind ranges over all the towns and places where I have laboured in seasons of revival with peculiar delight. *I have feelings of inexpressible tenderness and compassion for all the young converts.* They will find much of them in 1st and 2d Thessalonians. My affectionate regards to all my relatives in North Killingworth. Tell them to prepare to follow me. I die among kind friends. Tell your congregation, and especially the young people, to seek an interest in Christ without delay. When I am buried on yonder hill, tell them to remember the evening when I preached to them from these words: '*Seek first the kingdom of God.*' Whenever they pass my grave, tell them, they will each one remember: 'There lies the man who talked to me about my soul.' I die in peace with all mankind. In great weakness,—Your affectionate friend and brother, A. N."

Notwithstanding his great weakness while at Durham, his labours were attended by a divine blessing.

God poured out His Spirit, and numbers were hopefully made the subjects of renewing grace.

In the summer of the same year, there was an interesting revival under his preaching at *Lexington Heights*, on the Catskill mountains. Between thirty and forty were, in the judgment of charity, called out of darkness into marvellous light.

While there, he wrote the following letter to Mr. Charles E. Furman, a member of the theological seminary at Auburn, afterwards pastor of the church in Victor, New York,—a letter that may be said to cast light on God's dealings with His servant, in sending him a time of weakness.

"MY DEAR FRIEND,—When I saw that the captivity of Zion was turned, I retired out of the region of news and noise among these mountains. The bear and the panther, the wolf and the wild-cat, it is said, are occasionally seen, or heard ranging the forests which surround the village and the mansion where I now reside. The deer I have seen leaping the fence and the mound, with a hound close to his heels. I have often been reminded of these words: 'And He was with the wild beasts: and the angels ministered unto Him.' When the apostles returned to Christ, and gave an account of their mission, He said unto them: 'Come ye yourselves apart into a desert place, and rest awhile.' Every itinerant preacher, especially if he has been engaged in a revival of religion, must feel the need of this last direction, or suffer greatly if he long neglect it. I could not advise any one to be employed in a powerful revival more than three months, without retiring into solitude for a short time to review the past, and to attend to his own heart.

He will find much to lament, and much to correct; and it is by deep and solemn *reflection* upon the past, and by this only, that he can reap the advantages of past experience. It is not by passing through many revivals of religion that we can gain any valuable experience on the subject. Many former, as well as some recent examples, prove the truth of this remark.

"The people where I reside are destitute of a settled pastor. I have preached a number of times to a very crowded, silent, and solemn assembly. I have met a number in deep distress of soul; and, recently, some are rejoicing in hope, and begin to sing 'Redeeming Love.' We have a most excellent choir of youthful singers,—some of whom are among the young converts. Last evening I saw two of the most gay and thoughtless of them, who I feared were going to be left, and found them in awful distress. I had noticed that they did not sing in the choir on the Sabbath, though they are favoured with the sweetest voices. On my visit, I found the reason might be given in the following beautiful lines:—

'How can my soul exult for joy which feels this load of sin;
And how can praise my tongue employ while darkness reigns within?
My soul forgets to use her wings, my harp neglected lies;
For sin has broken all its strings, and guilt shuts out my joys!'

"I have thought very seriously of requesting you to make us a visit, for I needed your help to write off tunes, and to aid in learning them. But my time here is so short that I could not request it. My health is feeble, though better than it was last summer. I have been advised by physicians to spend the winter at the south; and it is time to make my arrangements. I wish to hear from you soon. What is the state of things in

Auburn? My best regards to Dr. Richards and to all my friends.—Yours truly."

In the Fall of 1827, he went to the south for the benefit of his health. He spent the winter in *Virginia*, and was made the instrument of a great work of divine grace. Dr. John H. Rice, in a letter to Dr. Alexander, thus speaks of these labours :—

"When Mr. Nettleton had strength to labour, he soon was made instrumental in producing a considerable excitement. This has extended, and now the state of things is deeply interesting. Five lawyers, all of very considerable standing, have embraced religion. This has produced a mighty sensation in *Charlotte*, *Mecklenburg*, *Nottaway*, *Cumberland*, *Powhattan*, *Buckingham*, and *Albemarle*. The minds of men seem to stand a-tiptoe, and they seem to be looking for some great thing. Mr. Nettleton is a remarkable man, and chiefly, I think, remarkable for his power of producing a great excitement, without much *appearance* of feeling. The people do not either weep, or talk away their impressions. The preacher chiefly addresses *Bible truth* to their *consciences*. I have not heard him utter, as yet, a single sentiment opposed to what you and I call orthodoxy. He preaches the Bible. He derives his illustrations from the Bible."

Mr. Nettleton remained in Virginia, labouring in different parts of that state, as his health and strength would permit, and with no inconsiderable success, until the spring of 1829.

The following letter to his friend Mr. Cobb, will give some idea of his labours in Virginia, and their results :—

"New York, *Feb.* 17, 1831.

"My dear Brother,—Your very welcome letter of the 15th is just received. It awakened in my mind the most tender recollections of scenes that are past—the years of the right hand of the Most High, never to be forgotten. I rejoice to hear that the subjects of the last revival in your society so generally run well. My most affectionate regards to every one of them, and tell them how I should rejoice to see their faces once more in this world.

"Many things have transpired in my own history since I saw you last, and some deeply interesting. My turns of faintness increased until 1827, when the physicians despaired of my life; and, as the last resort, I was advised to go to a southern climate. For three winters I have been in the southern states, and my health has wonderfully improved, so that I have been able to labour almost incessantly. The scene of the deepest interest was in the county of *Prince Edward*, Virginia, in the vicinity of the Union Theological Seminary, and Hampden Sydney College. Our first meeting of inquiry was at the house of Dr. Rice—the very mansion containing the theological students. More than a hundred were present, inquiring, 'What must we do to be saved?' Among the subjects of divine grace were a number of lawyers—six or seven—and some of them among the leading advocates at the bar. Some were men of finished education, who are soon to become heralds of salvation.

"During my residence in Virginia, I took a tour across the Alleghany Mountains, about two hundred miles, to spend a short time during the warm season. On my way, I spent a few weeks at a place called

Staunton, where I left a pleasant little circle of young converts. On a certain Sabbath, as we were almost destitute of singers, I noticed a female voice, which, from its fulness, and sweetness, and wildness, all combined, attracted my attention. On arriving at my lodgings, I inquired of a young lady whose voice it could be, and whether we could not catch and tame it, and enlist it in our service? The name, I was informed, was S—— L——. 'Will you not invite her to call and see us?'—'Oh! she is a very gay and thoughtless young lady, was never at our house, and we have no acquaintance with her.' 'Tell her from me that I wish to see her—that I want the aid of her voice.' N—— went out, and, in a few moments, returned with the interesting stranger, who sat down with a pleasing, pensive countenance, which seemed to say: Now is my time to seek an interest in Christ. And so it was, that she and her sister, and fifteen or twenty others, became deeply impressed, and soon became joyful in Christ. This little circle would call on me daily, linking hand in hand, and, smiling through their tears, would sing 'Redeeming Love.'

"I bade them farewell—and now for the sequel. I have received a letter from Dr. Wardell, the worthy physician of that place, at whose house I resided, from which I will give an extract: 'We have had several instances of death from typhus fever since you left us. The only individual whom you know, included in this number, was one of your *little circle*, S—— L——. It will be no less gratifying to you than it is to her friends here, to learn that she gave abundant evidence of the genuineness of the Christian profession. To go a little into detail. She had been complaining for several days before she would consent to lie by; and even then did not call in medical aid for some days. I first saw her six days from her first attack, when she was entirely prostrate. She said she believed she should not recover; nor had she any desire to live longer. So far from being dismayed at death, she seemed to view it as one of the most joyful events. I was in some perplexity to ascertain whether these were the feelings of a sound mind, and the vigorous exercise of faith; and closely watched for some *incoherences* which might settle the inquiry; but there was nothing of the kind. She was too weak to converse much; but had her friends summoned around her, to give them a word of exhortation; expressing a strong desire to be the means of leading one soul to heaven. She took great delight in gazing on those whom she had been accustomed to meet in your *little religious circle*, because she expected to meet them in heaven. She often spoke of you and your little social meetings, prayed for you, and said she should meet you in a larger circle in heaven than she had ever done in Staunton. In order to test the correctness of her apprehension, I asked her if she would feel no diffidence in being admitted into the presence of a holy God, and the holy beings who surround His throne? She had strength only to reply: "But I am washed—I am washed!" She lived fourteen days after I saw her first. I have been thus particular, because she requested that some one would inform you of her death.'

"You will pardon me for sending you this little story. It cannot touch your feelings as it does my own. You may read it to your young people as a token of affectionate remembrance from—Their unworthy friend."

While Mr. Nettleton was in Virginia, he wrote the following letter to the Rev. Lavius Hyde; and although it contains but little respecting his labours, it will be read with interest on other accounts. It will give the reader some idea of Mr. Nettleton's exquisite sensibility to the beauties of poetry:—

"STAUNTON, VIRGINIA, *March* 4, 1829.

"MY DEAR BROTHER,—So many things have transpired since I left the north, that I am really at a loss how to begin my letter, or what to say. Indeed, I should not probably have sent you even this, had not the biography of our departed friend, Carlos Wilcox,* to my surprise, found its way over these mountains, into the interior of Virginia. I have read it with no common interest alone—also in company with a number of ministers and Christians, who were greatly delighted. Some part of it, I mean the poetic part, I have read frequently in a circle of young converts in this place. 'The Religion of Taste' has set them all weeping; especially from the 79th to the 91st verse inclusive. A few Sabbaths since, seventeen persons made a public profession of religion in this place: and as they all stood in a single row, side by side, in front of the pulpit, while the minister was addressing them, they affectionately grasped each other by the hand. With wonderful adroitness, the minister seized this circumstance, and observed that he considered it as a signal of the union of their hearts. A

* Mr. Hyde was the author of this biography.

few days after, while sitting in a circle, linking hand in hand, I read to them, for the first time, the 'Religion of Taste.' When I came to the 87th verse, the effect I cannot describe. Others were present who were without hope, and anxious for their souls. And, oh! you cannot imagine how solemn it was, when I came to these words:—

> 'I only wandered on, with none to meet,
> And call me dear, while pointing to the past,
> And forward to the joys that never reach their last,
> I had not bound myself by any ties
> To that blest land.'

"I do think this piece contains specimens of exquisite painting. The fourth verse I have often read to my friends as specimens. The 98th and 101st are favourites. How I should like to read and enjoy the whole of this and Pollok with you and Mr. Hyde! While reading the latter, how often has the thought crossed my mind: What would friend Carlos have said had it made its appearance in his lifetime?

"I have no time to give you an outline of my own sorrows or joys.

> 'What matter whether pain or pleasure fill
> The swelling heart one little moment here!'

"Providence permitting, I start for Prince Edward within a few days, and hope to visit New England in the spring. My best regards to all your family.—Yours truly."

The following letter, from a highly respectable clergyman in Virginia, furnishes information in reference to Dr. Nettleton's labours in Virginia, and the estimation in which those labours were held by Christians here:—

"CUMBERLAND COUNTY, VIRGINIA,
July 17, 1844.

"It was my privilege, while a young man in the ministry of the Gospel, to share his confidence and his friendship, during his first visit to Virginia in 1828, and the beginning of '29; and I had, on two occasions, afterwards, an opportunity for intimate and most delightful intercourse with him. During the winter of 1828, he spent two weeks in my study at Buckingham, C. H.; to which place I had just been called as the pastor of the small Presbyterian church there, and which had enjoyed the privilege of his ministry for a few weeks during the summer of that year, with the manifest blessing of the Head of the Church on his labours. He was then resting from the severe and exhausting labours which he had undergone during the summer and Fall, at Hampden Sydney, Prince Edward Co., at Buckingham, C. H., and in the Valley of Virginia. During those two weeks I had the highly-prized opportunity of full conversation with him about his views in theology; with the doctrinal history of which he was uncommonly well acquainted; about the whole subject of revivals of religion; the proper manner of presenting divine truth to the understandings and consciences of men, in connexion with a spirit of prayer, and a feeling and entire dependence on the Spirit and grace of God to make the truth effectual; and plans for building up the kingdom of Christ. On all these subjects he was the most interesting and instructive individual with whom I have ever had intercourse; and, on the subject of *revivals of religion*, incomparably the *wisest* man I ever saw. It was a subject which he had thoroughly studied in the light of revelation and ecclesiastical history, and on which he had an amount of experience and observation probably beyond any man living. You will render most important service to the cause of Christ if you succeed, as I trust you may, in getting before the public mind a full exhibition of his views on this subject.

"He was introduced into Virginia by the Rev. Dr. John H. Rice, then Professor of Christian Theology in Union Theological Seminary, Prince Edward Co., and very soon began his labours with the Presbyterian church in the immediate vicinity of the seminary and Hampden Sydney College. The Spirit of God accompanied his exhibitions of divine truth, and soon a most interesting and precious revival of religion was enjoyed with the church there. He was deeply interested in this revival of religion, and so were many others, because of the number of educated gentlemen, especially lawyers of high standing and extensive influence, who were hopefully converted during this blessed season of divine influence. Not many gentlemen of this profession had, up to this time, been members of any church in this section of country. Those referred to were from several adjoining counties; and this circumstance attracted no little attention, and sent out an extensive and most salutary influence on the surrounding country, especially the county of *Buckingham.* This county, in execution of his ordinary plan of making the scene of a revival a centre of influence for the surrounding country, he took an early opportunity to visit. He preached at the court-house for a few Sabbaths, to a small church which had been organized a few years before; and here his ministry excited great attention, and was accompanied with the special blessing of Heaven. The revival at this place was not extensive, but it laid the foundation, as I had occasion to know, for building up quite a flourishing Presbyterian church in that region. I had on the ground an interesting opportunity to observe the practical effects of a genuine revival of religion, conducted on true scriptural principles, as I began to minister to that community in the beginning of the winter of that year. The views of religion which he presented were so scriptural and rational, commending themselves to every man's conscience, and the sympathies of the community, in the midst of deep interest and intense feeling, were so wisely managed, avoiding everything like extravagance and fanaticism, that the sober and well-balanced minds of *those without*, could find no occasion to object to anything that was said or done. When Dr. Nettleton went away, the consciences of the people were left on the side of rational and intelligent piety. The young people, too, grew up under the impression that revivals of religion are blessed seasons; so that, when another revival came, the obstacles in the way seemed to be small. That church has been emphatically one of revivals ever since, and has been mainly built up by them. The same impression, as I have had opportunity to know, was left on the public mind by the revival in *Prince Edward Co*, as indeed, it always will be when a genuine revival of religion, properly conducted, is enjoyed.

"Towards the close of the summer of that year, Dr. Nettleton's health, which was quite feeble when he came to Virginia, rendered it proper, as he thought, that he should visit the mountains and the mineral springs located among them. He could not, however, during his excursion, debar himself the privilege of preaching the Gospel. He laboured for a few weeks, with the blessing of God, (but not to the same extent as at Prince Edward and Buckingham C. H.,) at *Lewisburg*, Greenbrier County, and at *Staunton*, Augusta County.

"These trips gave him an opportunity for extending his acquaintance and his influence with the clergy of Virginia, by whom he was everywhere received with the utmost cordiality and Christian affection. The report of the blessing of God on his labours for Christ, which preceded him, opened the hearts of all our ministers and people towards him. You, doubtless, had an opportunity to know how the cordiality and Christian affection of his Virginia brethren affected him. On their part, (I had many occasions to know,) they regarded his visit to Virginia as a great blessing to our churches. I have always thought that Dr. Nettleton's sojourn among us was worth more to the cause of Christ, from the influence which he exerted on the *minds of ministers*, than in any other point of view. He certainly exerted no little influence on the manner of preaching the Gospel in this part of the state; but, probably, yet greater good resulted from the interest which he excited on the subject of genuine revivals of religion. Our churches had been blessed with such seasons of refreshing before; but the subject had not been anything like so well understood. The views which followed his visit have powerfully influenced the minds of ministers and Christians generally ever since; and their hallowed influence, we may reasonably hope, will go down upon the Church for many years to come. He felt great interest *in the students of our seminary,* who were soon to be in the field of ministerial labour; and cordially co-operated with good Dr. Rice in efforts to imbue them with the right spirit for the great work of preaching the Gospel. I well knew how high a value Dr. Rice placed on his visit to the seminary, and on the opportunity which his young men enjoyed for witnessing his manner of presenting divine truth, and conducting things in a revival of religion.

"His interest on the subject of revivals was intense; and as he regarded them as the great means, in connexion with the pastoral office, in building up the kingdom of Christ, and saving a lost world, he was most deeply solicitous that correct views on the subject should prevail. He took great pains in explaining his views to those whom he regarded as being judicious, and *trusty;* and guarded with extreme caution against everything wild and fanatical. He had abundant reason to be deeply solicitous on this subject, as individuals at the north, and especially in western New York, had run revivals into extravagance; and then, as he said, attempted to plead the authority of his name and example for their ultra and extravagant proceedings. I never saw him so deeply excited on any subject as in conversation about these abuses. His *measures*—if it be proper thus to characterize the means which he used in connexion with revivals of religion—were new in this region, and excited great interest. The fact, however, was, that there was nothing new about his plans, except that he brought people together who were concerned about their soul, and had made up their minds to attend at once to the subject of religion, into a general *inquiry meeting,* and sometimes into smaller meetings of the same kind in private houses, in the more distant parts of a congregation, for the purpose of personal conversation and instruction adapted to the peculiar cases of individuals. At these meetings young converts were kept with those who were anxious. These plans were suggested by common sense and the necessity of the case, and were approved by the most judicious ministers amongst us. Some, however, were disposed, as had been done elsewhere, to try to improve on his simple plans; and as he knew that *imitations* were likely to rise up here, as in other places, and plead his authority for measures which he could not approve, he was reserved in communicating his views, unless to persons who, he was convinced, were opposed to running revivals into extravagance and contempt. This, in some instances, brought against him the charge of being reserved and *queer*,—often because he would not sit down (when his time was directly needed for the Lord's work) to explain all his views and plans to every individual who chose to visit him,—or because he could not go to preach at several places at the same time, to which he was invited. It is enough to say, that he had the cordial approbation of the most judicious ministers and intelligent laymen in the region, and that his visit was regarded with special gratitude to the great Head of the Church.

"It was not to be expected that the devil would be still when he saw so much done to make his strongholds in this part of the country *tremble from turret to foundation-stone.* Accordingly, one of his agents at Cartersville, in the lower part of this county, when I was there preaching as a licentiate, imported some stale slanders from Connecticut about Mr. Nettleton. The name of this man was O—— G—— W—— from Connecticut; and he attempted to gain currency for his stories by the aid of a letter from R—— S—— H——, also of Connecticut. All these slanders were silenced by an overwhelming mass of testimony from a number of the first men in New England.

"Dr. Nettleton paid several other visits to Virginia in later years; but generally in such poor health, that he attempted very little in the way of preaching the Gospel. To the last he retained the confidence and affection of those who had known him in the days of his greater vigour to labour for Christ and the salvation of souls.—With Christian regard, your brother in the Gospel, JESSE S. ARMISTEAD."

During the summer of 1829, he preached in several different places in New England; in all of which, I believe, he was instrumental in the conversion of some souls. I know not that there were extensive revivals in any of these places, except in *Monson*, Massachusetts, where he laboured a short time amid scenes of great interest. The following is an extract of a letter from the Rev. Dr. Ely, pastor of the church in Monson, written June 4, 1844:—

"Dr. Nettleton was among the few whose memory will be long cherished by the churches as an eminent instrument, in the hands of God, of reviving His work, and of bringing multitudes to embrace the Saviour for righteousness and life. He seems to have been raised up by the great Head of the Church to accomplish His purposes of mercy in the revival of pure religion, and in the conversion of sinners. His influence upon the ministry, and upon the churches where he laboured, was peculiarly happy. *He always left behind him a sweet savour of Christ.* Harmony and Christian affection between pastors and people, were the result of his labours, even where they had been most successful in the conversion of souls. His zeal and earnestness in preaching the Gospel, where Christ was named, were so tempered with practical wisdom and singular prudence, that he was received, and loved, and remembered, as a messenger from God sent to bless the people.

"His labours among us, in the year 1829, are recollected with affection and gratitude. The revival with which we were favoured that year, commenced about the middle of July. It was unusually powerful and still, and rapid in its progress. There was less animal excitement, convictions of sin were more thorough, and conversions were more clear and decided, than in some other seasons of revival which we have enjoyed. We had little to do, but to stand still and see the salvation of God. Mr. Nettleton, if I mistake not, was then preaching at *Enfield*, Massachusetts. By my request he came and spent a week with us about the first of September, and preached frequently to the most solemn and attentive assemblies I ever witnessed. He then left us, and returned again in about ten days, and spent another week. He preached on one Sabbath only. On that day I supplied his place at Enfield. He preached and held inquiry meetings in the evenings of the week, and visited the families with me in the daytime. His labours were very acceptable, and eminently useful; and I bless God for his aid. Many were awakened under his preaching, and some hopefully converted; and those who entertained hope, were greatly enlightened and strengthened. He is remembered to this day with much affection.

"The chief excellence of his preaching seemed to consist in great plainness, and simplicity, and discrimination—in much solemnity and affectionate earnestness of manner—in the application of the truth to the heart and conscience—in taking away the excuses of sinners, and leaving them without help and hope, except in the sovereign mercy of God. In short, it was conformed to the work for which the Spirit was sent into the world,—viz., to reprove or convince the world of Sin, of Righteousness, and of Judgment. This characteristic was most striking. His manner of dealing with awakened sinners was peculiar. While it served to deepen their convictions, and lead them to Christ, it gained their confidence, and secured their belief of the truth. He knew, too, how to search those who expressed hope. And while he detected the hypocrite, and encouraged the desponding, he was regarded by all with affection and reverence.

"A large number of the subjects of this revival were young people, belonging to the first families in the place. Of about one hundred who expressed hope at that time, more than sixty belonged to the centre district. Numbers of them have removed to other places, and others have died in the joyful hope of glory. Frequently have I heard them express their remembrance of Dr. Nettleton's labours, and of their obligations to him as the instrument of leading them to Christ. Some, on examination for church fellowship, dated their awakening and conversion to his labours. Of the number admitted to the church that year, only four have apostatized. They have generally maintained the Christian character; and some of them are eminently useful in the Church. His labours, though short with us, were *greatly* blessed; and I shall ever remember them with gratitude to the great Head of the Church, who disposed him to come and help us."

In the Fall of 1829, he went again to the south for the benefit of his health. He spent some time in *Charleston*, S. C. He then repaired to North Carolina, and preached considerably, during the months of February and March, at *Chapel Hill*, *New Hope*, and *Hillsborough*. In all these places, it is understood his labours were crowned with success; but to what extent, we have no means of ascertaining.

The summer of 1830 he spent in New England, preaching occasionally in different places, as his strength would permit. During the winter of 1830-31, he preached in *Newark*, N. J., and in the city of *New York*, assisting the Rev. Baxter Dickinson, and the Rev. Drs. Snodgrass and Spring, while God was pouring out His Spirit on their congregations. Still, as before, to the extent of his bodily strength, he entered wherever the Lord opened a door, and seemed to send him.

Dr. Humphrey, President of College, Amherst, says of him in a letter to his biographer:—

"It is as clear to me that God raised him up to spend his best days in promoting revivals of religion, as that he raised up Whitefield for the same service on a wider theatre. They were as unlike, in many respects, as any two great revival preachers could be; but they had 'one Lord and one faith,'—the same love for souls, and the same irrepressible desire to win as many of them as possible to Christ. Each was fitted for the age in which he lived, and for the work to which he was called;—Whitefield, to blow the trumpet over the dead and buried formalism of the churches both in Great Britain and America; Nettleton, to 'strengthen the things that remained and were ready to die' in destitute churches of Connecticut, Massachusetts, New York, and Virginia; and to help the brethren in gathering their spiritual harvests."

The days in which he had health and strength to engage in arduous labour, were emphatically days of the right hand of the Most High. They will long be remembered on earth, and never be forgotten in heaven.

CHAPTER XI.

VISIT TO GREAT BRITAIN IN 1831—HIS METHODS—CHARACTERISTICS OF REVIVALS UNDER HIM.

THE sovereignty of God in blessing when and where it seemed good to Him, was never more acknowledged by any one than by Mr. Nettleton; and as if to teach him this doctrine by experience, at a time when revivals seemed to appear wherever he laboured, the Lord first visited him with sickness, and then gave him a change of scene and of effects.

In the spring of 1831 he took a voyage to England for the benefit of his health. Before sailing, he thus writes to a friend:—

"I have but a few moments to write, and I never wrote with such fulness of heart. Drs. H—— and G—— and others you know, contemplate a voyage to England. My friends have arranged for me to go with them, without any agency of my own. But if I go, it is not to labour, and it is entirely at my own expense. If you hear that I am on the great waters, do remember me. I never loved my friends so ardently as since I have been thinking of this voyage. I cannot tell you on paper the ten thousand tender recollections that have crowded on my mind."

He reached England, and visited various parts of

Scotland and Ireland also. He was more than a year in the United Kingdom.

He had gone thither to rest, not to labour, according to his own words in the letter given above; but he was not permitted to remain idle; nor were his labours altogether in vain. At the same time, there was nothing apparent of that singular success that had attended his labours at home.

He kept a very brief journal, in which he noted down the places which he visited, and the texts from which he preached, together with a few occasional remarks. It appears from this journal, that he travelled extensively, and preached frequently. No doubt, however, his vigour of body was not what it had been, nor could his mental energy be equal to what it was in the days of strong health; and this may account, in some measure, for the impression made by his preaching having been far less than was expected. Besides, he was unable to hold any *series* of meetings, a measure to which he attached much importance. At the same time, the Lord may have intended to prevent His people attaching too much importance to any instrument; and to this cause, as much, at least, as to anything in his style not being so suitable to this country as to America, may be ascribed the comparative inefficiency of his preaching.

In *Edinburgh* he preached a sermon that made a most powerful impression on all present. While he was speaking, a pious woman, who sat in a remote part of the house, was so affected, that, leaving her seat and walking up in front of the pulpit, she thus addressed the preacher: "Dear Sir, don't forget that 'God so loved the world that He gave His only begotten Son, that whosoever believeth on Him might not perish, but have everlasting life.'" The following notes of the close of that sermon have been preserved:—

"But what must be the state of every sinner out of Christ? Sinner, in what court will you plead? At the tribunal of justice or of mercy? It is with the kindest intention that you are now called upon to hear that the sentence of eternal death is pronounced upon you, and that this sentence is holy, just, and good. Let the miseries of this life—let the messenger of death, and the dark world of woe, rise up to your view, and testify how awful is that law which condemns you! To vindicate the honour of this broken law, everlasting fire is prepared for the devil and his angels. Here they dwell in endless torments. These, O sinner! were once angels of light, and dwelt in the presence of God. But how are they fallen, no more to rise! They sinned against that God whose law now condemns you. 'The inhabitants of the old world, and of Sodom, are set forth for an example, suffering the vengeance of eternal fire.'

"Out of Christ, you are condemned already, and the wrath of God abideth on you. Out of Christ, all your actions hitherto are scanned by this perfect law, and not one sin is pardoned. Out of Christ, you stand this moment in awful hazard of losing your immortal soul, and suffering for every failure of perfect obedience to this holy law. Out of Christ, nothing but the mere mercy of that God in whose hand is your life—the mercy of Him whom you are continually provoking by your sins, this moment holds you from dropping into the flames of hell. What, then, must be the weight of your guilt? If one sin must send an angel of light into the bottomless pit—if, in consequence of Adam's sin, he, too, with all his posterity, might have been reserved in everlasting chains, under darkness, without one offer of pardoning mercy,—what must be your guilt, when every action is laid in the balance, and found wanting? Oh! that you might hear and tremble! When God in awful majesty pronounced this law from Mount Sinai, His voice then shook the earth, and they that heard entreated that the word should not be spoken to them any more; for the guilty world could not endure that 'which was commanded.' But this law still speaks, however deaf, and however careless the sinner may be—this law still speaks, and proclaims approaching vengeance near.

"But, stop! the uplifted arm of vengeance is yet stayed. The collected wrath yet waits a moment. A voice from the mercy-seat—a warning voice is heard. The Saviour calls. Haste, then, O sinner! haste to Christ, the only refuge from the storm, and covert from the gathering tempest. Then safe from the fear of evil, at a distance, you shall only hear the thunders roll; while pardon, peace, and eternal life are yours."

Much prejudice existed in both England and Scotland against revivals, caused by false information conveyed to this country as to modes of proceeding said to be adopted in America, and by Dr. Nettleton himself. He attended several meetings convened for the purpose of hearing his accounts of them.

While he was in Sheffield, he saw a letter which was written by an English clergyman who was travelling in America, and who had attended several protracted meetings. He makes from this letter the following extract:—

"Terrific sermons* and other means are artfully contrived to stimulate the feelings of ignorant people. In compliance with the call given at the period of the highest excitement, they repair to *the anxious seat* by scores. As their fears are soon aroused, they are generally as soon calmed; and in a few days many profess to entertain hope. Many such converts soon lose all appearance of religion; but they become conceited, secure, and Gospel-proof; so that, while living in the open and habitual neglect of their duty, they talk very freely of the time when they experienced religion."

After giving this extract, he remarked:—

"This man is said to be an excellent man, about fifty years old, having the confidence of Christians and ministers wherever he is known in this kingdom. I find they are losing confidence in our American revivals. And so the imprudence of a few zealous individuals is doing more mischief to the cause of Christ in this kingdom, than all the opposition of open enemies could ever effect. I am almost exhausted in my attempts to vindicate our revivals. I can only tell the good ministers here, that I do not, and never did, approve of the practice mentioned in the above letter; and those who adopt it must alone answer for the consequences."

At Glasgow, in Scotland, he makes the following note in his journal:—

* So far was this from being true in the genuine revivals, that Dr. Griffin, writing of an awakening among his people in 1799, says: "Little terror was preached, except what *is implied in the doctrines* of the entire depravity of the carnal heart, its enmity to God, its deceitful doubtings and attempts to avoid the soul-humbling terms of the Gospel, the radical defects of the doings of the unregenerate, and the sovereignty of God in the dispensation of His grace"—*New England Revivals.*

"Breakfasted at Mrs. Smith's, in company with the Rev. Mr. Russell of Dundee, and many others. I was questioned about American revivals—'anxious seats,' —as related by Mr. Colton and Mrs. Trollope. They said, they supposed that the practice of calling out the anxious was universal in American revivals. A long talk ensued about the propriety of the measure. The subject of anxious seats has evidently depreciated American revivals a hundred per cent. in this country. The practice of calling persons to the anxious seat, they said, existed in England only among the Methodists and Ranters. They seemed greatly surprised when I informed them, that this was not practised, nor approved of, by the best ministers in New England; and they wished me to hold a meeting to disabuse the public mind on that subject."

The following brief notice of a meeting of Episcopal clergymen, will be read with deep interest:—

"Attended a meeting of clergymen of the Established Church—principally evangelical—at the house of the Rev. Daniel Wilson, Islington. More than forty were present. I was called upon to give some account of American revivals. Commencing with the one in Yale College, in 1820, I was led to inquire if any one present could inform me of a young minister from America, who came to this country the last year for his health, and who, as I had been informed, died somewhere in the vicinity of London. I had often inquired for the house where he died, but as yet had found no one who could give me information. His name was Sutherland Douglass. Mr. Wilson, the moderator, whom I was addressing, lifted up his hands, and exclaimed: 'I knew him. I received a note informing me that a young minister from America, a stranger, dangerously sick, desired to see me. I visited him twice, and prayed with him. He died on the third day after I first saw him. I brought his remains and buried them in my churchyard.' My reply was: He was one of the subjects of that revival in Yale College, of which I was speaking. (Much weeping.)"

Among his papers are numerous letters written by persons in England and Scotland, from which it appears that he had warm friends in these countries. The writers of many of these letters express great obligations to him for the pleasure and profit which they had derived from his preaching and conversation. Several of them allude to cases which had come to their knowledge of the awakening and hopeful conversion of sinners under his labours.* He had good reason to believe that he had got some souls for his hire in Great Britain. Certainly, he was useful to many of the Lord's people.

But as the subject has been alluded to above, it may be right to shew at some length what was, or if anything could be said to be, peculiar in the method he used in conducting revivals. It is connected with the question that naturally occurs to every one interested in these revivals: What was the secret of his success?

Jones, of Creaton, somewhere says: "Ministers, above all other men, can never be too careful to steer clear of nervous complaints, or take too much pains to get rid of timidity." And yet that good

* A venerable minister in Edinburgh, who heard him preach there in Argyle Square chapel, says: "There was nothing in his address like an attempt at oratory: it was a calm, pointed appeal to the conscience."

man never for a moment supposed that, even when these hindrances were escaped, any but God alone could bless. Still, he was wisely careful, and scripturally anxious to use all means in his power to have the instrument fitly prepared. Such, also, was Dr. Nettleton. He was perfectly aware, that all human means are utterly powerless, unless made effectual by the agency of the Holy Spirit. He did not rely on his own strength. He knew that he was an earthen vessel; and that, when any success attended his labours, the excellency of the power was of God, and not of him. It was his firm belief of this truth, powerfully operating on his mind, and leading him to place no dependence on his own efforts, but to look to God in humble, earnest, persevering and confiding prayer, which constituted one principal reason of his signal success. If the question then be asked: Why Dr. Nettleton was so much more successful in winning souls to Christ than most other ministers?—the great comprehensive answer is: "Even so, Father; for so it seemed good in thy sight." This is the only answer which he was disposed to give. He attributed none of the glory to himself. Nor did any of it belong to him. He did not possess any power over the human heart which other men do not possess—he was only an instrument by which God accomplished His purposes. Nor was he selected as the instrument of such good to mankind because he was more worthy than others, or because he had done anything to entitle him to this honourable distinction.

But God, in accomplishing His purposes, not only makes use of means, but adapts means to ends. He raises up instruments, and fits them for the work which they are destined to perform. Although no labour of the husbandman will insure to him a harvest, yet he has no reason to expect a harvest without labour: nor has he a right to conclude that it is a matter of indifference what kind of labour he employs. He knows it to be important to till his ground, and to sow in it good seed. So, in the moral world, means must be adapted to the end to be accomplished. Although Paul plant, and Apollos water, God must give the increase; yet we are not to suppose that it is of no consequence what seed is planted, or how it is planted and watered. Although God might bring to pass different results, when the same means are used, and in the same manner, yet, ordinarily, when the results are different, there is some difference in the means or in the manner of employing them. Whitefield was not only a more successful preacher than others who were his contemporaries, he was also a different preacher—not that he preached different doctrines, but he preached them in a different manner.

That Dr. Nettleton possessed peculiar skill in presenting truth to the minds of men, and labouring in revivals of religion, will be admitted by most who are at all acquainted with his history. During that protracted period of conviction through which he passed before his reconciliation to God, he obtained a knowledge of the human heart which few possess. He could trace the secret windings of human depravity; he understood the refuges of lies to which sinners are prone to resort; and he knew how to meet and to answer the various excuses by which they attempted to shield themselves from blame.

The following extract of a letter written to one of

his brethren in the ministry, in 1823, shews his own views of the importance of following up an impression when made, and of making special efforts when there is evidence that the Spirit of God is operating upon the minds of the people:—

"It becomes every friend of Zion to prepare the way of the Lord through all the towns in this region. The fields are whitening all around us; and though God can create and gather the harvest without human instrumentality, yet we do not expect it. A revival *begun* is likely to subside, without the constant pressure of Gospel motives on the consciences of the awakened. It is obvious from experience, that God generally blesses far more extensively *the means for extending His work*, than He does for commencing it in the midst of surrounding darkness. As the conversion of one sinner is often the means of awakening every member of the family, and the impulse is again felt through every kindred branch, and through the village and town, so one town may be the means of a revival in another, and that in another. Though some ministers feel the truth of this remark, yet few, if any, realize its full force. There is as really a season of harvest in the moral as in the natural world. Now, every hand that can hold a sickle needs all its strength. The harvest *fully ripe*, neglected a few days, is for ever lost. Other fields may whiten, and the same field a second time, but the former neglected harvest is lost for ever. There is a crisis in the feelings of a people, which, if not improved, the souls of that generation will not be gathered. In the season of a revival, more *may* be done—more *is* often done to secure the salvation of souls, in a few days, or weeks, than in years spent in preaching at other times. One sermon in a revival often does more execution, than a hundred equally good, out of it. And I verily believe that more good may be *lost* for the want of that *one*, than can be done with it, and with a thousand like it, when the crisis is past. 'Say not ye, There are yet four months, and then'—— It is now, or never. And 'he that reapeth receiveth wages.'"

The success of Dr. Nettleton was not in every respect like that of Whitefield. Whitefield's power was chiefly in the pulpit. His eloquence was overpowering, and great multitudes were sometimes awakened by a single sermon. Dr. Nettleton did not expect such effects from a single effort in the pulpit. His success was the combined effect of preaching in the church and the lecture room, and of private conversation. His preaching was always solemn and impressive, and sometimes in a high degree eloquent. It was more instructive, and addressed more to the conscience, and less to the passions, than that of Whitefield. As a natural consequence, says his biographer, the revivals which occurred under his preaching were more pure—attended with less fanaticism, and a smaller proportion of temporary converts.

When he commenced his labours in any place, one of the first things which he attempted was, to make the impression on the minds of the people, that their help must come from above, and that they must place no dependence on an arm of flesh. When he found that they were placing undue dependence on him, he often suddenly left them, at least for a season. Until this state of feeling was destroyed he had no expectation of accomplishing any good.

It was a prime object with him, when he went into a place where there was no special seriousness, to awaken a proper state of feeling among the people of God. Knowing that when God pours out His Spirit He usually first revives His work in the hearts of His own people, and that He awakens and converts sinners in answer to their prayers, he endeavoured to impress upon their minds a sense of their responsibility. While the Rev. Fosdic Harrison was preaching in Roxbury, in 1813, just previous to his settlement there, Dr. Nettleton made him a visit. "There was, at the time," says Mr. Harrison, "more than usual attention to the means of grace. One evening he attended a meeting with me in a remote part of the town, where there were tokens of the special presence of the Holy Spirit; and yet, to his mind, indications that something was wanting. After many inquiries, he asked: 'Have you established a prayer-meeting, and urged the church to pray for a revival?' I replied: No, not yet. 'Oh!' said he, 'that is the difficulty. If I had known that, I would not have gone to the meeting. It is of no use to preach, if the church does not pray.' From that hint I immediately established a weekly prayer-meeting; after which we soon had cases of hopeful conversion." Among his first sermons in a new locality, he would sometimes preach from Rom. xiii. 11: "And that, knowing the time, that now it is high time to awake out of sleep." And sometimes from Psalm li. 12, 13:* "Restore unto me the joy of thy salvation; and uphold me with thy free Spirit. Then will I teach transgressors thy ways; and sinners shall

* A meagre outline of five pages is all that exists of this sermon. An extract of the sermon on Rom. xiii. 2, is given in chap. ix., p. 194.

be converted unto thee." But while he called on Christians with great plainness and fidelity to awake out of sleep, he never addressed them in a harsh and denunciatory manner. With kindness and affection he would remind them of their obligations and their sins, and present to them such considerations as were suited to humble them, and to excite them to a faithful discharge of their duty. He loved to see Christians deeply sensible of their sinfulness, and, at the same time, deeply affected with the condition of sinners who were perishing around them. When things began to assume a favourable appearance, he did not like to see professors of religion elated, and disposed to talk about it with an air of exultation. He knew that flattering appearances often suddenly vanish, and he had learned that it is apt to be so when Christians begin to rejoice prematurely. He frowned upon everything like ostentation, and discouraged the disposition, which too often prevails, to proclaim a revival upon the first indication of unusual seriousness.

His views on this subject are expressed by himself in a letter to the Rev. Mr. Aikin of Utica, dated Albany, January 13, 1827. Speaking of the interesting state of religious feeling which existed in Albany, he says:—

"But I have great fears that the disposition of some zealous Christians round about us to proclaim it abroad, and to run before their own hearts, and the real state of things, will run it out into noise. I have already felt the evil. I find that many are disposed to make ten times as much of the same state of things as I have been in the habit of doing, though they know but a small part of what I have seen in this place. Various reports have gone out concerning a revival in Albany, which have done us much mischief. If they would let us alone, I should expect a great work in this city. But amid so much noise and bluster of Christians, it promises fair to end in smoke. But, after all, the good people here are astonished at our stillness. My opinion is, that, had they been ten times as still, they would have witnessed ten times as much. Seven years ago, about two thousand souls were hopefully born into the kingdom in this vicinity, in our own denomination, with comparative stillness. But the times have altered. The kingdom of God now cometh with great observation."

Dr. Nettleton never held out the idea to churches, that they could "get up a revival," or that they could have a revival at any time. It is true, that he set before them the encouragement which God has given to humble and fervent prayer. But he always maintained, that a revival of true religion depends on the sovereign interposition of God. Nor did he believe in the notion of the prayer of faith entertained by some,—viz., that God will always grant the particular things for which we pray, if we only believe that He will do it.

His mode of preaching, both to saints and to sinners, was solemn, affectionate, and remarkably plain. His style was simple, perspicuous, and energetic. His illustrations were familiar and striking; such as rendered his discourses intelligible to persons of the weakest capacity; and, at the same time, interesting to persons of the most cultivated intellect. He always commanded the attention of his audience. Every eye was fixed, and a solemn stillness pervaded the assembly. There was an earnestness in his manner which carried conviction to the minds of his hearers, that he believed what he spoke, and that he believed it to be truth of everlasting moment. There was also a directness in his preaching which made the hearers feel that they were the persons addressed; and such was his knowledge of the human heart, and of the feelings which divine truth excites when presented to the minds of unsanctified men, that he was able to anticipate objections, and to follow the sinner through his various refuges of lies, and strip him of all his excuses. So great was his skill in this respect, that it often seemed to individuals while listening to his preaching, that he must know their thoughts. And, in a certain sense, it was true. By knowing his own heart, he knew the hearts of others; because, "as in water face answereth to face, so the heart of man to man." He understood from his own experience what thoughts and feelings would be excited in the minds of sinners by the contemplation of particular doctrines. When, therefore, he exhibited these doctrines in his preaching, and perceived that the attention of his hearers was fixed upon them, he *did* know, to some extent, what were their thoughts and feelings; and this enabled him to adapt his instructions to their circumstances, and to give to each one a portion in due season.

This was particularly true of his preaching in the lecture room. Here he was at home, and enjoyed the greatest freedom. Here he seemed to come in direct contact with the minds of his hearers. He watched every countenance; and in this way he was assisted in judging of the effect of his preaching on the minds of different individuals. In establishing his positions, his reasoning was so clear and forcible as to be irresistible; and conviction came upon the mind like a flash of lightning; and, as one said, "like a stream of light." And the truth was urged home upon the conscience as a matter of personal and infinite interest. Here it was that those scenes of deep distress, occasioned by a vivid sense of guilt and the apprehension of the wrath of God, so frequently occurred. It often happened in the lecture room, that sinners were so overwhelmed with a sense of their lost condition, that it became necessary to remove them to a neighbouring house.

It was never the object of Dr. Nettleton to produce mere excitement, by working upon the imagination and sympathy of his hearers. All excitement which was not the result of clear apprehensions of divine truth, he considered not merely useless, but positively injurious. The cases of deep distress which occurred under his preaching, were not the effect of mere sympathy, but of clear conviction of sin.

One thing which contributed greatly to Dr. Nettleton's success, was his faithful *private conversation.* Many were, by this means, awakened from their stupidity, and excited to attend to the concerns of their souls. He had a talent which few possess, of introducing religious conversation with individuals of every description. He was rarely abrupt; never harsh, but always kind and affectionate. His first object was to secure the confidence of the individual with whom he was conversing, and to lead him on gradually to a consideration of the importance of religion in general, and then to a more particular consideration of his own spiritual state. When he perceived that an impression had been made, he would follow it up, and watch its progress with intense assiduity. He could easily introduce religious conversation with persons of every grade in society, from the highest to the lowest. To a lawyer he once said: "I have often thought that persons in your situation —persons of liberal education and high standing in society—are in peculiar danger of losing their souls: and for this among other reasons, that everybody is afraid to converse with them." This remark opened the way for a perfectly free conversation, in which he was as faithful as he would have been to any individual in the humblest walks of life.

In conversing with awakened sinners he exhibited great wisdom. There was no part of the ministerial work in which he excelled more than in this. It was not his custom to converse *much* with awakened sinners. He has often remarked, that a great deal of conversation has a tendency to confuse the mind, and to dissipate, rather than to deepen, religious impressions. He would converse with them enough to keep the subject before their minds, and to correct any false notions which they might have imbibed. He did not like to have awakened sinners spend their time in running from one individual to another, to seek sympathy and instruction, lest they should "weep and talk away their impressions." He was desirous that they should be much alone, engaged in reading the Scriptures, serious meditation, and prayer. Mr. Brace, in his account of the revival in Newington, after describing the solemnity which pervaded the assembly at the close of one of Dr. Nettleton's meetings, says: "He requested them to retire without making a noise. 'I love to talk to you, you are so still. It looks as though the Spirit of God was here. Go away as still as possible. Do not talk by the way, lest you forget your own hearts. Do not ask how you like the preacher; but retire to your closets—bow before God, and give yourselves to Him this night.'" He frequently gave such advice.

In his conversation with awakened sinners, he was careful never to flatter them, or to say anything suited to allay their fears. He never expressed to them the opinion that their condition was hopeful. On the contrary, he gave them to understand, that, while they remained impenitent, there was an awful uncertainty whether they would be saved. He urged the duty of *immediate repentance*, and shewed them that they could do nothing short of repentance, which would in the least degree improve their condition. He endeavoured to destroy all their dependence on their own works—to shew them that all their religious services were selfish and sinful, and that God has made no promise of pardon to anything short of faith and repentance.

Sometimes, instead of entering into particular conversation with individuals who were under concern of mind, he would drop a single remark suited to awaken in their minds profitable trains of thought, such as the following:—

"If your heart is so hard that you cannot repent now, what will you do when it becomes a great deal harder?"

"What reason can you assign why you should not love God?"

"Oh! what a hard heart you have!"

"What reason have you to think that you ever shall repent?"

It was not uncommon for awakened sinners to feel as if he could give them relief; but when he found that they were relying on him to save them, he would treat them with neglect. This often called into exercise the enmity of their hearts, and thus served to deepen their conviction, by shewing them their utterly lost condition.

His feelings were often severely tried by the injudicious directions which some professors of religion were in the habit of giving to awakened sinners. He has been heard to say, that he apprehended more evil from this source, than from all the opposition of the avowed enemies of religion. He usually occupied one meeting in considering these injudicious directions. A sketch of the address delivered on these occasions is found among his papers, of which the following is an extract:—

Injudicious Directions.

"1. *Wait at the pool. You must not be discouraged, for we read of one who waited thirty and eight years.*

This text is used by way of accommodation. The impotent man was waiting at the pool, not for the pardon of his sins, but to be healed of a bodily disease. We may accommodate passages of Scripture for the purpose of illustrating acknowledged truth; but we must not trace analogies too far. In many respects there is a striking analogy between a depraved heart and a diseased body; but there is one important point in which the analogy does not hold—the one is criminal, the other is merely calamitous.

This use of the passage contradicts many plain declarations of the Bible—particularly all those which enjoin the duty of immediate repentance. Suppose a person should address sinners in this manner: Behold, now is the accepted time! Behold, now is the day of salvation! *But wait at the pool.* Choose ye this day whom ye will serve; *but wait at the pool.* God now commandeth all men everywhere to repent, *but wait at the pool.* The effect of this direction is, to make the impression on the sinner's mind, that he is not under obligation to obey God immediately; and, of course, it counteracts the influence of every command of God on the sinner's conscience.

The sinner is told that he must not be discouraged, for the impotent man waited thirty-eight years. This, however, is not said. It is said that he had an infirmity thirty-eight years; but it is not said that he had waited a day. Be this, however, as it may, he was not healed by the pool after all, nor is there any evidence that he would have been if he had waited all his life.

2. *Be patient and wait God's time.*

What is the meaning of this direction when given to an awakened sinner?

Be patient! Is the sinner to understand that he is too anxious for the salvation of his soul, and that he ought to wait patiently in his sins till God shall see fit to change his heart? To tell the anxious sinner to be patient without a new heart, is the same as to tell him to dismiss all his anxiety, and to go back to a state of stupidity. *Patient* in his sins! Rather let him be more and more impatient with himself and with his deplorable condition. Let him tremble in view of a judgment to come, and weep and howl for the miseries that are coming upon him.

What is meant when the sinner is directed to wait God's time? Is it meant that God is not now ready to receive the sinner? Is it meant that the sinner is willing to do his part, and that he must wait for God to do His? If so, why not speak plainly, and tell the sinner: I know you are ready and willing to be a Christian, but God is not yet ready and willing to receive you. But if God is not ready now to receive the returning sinner, what evidence is there that He ever will be ready?

But when *is* God's time? Do those who direct sinners to wait God's time, mean that it is not their duty to repent and believe till God grants them repentance and faith? Then it never was the duty of those sinners to repent who have gone to destruction, and it never will be. They waited all their lives, and are waiting still, and will wait to all eternity. And it has never yet been the duty of any sinner, who is now impenitent, to repent; and if God should not grant him repentance, it never will be. But this directly contradicts the Scriptures.

The sinner under conviction is distressed with a sense of his obligation to comply with the terms of salvation without delay. And there is no way to relieve him from his distress while impenitent, but to release him from his sense of obligation to repent. To direct him to wait God's time is directly calculated to produce this effect, and to counteract the operations of the divine Spirit. It is to plead the sinner's cause against God.

But is it not hard to distress the sinner by pressing him with his obligations? It is painful, but it is necessary. It is painful to the surgeon to probe to the bottom a dangerous wound; but it must be done, or the patient will die. If, through false pity, we console the sinner under these circumstances, there is reason to fear that his blood will be required at our hands. If we direct the sinner to wait, we direct him to run the awful hazard of losing his soul.

3. *It is sometimes said to the sinner, under deep distress, Don't despair.*

This expression not unfrequently produces a bad effect upon the sinner's mind.

It is sometimes the case, that sinners speak of the greatness of their sins and the hopelessness of their condition, on purpose to be flattered and consoled. And when they do not, it is always best to admit that their case is quite as bad as they represent it. It is proper to hold up the fulness of the atonement, and the readiness of God to forgive all who repent. But this the sinner generally does not doubt. The thing that distresses the convicted sinner, is the fear that he never shall repent. From his own experience he has full conviction that it will never be easier to repent than now. His sins are increasing, and his heart is becoming more and more perverse. God has said: 'Except ye repent, ye shall all likewise perish.' He believes it. He despairs of obtaining salvation without repentance; and of this he ought to despair.

4. In every case of clear conviction there is in the mind of the sinner a painful sense of obligation to repent, and a fearful apprehension that he never shall repent. In this state he sometimes inquires: *Do you think there is any hope in my case? Do you think I ever shall become a Christian?* This is a most interesting crisis; and a little flattery here may ruin the soul.

The proper answer to these inquiries is: 'I do not know. It is altogether uncertain. One thing is certain, however great your sins may be, if you will repent they shall be pardoned; but whether you ever will repent, is altogether uncertain. Sinners as anxious as you, and perhaps more so, have returned to stupidity, and their last state has become worse than the first.' When sinners are in this state of mind their friends are exceedingly prone to flatter them. '*Oh! don't despair—Be patient—Wait God's time—You will, doubtless, find relief.*' Such language is exceedingly dangerous. Every word takes it for granted that the sinner's concern for his soul is without foundation. One of two things is true—either such directions are wrong, or the sinner is not under conviction; for if he is under real conviction, the Spirit of God is shewing him his true condition. His apprehensions are well founded, and if we attempt to remove these apprehensions, we directly counteract the operations of the Holy Spirit."

The foregoing extract will give the reader some idea of the manner in which Dr. Nettleton was in the habit of dealing with awakened sinners. He did not heal the heart of sinners slightly, nor cry "Peace, peace," when God had not spoken peace.

He discouraged everything like confusion and disorder in religious meetings. Whenever he saw any tendency to wild enthusiasm and extravagance, he exerted all his influence to check it. This is evident from the extract of a letter to the Rev. John Frost, inserted in a former chapter, in which he gives some account of the commencement of the revival in Salisbury, Connecticut.

He studiously accommodated his arrangements to accomplish the end in view—avoiding whatever might stir prejudice, and enlisting the imagination and sympathy of his audience. "He seemed," says one who often met with him in Scotland, "to do nothing, were it no more than crossing the floor of the apartment, without some deep-based aim at impression. While none leant more than he on divine sovereignty—none more carefully used the best means, philosophically adapted to gain his end."

He never adopted the anxious seat, nor any of its kindred measures. He never requested persons to rise in the assembly to be prayed for, or to signify that they had given their hearts to God, or that they had made up their minds to attend to the subject of religion. He never encouraged females to pray and exhort in promiscuous assemblies. He never held his meetings to a late hour in the night; nor did he encourage loud praying and exhorting. He did not encourage young converts and others, who had more zeal than discretion, to take the charge of religious meetings, or to go forth as public exhorters. He was never personal in his prayers and exhortations, nor did he countenance this practice in others. He did not allow himself to denounce ministers and professors of religion as cold and dead, and as the enemies of revivals. He entirely disapproved of all such measures, and considered them as fitted to mar the purity of revivals, and to promote fanaticism and delusion. It was against such measures as these, introduced in the western revivals, that he set his face in 1826, as we shall see in the sequel.*

* He says in a letter to a friend, written in 1835: "I did not oppose these measures because they were *new*, but because of the mischief which they

His meetings were regular and orderly, characterized by great stillness and solemnity. They were, it is true, sometimes interrupted by the overwhelming distress of a convicted sinner. But when this was the case, the individual was immediately removed to a neighbouring house, and means were adopted to check the effect of mere sympathy on the occasion. At Waterbury, at an evening meeting, a man was so overcome with distress, that it became necessary to remove him from the house. For a moment the congregation was greatly agitated. Dr. Nettleton requested a physician who was present to attend to the case, and then desired the congregation to be seated, and to attend to the discourse. Immediately the assembly was as still as if nothing special had occurred.

Dr. Nettleton was in the habit of appointing *meetings of Inquiry* for those who were under religious concern; and these meetings, under his management, were eminently useful. They were usually conducted in the following manner:—After a short address, suited to produce solemnity, and to make all who were present feel that they were in the presence of a holy and heart-searching God, he would offer prayer. Then he would speak to each individual present in a low voice, unless the number was so large as to render it impossible. When that was the case, he would sometimes have one or two brethren in the ministry to assist him. He would converse with each one but a short time. The particular object of this conversation was to ascertain the state of each one's mind He

had done in bringing the very name of a revival into disgrace. And up to this day, I have in *no instance* called on sinners to take a separate or *anxious seat.* Nor was I ever present to witness the scene as practised by others would then make a solemn address, giving them such counsel as he perceived to be suited to their condition; after which he closed the meeting with prayer. He usually advised them to retire with stillness, and to go directly to their closets.

He was very careful to warn those who were anxious, and those who were indulging hope, against the danger of self-deception. He reminded them of the deceitfulness of the human heart, and of the unremitted efforts of the great adversary to delude unwary souls. On entering a house one morning, in New Haven, in the revival of 1815, a person said to him: "Here are three more rejoicing." He replied: "If I knew as well as the angels whether they have truly repented, I should know whether to rejoice with them." He was very cautious not to encourage premature hope. He never told a person that he thought he had experienced religion; but he often advised persons to give up their hopes.

He took great pains to *instruct young converts* in the fundamental principles of the Christian religion. He would often appoint meetings for their special benefit. In these meetings he was wont to explain and enforce, in a familiar manner, the doctrines of the Gospel. Hence the young converts became rooted and grounded in the truth, and continued stedfast in the faith. In this way, also, they became acquainted with one another; and receiving the same doctrines, and drinking into the same spirit, they became united as a band of brethren.

He felt it to be of the *first importance* to *preach the doctrines of grace* with great plainness in revivals of religion. He had no confidence in those revivals in which these doctrines could not be preached. His opinion was, that while the preaching of divine sovereignty and election, with their kindred doctrines, was eminently fitted to check fanaticism, and put a period to a spurious religious excitement, it was equally adapted to promote a genuine revival of religion. In Dr. Porter's *Lectures on Homiletics*, may be found the following reference to Dr. Nettleton's opinion and practice in relation to this subject:—

"The minister of Christ, whose experience and success in such season have been greater than those of any other man in modern times, observed to me: 'I have seen churches run down by repeated excitements, in which there was *emotion* merely, without *instruction*.' 'In the first stage of a revival,' said he, 'while depravity is yet ascendant, and conscience asleep, I would preach the Law, with its awful sanctions and solemn claims on sinners to be holy, and that immediately. But when the first moments of a revival are past, and sinners are settling down on presumptuous confidences, I would preach Election. Conscience is then roused enough to make a cord which sinners cannot break. Their own convictions are on my side, so that they cannot escape; and I would hold them fast, and repeat my strokes under the fire and hammer of divine truth.'"

He was cautious in admitting persons to the Church. He would not encourage any to make a profession of religion till they gave satisfactory evidence of a change of heart. His fidelity in this respect is illustrated by the following fact:—In the town of W——, where there had been an extensive revival under his preaching, a meeting was appointed for the examination of those who were desirous of making a profession of religion. A man and his wife attended this meeting, who had, till a short time before, belonged to another religious denomination. They were persons of great respectability, and of a blameless life; but they gave no satisfactory evidence of having experienced a change of heart. The deacons and committee of the church were in favour of admitting them. They knew not how to reject persons of their character and standing in society. But Dr. Nettleton would not consent. The next day he called on these individuals, and in a kind and affectionate manner informed them of his fears respecting their religious experience, and pointed out to them the danger of making a profession of religion without the requisite qualifications. They immediately withdrew their application. Soon after this, Dr. Nettleton left the town; but within a short time he was informed by letter, that these individuals had both become the hopeful subjects of divine grace. Some months afterwards, on a visit to the place, he called on this family. The man and his wife both met him at the door, and with tears in their eyes they seized him by the hand, and broke out in strains of the most unfeigned gratitude. "Oh!" said they, "if it had not been for your faithfulness we should have lost our souls." Let this example stimulate all ministers to faithfulness and caution in admitting members to the communion of the Church.

Dr. Nettleton had but little confidence in the conversion of persons who had been in the habit of using spirituous liquors, unless they entirely abandoned the habit; and he was very unwilling to admit such persons to the Church. His views on this subject are expressed in a letter which was written to Dr. Beecher, in May 1822, and which was afterwards published in the *Spirit of the Pilgrims*:—

"My dear Brother,—I hear frequently from many places where God has, of late, poured out His Spirit and revived His work. My friends residing in these places, far and near, either visit me or write to me, and tell me all their joys and sorrows. For a number of years I have kept a list of the names of those who have hopefully experienced religion, and made a profession of it, in these revivals. When far from them, in my retired moments, I have often read over their names, and pondered on them, and on the scenes they have awakened, with emotions too big for utterance. I have watched them with anxious solicitude, and have made particular inquiry about the spiritual welfare of each one, as opportunity presented. My heart has often been refreshed when some Timothy has brought me good tidings of the faith and charity of the young converts. No tidings have been more refreshing. I have often had occasion to adopt the language of Paul on this very subject: 'What thanks can we render to God again for all the joy wherewith we joy for your sakes before our God?'

"During the leisure occasioned by my late illness, I have been looking over the regions where God has revived His work for the two years past. The thousands who have professed Christ in this time, in general, appear to run well. Hitherto I think they have exhibited more of the Christian temper, and a better example, than the same number who have professed religion when there was no revival. With hundreds of these I conversed when anxious for their souls, and afterwards, when rejoicing in hope. Some of them I have followed through life, and down to the grave. *If genuine religion is not found in revivals, I have no evidence that it exists in our world.* Some few, indeed, have dishonoured their profession, have opened afresh the wounds of the Saviour, and caused the hearts of His friends to bleed. Bunyan says: 'If at any time I heard of such instances of apostacy among those who had been hopefully benefited by my ministry, I feel worse than if I had followed one of my own natural children to the grave.' I have lost near and dear relations, but the tidings of which Bunyan speaks have sometimes struck me with deeper sadness. Of the few who have finally apostatized, you may wish to know the cause. I have made particular inquiry, and find that the declension of some has commenced with an undue conformity to the world; but the sin of *intemperance* has caused more trouble, and done more dishonour to the cause of Christ, than any other that can be named.

"Though some have confessed, and doubtless repented of other crimes, yet few, if any, excommunications have hitherto taken place for any crime except intemperance. I have heard from S—— county, that of the hundreds who professed religion there two years ago, a few only have been called to a public confession, and these have been restored.

"I have heard of one excommunication. He was an acquaintance of mine, a man about thirty-five years of age, in the town of M——. He had been a little inclined to intemperance. He was anxious with others; his conversion was considered interesting; and at the time he professed religion, it was thought that his habit was broken. But before I left that place he ventured to drink a little. On a public occasion he became boisterous, and charged one man with lying; and that led on to an angry dispute, in which all present considered him the aggressor. This was soon noised through the place. It gave a general shock to all the young converts. I well remember the effect. Each one began to tremble lest he too should wound the cause which was dearer to him than life. I shall not forget what tenderness of conscience the young converts manifested. Each one seemed to tremble most of all for himself. The next morning Mr. H—— became sober, and now he felt exceedingly chagrined on remembering what he had said and done. He told me that his first thought in the morning was, that he had dishonoured religion; and he could not bear to be seen. He was almost tempted to leave his family and friends, and abscond. He however confessed his fault and appeared penitent. But, sad to relate, he drank again; and, as I have been informed, is now cut off and utterly abandoned.

"A Mr. T——, in the town of B——, was under conviction, hopefully experienced religion, and made a public profession, with about sixty others. He appeared well, with the exception of this circumstance, that, previous to his convictions, he had been a little inclined to intemperance. In the judgment of charity, he had reformed and become a new man. He forsook his wicked companions, prayed in his family, and appeared to be much engaged in religion, and continued for a number of months to adorn his profession. But he began by slow and cautious steps (as he thought) to *sip a little* only for his health. Though not drunk, he became foolish; and this led on to other things, until he dishonoured the cause of religion. He made a public confession of his fault, and for awhile appeared penitent. But he drank again, and this led to other unchristian conduct, which demanded Christian satisfaction. His brethren began, a few days since, their endeavours to reclaim him. But he removed in the night, with all his family, and has left the state to avoid another confession. We consider him a ruined man.

"In the town of K——, a promising young man hopefully experienced religion during the recent powerful revival there, and made a public profession on the same day with a hundred and six others. I believe he was never considered at all inclined to intemperance. He left K—— and laboured in company with others, who made free use of ardent spirits. He soon contracted a taste for it; and we have heard of the public disgrace which he has brought on the cause of religion. With taunting voice the enemies have been heard to say around him, 'There is one of Mr. K——'s converts.' Brother K—— went after him to a neighbouring place; and the young man has just made a public confession of his fault, and appears penitent. I find that all are flattering themselves that he will never offend again. I should think and rejoice with them, if I had not so often been disappointed. Of the whole number who professed religion in that revival, this, I think, is the only instance of an offence demanding a public confession.

"When I look back on revivals which took place ten or fifteen years ago, I have been agreeably surprised to find so many of the subjects of them continuing to adorn their profession. Take the whole number who professed religion as the fruit of these revivals, and take the same number who profess religion when there was no general revival, and I do not think the former have outshined the latter. I have not made a particular estimate; but from what I have seen, I do believe the number of excommunications from the latter is more than double in proportion to the former. And I find, all along, that more excommunications have taken place in consequence of intemperance, than for any other crime.

"A Mr. H——, a member of brother T——'s church, was thought to have experienced religion in L——, in the days of your predecessor. He was a promising, active young man, much beloved and highly esteemed by Christians, and never suspected of intemperance until about a year since. The disclosure of this fact not only grieved Christians, but surprised and astonished everybody. Though he was not suspected of intemperance, it was afterwards ascertained that he had been in the habit of drinking a little in private. This is one method of covering sin. Whoever does it is privately working out the ruin of his soul. But Mr. H—— made a public confession, appeared penitent, and all rejoiced in his reformation. This, I said, was about a year ago. When I was last in N—— he called at brother T——'s on an evening visit. It was evident he had been drinking. The next day brother T—— warned him in the most solemn manner; but all to no purpose. He was past fear, and past shame; and all have given him up as lost. He had accomplished his ruin by drinking in private, before his friends had any chance to prevent it. I could name a number of individuals, in different towns in this state, whose case is similar to this.

"Now, my brother, what shall be done? I do not ask what shall be done to reclaim those who have so grievously offended. For these nothing, ordinarily, can be done. Their case is hopeless. My inquiry is, What shall be done to prevent the future disgrace of the cause of Christ? As for those who have confessed their fault, and have been restored to fellowship, they must remain where they are until the next offence cuts them off. But a public confession for intemperance, I think, is about nothing, and ought to go for nothing. *The only evidence of repentance, in such cases, is* A CONTINUED COURSE OF ENTIRE ABSTINENCE FROM ARDENT SPIRITS OF EVERY KIND.

"As for those who think they have experienced a change, if their habits are bordering on intemperance, we ought to be cautious how we admit them to a public profession. If they have been in the habit of drinking freely, though not to intoxication, however clear in other respects, this circumstance alone renders the evidence of their conversion very doubtful. From what I have seen, I do believe no class of persons are more likely to be deceived with false hopes than the intemperate. If, while under conviction, a person allows himself to sip a little, or raises his sinking spirits in the least, he is sure to grieve away the Spirit of God.

"During the revival at S——, two years ago, I witnessed an instance which, if you please, I will relate. Mr. A—— was one of the most respectable men in that village, about thirty-five years of age, who kept a large boarding house. His wife was under deep conviction, and soon was rejoicing in hope, and prayed with and for her husband. This was the means of his conviction, though at the time it was not known. Report said that he was confined to bed, and was dangerously ill. Hints were privately circulated that he was anxious for his soul, and was ashamed to have it known. It was late in the evening when brother G—— went to his house, and found him in a bed-room, in a remote corner, in the greatest agony. 'What is the matter?' said brother G——. 'Oh! I am sick; I am in such distress.' 'But your pulse is regular, where is your pain?' He made no reply, but with violence smote upon his breast. He asked: 'Is it there?' 'It is,' he replied. The next evening, I called and found him in the same distress. His convictions appeared to be deep. But when I returned I suggested to brother G—— a suspicion of the smell of ardent spirits. I then related a number of anecdotes of false conversions, connected with his suspicious scent. 'Mr. A—— is a very moral man,' said he, 'and far from suspicion on that point.' But for fear, he sent me back to give him a solemn caution. I returned, and, with much delicacy, warned him not to taste, lest —— He seemed startled at my suggestion, and assured me he was far from the habit. I requested his wife to watch him, and learned from her, that through his distress his strength had greatly failed; and that he had taken a *very little only*, to prevent his sinking entirely. I returned and observed to brother G——, that I feared Mr. A—— was a ruined man. His concern continued for a few days, when he became exceedingly joyful. His conversion was considered wonderful. But my joy was checked. I could not forget the smell of ardent spirits. I called and found him much elated with joy. But when I cautioned him he seemed surprised, and somewhat offended, and observed: 'I think I have been distressed enough to experience religion!' 'Ah!' said I, 'now I doubt more than ever whether your heart has ever been changed. Do you think there is any merit in the distress of an awakened sinner? Suppose you had been to hell and endured the torments of the damned—what then? It is not distress, but love to God, and a change of heart, which alone can fit the sinner for heaven.'

"After a little conversation, his heart rose in such opposition, that he relinquished his hope—his distress returned in a moment—and he cried out: '*What shall I do?*' His heart was evidently unrenewed, and quarrelling with the justice of God. From some expressions, I caught a glimpse of his heart; and that, if he should ever experience religion, it was his secret purpose never to make a public profession of it. He was evidently unhumbled—*like a bullock unaccustomed to the yoke.* I put into his hands, Edwards on *The Justice of God in the Damnation of Sinners.* Shortly he again found relief. He wished to profess religion with others; but prudence led us to wait; and the result was, that in process of time he became a sot. I know not of a more hopeless being on earth. He does no business; has drunk himself out of his property, and almost out of his reason; and, as brother G—— says, he has become a brute.

"I could fill sheets with the relation of facts of a similar character, all of which lead to the conclusion, that persons of intemperate habits, though deeply convicted, are far more likely to rest in a false hope than others. However distressed a person of this character may have been, or however joyful in hope, I think we may set it down as a probable sign of a false conversion, if he allows himself to *taste a single drop*. If he does not give evidence that he intends to abstain wholly and for ever, I feel decided that he ought not to profess religion. If he cannot be willing to do this, he can have no sufficient evidence of his own repentance or conversion; and his hope is a spider's web. Brother T—— preached an excellent sermon not long since from these words: 'Cleanse thou me from secret faults: keep back thy servant also from presumptuous sins.' In the class of presumptuous sinners he placed the person of intemperate habits. 'The person who has drunk to excess, and has been warned, cannot venture to drink again, at all, without sinning presumptuously. He sins deliberately and with his eyes open. *Let him remember that he drinks damnation.*' I felt the justice of this last sentence. It was attended with a thrill of horror. I am satisfied that he who cannot break off entirely, and at once, can never do it. And without it we can have no evidence of his piety. Every time he tastes, he is putting fire to tinder and powder. If he really thinks he can drink a little, and yet not become a drunkard, his danger is so much more the greater. This confidence evinces his consummate ignorance of his own heart. This confidence, if not destroyed, will damn him. '*He that trusteth in his own heart is a fool.*'

"I wish that all the young converts who make a profession of religion, would make it a point of conscience not to taste of ardent spirits. This is the way in which many have dishonoured the cause of Christ on public occasions. In this way thousands have become drunkards. I scarcely expect that any drunkard will be reformed by any measures that can be adopted. The only successful method of preventing this kind of disgrace to religion in future, is to begin with the temperate. Though the plague cannot be cured, it may be shunned. Had all young converts seen what I have, they would need no other motives to induce them to adopt the resolution to abandon the use of ardent spirits for ever. Could I learn that all the young converts in your parish had jointly adopted this resolution, it would be to themselves, to you, and to me, a most delightful evidence of the sincerity of their Christian profesion, as well as of genuine conversion. '*Dearly beloved, I beseech you, as strangers and pilgrims, abstain from fleshly lusts, which war against the soul.*'—Yours, as ever."

There was a striking resemblance between the revivals which occurred under Dr. Nettleton's preaching, and those which occurred at the close of the last, and at the beginning of the present century. Let any one read with attention the narratives published in the first three or four volumes of the *Connecticut Evangelical Magazine*, and he will obtain a very correct idea of the revivals of which we are speaking. If there was any difference, it was this—that the latter were more powerful and more extensive,—that is, they were characterized by more clear and distressing conviction of sin, and, in some instances, embraced a larger number of subjects. As to the *doctrines which were preached*, *the means employed*, and the character of the religious exercises, both of awakened sinners and hopeful converts, there was a marked coincidence. The same may be said as to the permanency of their fruits. A large proportion of the hopeful converts in all these revivals continued to adorn the Christian profession.

These revivals were characterized by great solemnity. Christians were solemn. They were not merely excited, and filled with great animation for a season; but they were deeply humbled in view of their past neglects of duty. They mourned over their backslidings, and returned to God with deep contrition. Sensible of their great sinfulness, and of the alarming condition of sinners around them, they felt deeply solemn, and walked humbly with God. Their minds, it is true, were sometimes filled with great joy; but it was a joy mingled with reverence. They felt that they were in the presence of God, and had no disposition to indulge in vain mirth. They carefully abstained in their conversation from everything suited to produce levity, or to banish serious thoughts from the minds of the impenitent. The things of eternity lay with great weight on their minds, and had a commanding influence upon all their conduct. When they looked around them, and saw so many of their fellow-men perishing in sin, their eyes affected their hearts. They felt, in some measure, as did the weeping prophet, when he said: "Oh! that my head were waters, and mine eyes a fountain of tears; that I might weep day and night for the slain of the daughter of my people!" With these feelings they could not but be solemn.

Sinners were solemn. Those who were under conviction were bowed down with distress. They felt like criminals under sentence of death. In some cases, as we have seen, their distress was exceedingly great. And when a revival had become somewhat extensive in a parish, the whole community was more or less solemn. The Rev. Dr. Porter of Farmington, speaking of the revival in that town, says: "The state of feeling which at this time pervaded the town, was interesting beyond description. There was no commotion, but a stillness in our very streets; a serenity in the aspect of the pious, and a solemnity apparent in almost all, which forcibly impressed us with the conviction, that in very deed *God was in this place.*" What is here stated might be stated with truth in reference to most of the places where revivals became extensive under Dr. Nettleton's labours.

These revivals were characterized by deep and clear convictions of sin. Dr. Nettleton had no confidence in those revivals which dispense with the "law work." *He did not, however, suppose that the work of conviction need be of long continuance.* Although in his own case it was protracted through many months, he did not suppose it was always so in cases of genuine conversion, nor ordinarily, when the doctrines of the Gospel are fully and plainly preached, and when the obligations of sinners are faithfully pressed upon their consciences. Under his preaching convictions were generally of short continuance; but they were clear, and frequently exceedingly distressing. Sinners were not brought to entertain the hope of salvation without being awakened to a sense of their lost condition by nature. Nor were they merely alarmed by some vague sense of danger; but they were convinced of sin. They saw themselves in the light of divine truth. Like Peter's hearers on the day of Pentecost, "they were pricked in the heart." "The commandment came, sin revived, and they died." They saw what the law of God required. They saw, also, that they never had obeyed it in a single instance, and that their hearts were at enmity against God, and not subject to His law.

There was, it is true, a difference in the dealings of God with different individuals, in respect to the degree and continuance of their convictions, and the strength and bitterness of their opposition. But, in general, the convictions of awakened sinners were distinctly marked. In the first stages of their concern, they were usually filled with alarm on account of their past lives. Seeing themselves in danger, they went about to establish their own righteousness, hoping, by their abundant religious services, to appease the anger of God, and to secure an interest in His favour. But they were soon convinced of the futility of these efforts. The more they strove to make themselves better, the more they saw the worthlessness of their own works. They were brought to see that they were actuated in all that they did by unholy motives; and that, so far from growing better, they were adding sin to sin, and sinking deeper and deeper in guilt and wretchedness. Thus they were convinced of their utterly lost condition, and of their entire dependence for salvation on the sovereign mercy of God.

While in this state they were frequently sensible of the most dreadful heart-risings against God. Although they were convinced of the exceeding sinfulness of such feelings, they found themselves disposed to accuse their Maker of injustice in His commands and threatenings, and of partiality in the dispensation of His grace; and when they saw others brought to rejoice in hope, while they were left, it sometimes filled them with the bitterest opposition. These discoveries of the desperate wickedness of their hearts occasioned the most acute distress. In some instances the mental agony was overwhelming. Such extreme distress was generally of short continuance, and in most cases it was succeeded by joy and peace in believing.

In proof of the deep feeling which occurred under Dr. Nettleton's preaching, the reader is referred to the sketch of the revival in Nassau, inserted in the former chapter.

But while Dr. Nettleton considered conviction of sin essential to genuine conversion, and while his preaching and conversation were adapted to give sinners a clear and distressing view of their true character and condition, he, at the same time, endeavoured to check all *violent manifestations* of feeling, by shewing that they had in them nothing of the nature of religion; and when he discovered any tendency to such manifestations in a religious meeting, he would generally dismiss the assembly, and advise the people to retire in silence to their homes.

The converts in these revivals were led in a way they knew not. Darkness was made light before them. They did not feel that they had made themselves to differ from others by any efforts of their own. They did not suppose that they had gone through a process of means while unrenewed, by which they had made themselves new hearts. On the contrary, they knew that they had resisted every overture of mercy, and that all their feelings and moral actions were sinful, to the very moment when their hearts were renewed by the power of the Holy Ghost. Consequently they took none of the glory to themselves. They had no doubt, that if they were the children of God, it was owing wholly to His distinguishing grace.

As might be supposed from what has just been stated, the converts in these revivals cordially embraced the doctrines of grace, and were stedfast in their belief of them. They received them, both because they appeared to be clearly taught in the Scriptures, and because they were in perfect harmony with their own experience. "They were born into the truth." The knowledge which they had obtained of their own hearts while under conviction, and the wonderful change which had taken place in their views and feelings in relation to divine objects, were all in accordance with the evangelical system, and entirely at variance with the views of those who deny the doctrines of grace. It was no matter of doubt with them whether the natural heart is totally depraved, and unreconciled to God. They *knew* it to be true in reference to themselves, for it had been matter of painful consciousness. They were, of course, convinced that salvation must be by grace through the redemption of Christ. They trusted alone in His righteousness for justification, and counted all things but loss for the excellency of the knowledge of Christ Jesus their Lord. They were fully convinced of the necessity of regeneration by the special agency of the Holy Ghost; for they knew, that if they had passed from death unto life, they had "been born, *not of blood, nor of the will of the flesh, nor of the will of man, but of God.*"

They were also convinced, that unless God had from all eternity determined to make some of mankind the trophies of grace, not an individual of the human race would obtain salvation. The doctrine of eternal and particular *election*, therefore, appeared to them to lie at the foundation of all hope in regard to the salvation of man; and they rejoiced in the assurance, that God hath from the beginning chosen some to salvation through sanctification of the Spirit and belief of the truth—and in the promise that all true believers shall be kept by the power of God through faith unto salvation. The converts were generally so stedfast in their belief of these doctrines, that their faith could not be shaken. They possessed, in an unusual degree, stability of character. They were not carried about by every wind of doctrine, nor often led astray by those who lie in wait to deceive. The religious exercises of the subjects of these revivals, so far as they could be known, were generally such as indicated a radical change of character. The whole current of their moral feelings seemed to be changed. What they had hated, now they seemed to love. Those objects which had awakened in their bosoms feelings of enmity, were now contemplated with supreme delight. Their affections were not such as could be traced to the operation of any natural principle of the human mind—such as self-love or natural gratitude. They did not love God merely on account of His kindness to them, but on account of the supreme excellency of His character. Their first consolation did not arise from the belief that God had pardoned their sins, and received them to favour; for, in most instances, when they first found peace they had no apprehensions that their sins were pardoned. When divine objects appeared to them in a new and pleasing light, they scarcely thought of their personal safety, or whether they were or were not converted. They discovered a relish for divine objects to which they had been total strangers; and the truths of the Gospel with which they had been contending were now objects of complacency. It was no uncommon thing for persons, whose chief distress had arisen from the thought that they were in the hands of God, to find themselves unexpectedly rejoicing in that very thought, contemplating the glory of God as an object of higher importance than their own salvation; and all this, while as yet they had no idea of having experienced a change of heart. It thus appeared, that "the first objective ground" of their religious affections, was the "transcendently excellent and amiable nature of divine things, as they are in themselves, and not any conceivable relation they bear to self, or self-interest."

What Edwards says of the converts in Northampton, was equally true of those of whom we are speaking: "It has more frequently been so among us, that persons have had the Gospel ground of relief for lost sinners discovered to them, and have been entertaining their minds with the sweet prospect, while they have thought nothing at that time of their being converted. There is wrought in them a holy repose of soul in God through Christ, and a sweet disposition to fear and love Him, and to hope for blessings from Him in this way; and yet they have no imagination that they are now converted; it does not so much as come into their minds."

There are religious affections, and they sometimes rise to a high degree, which are founded on self-love.

Persons may think they love God, when their love arises entirely from the belief that God loves them, and that He has pardoned their sins, and given them a title to heaven. But such love is natural to the human heart, and affords no evidence of a supernatural change. "Sinners also love those that love them." Persons may be filled with joy because they have persuaded themselves, without any good reason, that their immortal interests are secured; but such joy is selfish, and partakes not of the nature of holiness. Sinners may be convinced, that *in order to be happy* they must become the servants of God; and they may resolve, for the sole purpose of securing their happiness, to devote themselves to the service of God; and having adopted the opinion that such a resolution is a change of heart, they may experience pleasurable emotions in the thought that they are interested in the divine favour. But such conversions imply no radical change of character, and will not endure the test of the judgment day.

The conversions in these revivals (says his biographer) appeared to be widely different from these. If any cases occurred which appeared to be of this description, they were treated as spurious. If any persons professed to have experienced a change of heart, and gave no other evidence than what is afforded by such religious affections as, to use the language of Brainerd, "have self-love for their beginning, centre, and end," they were advised to abandon their hopes without delay.*

* On this subject a wise statement is made by Doolittle: "This love chooseth Christ for *Himself, and for the excellency of His own person, though not with the exclusion of our own benefit and salvation* by Him. Our own benefits by Christ might be looked at by the returning soul at

The converts in these revivals were not bold, forward, self-sufficient, and censorious; but humble, meek, gentle, and docile. When we see those who profess to have entered recently upon the Christian life, lifted up with pride—wiser in their own estimation than their teachers—disposed to put themselves forward as leaders—abundant in their censures of old professors—full of self-complacency and self-commendation, there is reason to fear that they know not what manner of spirit they are of. Such is not the spirit of the Gospel. "The wisdom which is from above is first pure, then peaceable, gentle, and easy to be entreated, full of mercy and good fruits, without partiality and without hypocrisy."

These revivals exerted a most benign influence upon the churches. They did not divide churches, and dissolve the relation between pastors and their flocks. On the contrary, they built up churches—healed divisions where they had previously existed—promoted union and brotherly love among the members, and greatly strengthened the hands of pastors.

One striking effect of these revivals was to elevate the standard of orthodoxy. Dr. Nettleton preached with great plainness the *doctrines of Calvinism.* Under his preaching, these doctrines were seen to be the

first. The soul might first be allured and drawn to look after Christ, and to love Him, by the consideration of the matchless good and benefits it might have by Him, which the convinced sinner seeth he can find in no other. But, in process of time, and in his progress in the way to heaven, he learns and sees such excellency and beauty in Christ, that He is in himself more amiable than all the objects of his former love. To ask, therefore, whether we are to love Christ *for himself*, or for *the benefits we have by Him*, is to propound a question which yet I have not observed in Scripture, nor disjunctively answered therein; for the one is *subordinate* to the other, not *opposed*," &c.—*On Love to Christ*, i., 9. We love Him, in short, because He is both *loving* and *lovely*.

power of God unto salvation. It was in vain to object that they tend to paralyze effort, and to harden men in stupidity. They were seen to produce the opposite effect. Sinners were pricked in the heart and brought to repentance. Saints were quickened and comforted, and incited to fidelity in their Master's service. The converts, as we have seen, cordially embraced these doctrines, and were confirmed in their belief by their own religious experience. If creeds were altered, it was for the purpose of making them *more Calvinistic.* In many instances, where violent prejudices had existed against the Calvinistic system, they were overcome; and some churches, which had been very lax in doctrine, became sound in the faith.

These revivals exerted a salutary influence upon society at large. They checked the prevalence of vice, raised the tone of moral sentiment, and elevated the standard of morals. So striking was the evidence that they were not the result of mere human agency, that few could resist the conviction that they were the work of God. In those days, such was the state of the public conscience, that the very name of a revival had wonderful power. Announce to a congregation that a revival had commenced in a neighbouring town, and it would produce great solemnity on the whole assembly. The general feeling seemed to be: "God has come nigh to us, and is calling upon us, in solemn accents, to prepare to meet Him." This state of the public mind resulted from the general agreement that existed as to the true effects of these revivals. They were seen to be good.

Once more. The salutary fruits of these revivals were permanent. These were not temporary excitements, which were soon over, followed by a melancholy reaction. No; the good effects were abiding. The converts generally continued to adorn their profession. There were but few apostacies.

Dr. Nettleton, in his letter to Dr. Beecher, already given, says: "For a number of years I have kept a list of the names of those who have hopefully experienced religion, and made a profession of it in these revivals. I have watched them with anxious solicitude, and have made particular inquiry about the spiritual welfare of each one as opportunity presented. The thousands who have professed Christ in this time, in general appear to run well. Hitherto, I think, they have exhibited more of the Christian temper, and a better example, than the same number who have "professed religion when there was no revival."

If the reader will recur to the accounts given by ministers of revivals among their own people, under Dr. Nettleton's ministry, (inserted in the preceding chapter,) he will perceive that they all bear testimony to the permanent good effects of his labours. And such testimonials might have been multiplied to a great extent.

CHAPTER XII.

BLESSED AGAIN—PROFESSOR OF PASTORAL DUTY—DEGREE OF D.D.—OPPOSED TO NEW MEASURES AND NEW DOCTRINES—MR. FINNEY.

After his return from England, which was in August 1832, he preached in a number of different places in New England and in the middle States—with what success we are unable to state. In the autumn of 1833, there was an interesting revival under his preaching, in *Enfield*, Connecticut.

The following is an extract of a letter from the Rev. Francis L. Robbins, pastor of the church in that town:—

"I have not known the man who, in my deliberàte judgment, has been the honoured instrument of Heaven in turning so many sinners to the knowledge of the truth, and saving souls from death, as the Rev. Mr. Nettleton. As he was himself 'mighty in the Scriptures,' and 'fervent in the spirit,' he spake and taught diligently the things of the Lord, and was not satisfied unless men exhibited scriptural evidence of true religion. When he went into a place, remembering what was said of his Master, 'He shall not strive nor cry, neither shall any man hear His voice in the streets,'—he laboured, as far as practicable, without observation, striving to turn the eyes of his hearers in upon themselves, while they listened diligently to the Word. His meetings, therefore, whether on the Sabbath, or at other seasons, were singularly marked with stillness, order, fixed and solemn attention.

"My people were sensibly struck with the correctness of this statement in relation to his labours here. For in this place he had 'seals of his ministry' in a goodly number of hopeful converts, who regarded him as their spiritual father, and remembered him with high respect and gratitude. I refer to the revival of religion here in 1833, when several of the choice, active, and exemplary members of this flock, received deep impressions, and became, as we believe, in heart and spirit, the people of the living God.

"Mr. Nettleton came here in September of that year, at my solicitation, when my health was, and had been, for several months, in a very feeble and precarious state; and when some of our good people were fearful of the result, not only to myself, but to the interests of religion. When Mr. Nettleton came, it was like the coming of Titus, especially to myself. Many of God's professed people had left their first love, and were engaged in matters of 'doubtful disputation,' which tended more to alienate and distract their feelings than to quicken them in the work of the Lord.

"Mr. Nettleton continued with us nearly three months. Under his lucid and frequent exhibitions of divine truth, and by solemn addresses to the church, together with instruction given in the inquiry meeting, and by direct personal conversation, deep impressions were made on the minds of a number, which resulted in a disposition to renounce themselves, and humbly accept the salvation of the Gospel. As he laboured to instruct the people in the things of the kingdom of God, and establish them in the faith and order of the Gospel, he very generally secured their esteem and confidence, and left a salutary influence behind him.

"Not long after he left us, nearly twenty, mostly youth, who ascribed their conversion to the abounding grace of God, through his instrumentality, came forward, and made a public profession of religion. Several others, who entertained a hope at that time, clouded with many fears, have been revived and quickened, and prepared to profess Christ since that time; while others who were brought to serious consideration under the religious exercises conducted by Mr. Nettleton, never, I believe, lost their impressions, until, as objects of God's special remembrance, they were hopefully gathered in, in a subsequent revival. All of those who were brought hopefully from darkness to light, as the fruits of that revival, so far as I have knowledge, (for a few have removed to other places,) have walked worthy of their vocation, bearing the fruits of righteousness unto the praise and glory of God."

Many other places might be mentioned in which he preached occasionally, and in which there were some fruits of his labours that will abide when all earthly scenes shall have passed away. But his biographer has mentioned only those places in which his labours are known to have been attended with *very considerable success.*

In 1833 the Pastoral Union of Connecticut was formed, and the Theological Institute was established. These measures did not originate with him, as some have supposed; but they were measures which he cordially approved, and in which he felt a deep and lively interest.

When the seminary was organized he was appointed Professor of Pastoral Duty. He was at the time absent at the south. In reply to a letter informing him of his appointment, he says: "I hardly know what to say. I need not tell you how entirely I am interested in the whole concern. If it can be of any service to the seminary for me to sustain some official relation to it, I should be sorry to decline. But it has from the beginning seemed to me, that, on many accounts, I could plead its cause with more freedom and effect without sustaining that relation to it. My reasons I cannot fully state on paper. At any rate, I must see you and the trustees before I can give an affirmative answer. I have, too, some doubts whether my habits and the state of my health will permit me to sit down to close study, and to all the requisite preparation for that department. I have been wishing, for some time past, to shun public observation, and to retire more into solitude."

He did not accept. But although he chose to sustain no official relation to the seminary, he took up his abode at East Windsor, and consented to deliver some familiar lectures to the students. His instruction was highly prized by the classes who enjoyed it.

During the last ten years of his life, although East Windsor was his home, he spent several winters at the south, and preached in several different places in New England, not without some success. But such was the state of his health, as to render him unable to endure much excitement or fatigue. In a letter to

Mrs. Parmele, dated Sept. 21, 1839, he says: "Your note came to hand this morning. Accept my best thanks for your kind invitation. It would, indeed, be very pleasant to spend a little season among my old friends in the still and retired town of Bolton, and once more talk over scenes that are past,—'pleasant and mournful to the soul.' And *possibly*, if life be spared, that time may come. But I have journeyed so long and so far in this wilderness world, and have passed through so many scenes of alternate storm and sunshine, that I am worn out with languor and fatigue, and have long since concluded to retire, and journey as little as possible, except so far as duty and the state of my health seem to demand."

In the year 1839, he received from two literary institutions* the degree of D.D. This was an honour which he did not covet, as appears from the fact, that it would have been conferred several years before, by one of the New England colleges, had not his own remonstrances prevented. When he first received the intelligence, he was quite disturbed; and he asked one of his brethren what he should do? All the advice which he received from that brother was contained in the following anecdote:—"A man once said to an aged clergyman, 'My neighbours are slandering me, and what shall I do?'—'Do your duty,' said the clergyman, 'and think nothing about it. If they are disposed to throw mud, let them throw mud; but do not attempt to wipe it off, lest you should wipe it all over you.'"

On reflection, says his biographer, he seems to have

* Hampden Sydney College, in Virginia, and Jefferson College, in Pennsylvania.

come to the conclusion to which his friend, the late Dr. Porter of Andover, came, under similar circumstances,—viz., "What shall a sober man do? If he refuses this title on general principles, because it is inconsistent with the spirit of the Gospel, he charges a long list of such worthies as Watts, &c., with wearing a public mark of pride or folly. If he refuses it on principles that respect himself only, he is liable to be charged with the ostentation of humility, and really needs much prayer and heart-searching to be certain that cursed pride is not at the bottom. Too much noise to get rid of this contemptible honour, 'resembles ocean into tempest wrought, to waft a feather, or to drown a fly.' A wise man would not kill a gnat by a blow that might fracture his leg."

He did not need, but assuredly he deserved, to be thus honoured by his fellowmen. Few ever won more souls to Christ, and few ever defended the truth more boldly and firmly against insidious error. Indeed, a man such as he was needed to resist successfully both the conduct and the doctrines which some were beginning to urge on all who would give heed to them.

Revivals have never been permitted by Satan to continue long without some direct effort, on his part, to counterwork them. And so it was to be now. The form this attack took was crafty; it was made by assuming the form of an angel of light. In the year 1826, there was a great religious excitement in the central and western parts of the state of New York, occasioned principally by the Rev. Charles G. Finney, who has been already mentioned,—an evangelist of great zeal, and of considerable native eloquence.

He had been a lawyer; and having, as he hoped, been converted to Christ, he entered the ministry with but little preparatory study. He was bold, ardent, and denunciatory in his manner. He rebuked, with harshness and great severity, not only open transgressors and impenitent sinners of every description, but professors of religion and ministers of the Gospel; and was not unfrequently very pointed and personal in his prayers. The consequence was, that he not only met with violent opposition from the open enemies of religion, but many of the most judicious ministers and private Christians felt unwilling to sanction his proceedings. Others became his warm friends and adherents; and, imbibing the same spirit, denounced their brethren as "cold and dead, and enemies to revivals." Some young evangelists, in particular, attempting to imitate Mr. Finney, became much more extravagant than their leader. A great excitement attended the preaching of Mr. Finney and his coadjutors; and multitudes were reported as the subjects of renewing grace. That very many of the reputed converts were like the stony ground hearers, who endured only for a time, few will at this day be disposed to deny. Yet it is believed that some were truly converted to Christ.

Connected with this excitement, various measures were introduced, similar to those which, in former times, had been the great instruments of marring the purity of revivals, and promoting fanaticism—such as praying for persons by name—using great familiarity in prayer—encouraging females to pray and exhort in promiscuous assemblies—calling upon persons to come to the *anxious seat*, or to rise up in the public assembly, to signify that they had given their hearts to God, or had made up their mind to attend to religion. The result was, that where this spirit prevailed, and these measures were introduced, there was division in the churches. Those who adopted these measures often appealed to the example of Dr. Nettleton, and made use of his name to sanction their proceedings. Those, however, who were acquainted with him, and his labours in revivals, knew that these representations were not true. They knew that he never had introduced such measures, nor countenanced such a spirit as was connected with them.

While these things were passing in the central and western parts of the state of New York, Dr. Nettleton, in very feeble health, was labouring in Jamaica, on Long Island. He was from time to time made acquainted with what was transpiring at the west, and was not without great solicitude as to the ultimate results. The lesson which he learned while labouring on the borders of Rhode Island, in those places which had been made desolate by the operations of Davenport and his coadjutors a century ago, had prepared him to resist everything which tended to corrupt revivals and promote fanaticism.

He heard, with inexpressible pain, that his own example was appealed to at the west, to sanction measures which he had always reprobated; still, although constantly urged by some of his friends to come out with a public testimony, he was very reluctant to do it; nor could he be persuaded to publish his views, till he was fully convinced that a regard to the interests of Christ's kingdom required it.

In the winter of 1826-7, at the earnest request of some of his brethren, he visited Albany, while Mr. Finney was preaching at Troy. He had two interviews with Mr. Finney, hoping that, by a free consultation, their views might be brought to harmonize, so far, at least, that they might co-operate in promoting the interests of Christ's kingdom. But in this he was painfully disappointed. Mr. Finney was unwilling to abandon certain measures which Dr. Nettleton had "ever regarded as exceedingly calamitous to the cause of revivals," and which, of course, he could not sanction. He perceived, also, that there could be no hope of convincing Mr. Finney of his errors, so long as he was upheld and encouraged by ministers of high respectability. After his second interview with Mr. Finney, he addressed a letter to the Rev. Mr. Aikin of Utica, a part of which is here inserted. It is dated Albany, January 13, 1827:—

"Seven years ago, *about two thousand souls* were hopefully born into the kingdom, in this vicinity, in our own denomination, with comparative stillness. But the times have altered. The kingdom of God now cometh with great observation. Opposition from *the world* is always to be expected. It is idle for any minister to expect a revival without it. But when it enters *the Church of God*, the friends of Zion cannot but take the alarm.

"There is, doubtless, a work of grace in Troy. Many sinners have hopefully been born into the kingdom; but it has been at an awful expense. Many of our first ministers have visited the place, to witness for themselves. Such men as Dr. Griffin, Dr. Porter of Catskill, Dr. Nott, Mr. Tucker, Mr.

Cornelius, and many more. Some of them have heard a number of sermons. After giving credit for preaching much truth, they uniformly say: 'I never heard the names of God used with such irreverence.' Dr. Griffin gave me a number of specimens. I do not wish to retail them. The church in Troy is greatly divided. Some have taken a dismission; others are consulting neighbouring ministers about the path of duty; and others are beginning to attend worship by themselves.

"But the worst is not told. The spirit of denunciation which has grown out of the mode of conducting the revivals at the west, is truly alarming. We do not call in question the genuineness of those revivals, or the purity of the motives of those who have been the most active in them. You, doubtless, are reaping and rejoicing in their happy fruits. But the evils to which I allude are felt by the churches abroad; members of which have gone out to catch the spirit, and have returned, some grieved, others soured, and denouncing ministers, colleges, theological seminaries, and have set whole churches by the ears, and kept them in turmoil for months together. Some students in divinity have done more mischief in this way than they can ever repair. I could mention names, but for exposing them. Some ministers and professors of religion have been to Troy, from the surrounding region, on purpose to catch the flame, and have returned home, saying: 'We do not want *such* a revival as they have in Troy.' . . . . .

"The evil is running in all directions. A number of churches have experienced a revival of anger, wrath, malice, envy, and evil-speaking, (without the knowledge of a single conversion,) merely in consequence of a desperate attempt to introduce these new measures. Those ministers and Christians who have heretofore been most and longest acquainted with revivals, are most alarmed at the spirit which has grown out of the revivals of the west. This spirit has, no doubt, greatly deteriorated by transportation. As we now have it, the great contest is among professors of religion—a civil war in Zion—a domestic broil in the household of faith. The friends of brother Finney are certainly doing him and the cause of Christ great mischief. They seem more anxious to convert ministers and Christians to their peculiarities, than to convert souls to Christ.

"It is just such a contest as I have sometimes seen, in its incipient stages, in New England, between some young revival ministers on the one side, and whole associations of ministers on the other. The young revival ministers, wishing to extend the work into all the churches, in their zeal would enter the limits of settled pastors, and commence their operations, and plead my example for all their movements; and so the war would begin—and all those ministers who would not yield the reins, and sanction their imprudences, would be sure to be proclaimed as enemies to revivals. Being thus defeated, these young ministers would come to me to make their complaints, and to work on my mind the conviction that all those ministers were enemies to myself—whereas the whole evil lay in a violation of all the rules of ministerial order and Christian meekness, or in the inexperience, ignorance, and imprudence of these young ministers. I am sorry to speak thus of my best friends; but it is due to my brethren to say, that those very ministers, who had been thus slandered by my young brethren, have since come to me with tears, urging me to visit their flocks. There is not one of them but would bid me a welcome, and would rejoice in a revival; but they would not invite these young ministers to preach for them, who had been so rash in their proceedings, and guilty of slandering them as stupid, and dead, and enemies of revivals. In this manner, some of the most promising young revival ministers have run themselves out, and lost the confidence of settled pastors and Christians in general.

"The spirit of denunciation which has grown out of these western revivals, seems to be owing to the implicit confidence which has been placed in the proceedings of just such young ministers as leaders. They dared not attempt to correct any of their irregularities, for fear of doing mischief, or of being denounced as enemies to revivals. This I know to be the fact. Brother Finney himself has been scarcely three years in the ministry, and has had no time to look at consequences. He has gone, with all the zeal of a young convert, without a friend to check or guide him. And I have no doubt that he begins with astonishment to look at the evils which are running before him.

"The account which his particular friends gave of his proceedings is, in substance, as follows:—He has got ministers to agree with him only by 'crushing,' or 'breaking them down.' The method by which he does it, is by creating a necessity, by getting a few individuals in a church to join him, and then all those who will not go all lengths with him are denounced as enemies to revivals. Rather than have such a bad name, one and another falls in to defend him; and then they proclaim what ministers, elders, and men of influence, have been 'crushed' or 'broken down.' This moral influence being increased, others are denounced, in a similar manner, as standing out, and leading sinners to hell. And to get rid of the noise, and save himself, another will 'break down.' And so they wax hotter and hotter, until the church is fairly split in twain. And now, as for those elders and Christians who have thus been converted to these measures, some of them are sending out private word to their Christian friends abroad, as follows: 'I have been fairly *skinned* by the denunciations of these men, and have ceased to oppose them, to get rid of their noise. But I warn you not to introduce this spirit into your church and society.' And so brother Finney's supposed friends, men of influence, are sending out word to warn others to beware of the evils which they have experienced. I heartily pity brother Finney, for I believe him to be a good man, and wishng to do good. But nobody dares tell him that a train of causes is set in operation, and urged on by his own friends, which is likely to ruin his usefulness.

. . . .

"Whoever has made himself acquainted with the state of things in New England, near the close of the revival in the days of Whitefield and Edwards, cannot but weep over its likeness to the present. It is affecting that the warm friends of Zion should unwittingly betray her best interests. But so was it then. The young itinerants, in their zeal to extend the work, began to denounce all those settled ministers who would not go all lengths with them. And then those members of churches who loved their pastors would assemble around to defend them; while those who favoured the itinerants assembled around them, and imbibing their spirit, of course lost all confidence in a settled ministry: and so the churches were split in twain. The Spirit of God took its flight, and darkness and discord reigned for half a century. And those preachers who had taken the lead, having cultivated such a spirit, began to fall into awful darkness themselves, when they saw the ruin that followed their labours. Some of them made and published their recantations to the world, which are now extant. But it was too late. A retribution followed. Some few of the young converts were called to order by David Brainerd, who passed through Connecticut at that time. But after their recantations these leaders were generally denounced hy their own followers. Could Whitefield, and Edwards, and Brainerd, and Davenport, now arise from the dead, I have no doubt they would exclaim: Young men, beware! beware!! . . .

"Some of brother Finney's younger brethren and friends may attempt to work on his mind the conviction that most of our ministers and churches are enemies to revivals, and unfriendly to himself. I feel it my duty to speak in their behalf. I know it to be a mistake. The best friends of revivals, as they have heretofore witnessed them, are certainly the most afraid to invite him into their churches, and are the most alarmed at the evils that are rising. And, I must say, that his friends are certainly labouring to introduce those very measures, which I have ever regarded as ultimately working ruin to our churches, and against which I have always guarded as ruinous to the character of revivals, as well as to my own usefulness.

"For example: whoever introduces the practice of females praying in promiscuous assemblies, let the practice once become general, will ere long find, to his sorrow, that he has made an inlet to other innovations, and entailed an everlasting quarrel on those churches generally. If settled pastors choose to do it on their own responsibility, so be it. For one, I dare not assume so great a responsibility. In this way churches were once laid waste; and it is by keeping out, and carefully avoiding everything of this kind, that some of them have again been built, others kept orderly, and the character of revivals, for *thirty* years past, has been guarded. If the evil be not soon prevented, a generation will arise, inheriting all the obliquities of their leaders, not knowing that a revival ever did or can exist without all those evils. And these evils are destined to be propagated from generation to generation, waxing worse and worse.

"The friends of brother Finney are afraid to interfere to correct anything, lest they should do mischief, or be denounced as enemies of revivals. 'Brother Nettleton, do come into this region and help us; for many things are becoming current among us which I cannot approve. And I can do nothing to correct them, but I am immediately shamed out of it, by being denounced as an enemy to revivals.' Thus my ministerial brethren from the west, whose views accord with my own, have been calling to me, in their letters during the summer past. 'There is religion in it, and I dare not touch it. I see the evil, and tremble at the consequences; but what can I do?' This is the language of many of his warmest friends. And so the bad must all be defended with the good. This sentiment adopted, *will certainly ruin revivals.* It is the language of a novice : it is just as the devil would have it. If the friends of revivals dare not correct their own faults, who will do it for them? *I know no such policy.* I would no more dare defend in the gross, than condemn in the gross. And those who adopt the former practice will soon be compelled, by prevailing corruptions, to take along with it the latter. The character of revivals is to be sustained on the same principles as that of churches, or individual Christians. *If we would judge ourselves, we should not be judged.* It is not by *covering*, but by *confessing* and *forsaking*, that pure revivals are to prosper. In this manner their character has long been sustained. Things have not been left to run to such lengths in our day. A strong hand has been laid on young converts, old professors, and especially on zealous young ministers, as many of them now living can testify.

"I have been afraid to kindle fires where there was not some spiritual watchman near, to guard and watch against wildness for which I might become responsible. Some students in divinity have caught and carried the flame into neighbouring towns and villages, and, no doubt, have been the means of the salvation of some souls. But I am sorry to say, that some of them have run before me into the most populous places, and have carried their measures so far, and have become so dictatorial and assuming, that, in the opinion of the most judicious and influential ministers of my acquaintance, they have done far more mischief than good. They have pleaded my example for many measures, which, as to time and circumstances, I utterly condemn. Some of the means which I have never dared to employ, except in the most interesting crisis of a powerful revival, they have caricatured in such a manner, and raised such prejudices against myself among strangers, that they have caused me much trouble. My plans have been laid to visit many towns and cities, and have been wholly defeated by these students in divinity thus running before me. I have been much grieved, and exceedingly perplexed on this subject. They assume an authority, unwittingly I allow, and adopt measures which no ordained minister could do without ruining his usefulness. Evils arising hence have uniformly been arrested in their progress by my taking the part of settled pastors among their flocks, at a great expense of feeling on the part of my young friends, no doubt; but the cause of revivals evidently required it.

"I have been anxiously looking and waiting, all summer long, for such men as yourself and Mr. Lansing, and others most intimately acquainted with brother Finney, to take hold, with a kind severity, and restore order; but in vain. It is not expected that a powerful revival can exist among imperfect beings, without more or less irregularity and opposition; but it is expected that these things will generally subside, and leave the churches in a more peaceful, happy, and flourishing state than ever. This has uniformly been the case where revivals have prevailed. But irregularities are prevailing so fast, and assuming such a character in our churches, as infinitely to overbalance the good that is left. These evils, sooner or later, must be corrected. Somebody must speak, or silence will prove our ruin. Fire is an excellent thing in its place, and I am not afraid to see it blaze among briers and thorns; but when I see it kindling where it will ruin fences, and gardens, and houses, and burn up my friends, I cannot be silent.

"Had the evil been checked in the commencement, it would have been an act of kindness to brother Finney, and great gain to the cause of revivals. He would have found ministers everywhere bidding him welcome. His help is everywhere greatly needed. For a settled pastor, the entire confidence of other ministers would not be so important. But whoever undertakes to promote revivals by running through the world in this age of revivals, must have the entire confidence of settled ministers generally; otherwise he will unsettle ministers, and desolate churches, wherever he goes. Without their hearty co-operation, he will certainly labour at great disadvantage: as if a mariner, steering his ship in a storm at sea, in his zeal should quit the helm, and ply his strength at the mast.

"The practice of praying for people by name, in the closet, and the social circle, has no doubt had a beneficial effect. But as it now exists in many places, it has become, in the eye of the Christian community at large, an engine of public slander in its worst form. I should not dare, in this solemn manner, to arraign a fellow-sinner before a public assembly, without his own particular request, unless my expressions were of the most conciliatory kind. And no Christian minister, whatever his character may be, can adopt the practice, without awakening the indignation of the world at large, and of Christians generally, against him: much less can it be done by anybody, and everybody, who takes it into his head positively to decide the question, and to tell God and the world that such and such persons are unconverted. I do not believe, whatever may be the effect upon the individual thus named, that God will regard such a prayer in any other light than as that of a proud, self-righteous Pharisee.

"There is another interesting topic that lies near my heart; but the time would fail me to express my views and feelings on the subject. That holy, humble, meek, modest, retiring form, sometimes called the Spirit of Prayer, and which I have ever regarded as the unfailing precursor of a revival of religion, has been dragged from her closet, and so rudely handled by some of her professed friends, that she has not only lost all her wonted loveliness, but is now stalking the streets in some places stark mad.

"Some, in their zeal on the subject of the *prayer of faith*, are tormenting others with their peculiar sentiments, which, if correct, everybody sees must equally condemn themselves; thus rendering themselves and their sentiments perfectly ridiculous.

"I have given you but an imperfect sketch of my own, and the views of our brethren abroad on this subject; but I assure you, as a whole, it is not overdrawn. How to correct these growing evils I cannot tell. Our brethren, far and near,—some of brother Finney's best friends at the west not excepted,—by letter and otherwise, have long been urging me to lay the subject fully before him. The evils which have existed abroad have certainly been very much concealed from him and his friends. It is certainly right that he should know something of the evils which have run from under him—and the feelings of the friends of Zion at large. I have nothing to say to him in the style of crimination or controversy. I have been too long on the field of battle to be frightened about little things, or to make a man an offender for a word. For Zion's sake, I wish to save brother Finney from a course which, I am confident, will greatly retard his usefulness before he knows it. It is no reflection on his talents or piety that, in his zeal to save souls, he should adopt every measure which promises present success, regardless of consequences; nor, after a fair experiment in so noble a cause, to say, I pushed some things beyond what they will bear. The most useful lessons are learned by experience.

"I wish I had health and strength to shew brother Finney my whole heart on this subject. I have long been wishing to correct some of his peculiarities, that I might invite him into my own field, and introduce him to my friends. Aside from feeble health, one consideration only has prevented me from making the attempt. Some of his particular friends are urging him on to the very things which I wish him to drop. I fear that their flattering representations will overrule all that I can say. And having dropped these peculiarities, his labours for awhile might be less successful; and then he would resort again to the same experiment. But I can inform him, that the same measures which he has adopted have been vigorously and obstinately pursued in New England, against the repeated advice of settled pastors, and that, too, by one of the most powerful and successful ministers that I have ever known, until, confident of his own strength, he quit them all, with this expression: 'We will see who will answer by fire'—a most unhappy expression, as he afterwards told me with tears. The result was, he lost his usefulness in our denomination. Some of his spiritual children, now excellent men in the ministry, have never dared to adopt his measures, but have uniformly opposed them. Others—some ministers and laymen—who followed him, became disorganizers; and the leader himself turned Baptist, and soon after died.

"There is another method of conducting revivals which may avoid these difficulties. Settled pastors occupy nearly the whole field of operation. They have, and ought to have the entire management in their own congregation. Each one has a right to pursue his own measures within his own limits; and no itinerant has any business to interfere or dictate. It will ever be regarded as intermeddling in other men's matters. If they do not choose to invite me into their field, my business is meekly and silently to retire. And I have no right to complain. But many young men are continually violating the rules of ministerial order and Christian propriety in these respects. Impatient to see the temple rise, they are now doing that which, it appears to me, will tend ultimately, more than anything else, to defeat the end which they wish to accomplish. They are now pulling down, in many places, the very things which I have been helping ministers to build up; and for which I have often received their warmest thanks. It is a sentiment which I have had frequent occasion to repeat to my young brethren in the ministry: 'Better forego the prospect of much present good, in your own opinion, than to lose the confidence of settled ministers, without which you cannot be long and extensively useful.'

"*There*, certainly, is another and a lawful point of attack on the kingdom of darkness, which, when you have taken, and it is seen, possesses wonderful advantages. It will give no offence to the Church of God. It will be sure to rally round you every faithful soldier of the Cross. Though it may seem too slow and silent in its operation, yet, being the lawful method of conducting this warfare, it will secure the confidence of ministers and Christians, the consciences of the wicked, and a crown of glory.

"And now, brother, I have ventured to lay before you the subject of my prayers and tears, and, I may add, the subject which brought me back to a region which I never expected to visit again. If you discover anything in this communication unchristian or unkind, you will pardon it. If, in your opinion, it can do no mischief, or will do any possible good, you are at full liberty to shew it to brother Finney, or any of the friends of Zion whom it may concern. We will lay the subject at the feet of our Divine Master, and there we will leave it.—Yours, in the best of bonds."

The letter from which the foregoing extracts are taken, with some other documents, was published, in a pamphlet, in 1828. In a note appended to it, Dr. Nettleton says:—

"The above letter was written some time last December, immediately after a second interview with Mr. Finney. From personal conversation with himself, but more particularly with his friends, I learned that they had adopted and defended measures which I have ever regarded as exceedingly calamitous to the cause of revivals.

"This letter was written originally as an expression of my own views, and the views of my brethren generally, on this subject, without intending to send it to any one. As my opinion was repeatedly solicited on this subject by the friends of Mr. F., I thought it best to give it in writing. Accordingly, this letter was read, at different times, to not less than twenty ministers, and to some who had adopted the measures in question. In this silent manner I laboured for a number of weeks, hoping to persuade the latter to drop them; but, to my surprise, I found that my own name was continually employed to give them sanction; nor was it in my power to prevent this perversion, without publishing my views to the world.

"As preparatory to publishing, and to cut off occasion for after complaints, it was thought best that I should delay no longer sending a communication to some one or more of our brethren in the Oneida Presbytery. The above 'document' is one, and only a small part of what I have written to the members of that body. What I have done in laying the subject before them, was not done without the knowledge and approbation of the watchmen of Israel—the long, the tried, the acknowledged friends of Zion."

The letter, although addressed to Mr. Aikin, was intended for the perusal of Mr. Finney and his friends. Soon after it was received, Mr. Finney prepared, and preached at Utica, a sermon on the text: "How can two walk together except they be agreed?" This sermon was understood to be a vindication of the things complained of in Dr. Nettleton's letter. It was afterwards preached in Troy, and published. Dr. Nettleton made some remarks on this sermon, in a letter addressed to the Rev. Dr. Spring of New York, which was first published in the *New York Observer*, and afterwards in the above-mentioned pamphlet. The following are extracts:—

"DURHAM, NEW YORK, *May* 4, 1827.

"MY DEAR BROTHER,—I have read brother Finney's sermon from the words: 'How can two walk together except they be agreed?' The principle on which it rests is contained in the following sentences:—

'If anything, even upon the same subject, that is far above or below our tone of feeling is presented, and if our affections remain the same, and refuse to be enlisted and brought to that point, we must feel uninterested, and, perhaps, grieved and offended. If the subject be exhibited in a light that is below our present tone of feelings, we cannot be interested till it come up to our feelings. If this does not take place we necessarily remain uninterested. If the subject be presented in a manner that is far above our tone of feeling, and our affections grovel and refuse to rise, it does not fall in with and feed our affections; therefore we cannot be interested—it is enthusiasm to us; we are displeased with the warmth in which our affections refuse to participate; and the farther it is above our temperature, the more are we disgusted. These are truths to which the experience of every man will testify, as they hold good upon every subject, and under all circumstances, and are founded upon principles that are incorporated with the very nature of man.'

"Now all this, so far as Christians and true religion are concerned, I take to be false in theory, contrary to fact, and dangerous in its consequences. Present to the mind of the Christian, whose holiness and flaming zeal shall equal that of Paul, the least degree of holiness in any saint, and he will not be offended, but interested. He would be greatly delighted with even 'babes in Christ.' And the higher the tone of his piety and holy feeling, the greater will be his delight, even 'upon the same subject.' Now, raise the tone of pious feeling up to that of the spirits of just men made perfect and holy angels, and still they will not lose their interest, 'even upon the same subject.' They will rejoice even over one sinner that repenteth, far more than will those whose feelings fall to the level of the penitent himself.

"Nor is it true that Christians are always better pleased with those whose tone of feeling is on a level with their own. The least saint on earth loves holiness in others, and rejoices in their growth in grace. And he loves those most whose tone of holy feeling is raised farthest above him; and, for the same reason, he loves the Saviour more than all. Every child of God who reads his Bible, is better pleased with the high-toned piety of Job, and Daniel, and David, and Isaiah, and Paul, than he is with that of other saints whose piety falls below theirs, or to the level of his own. What Christian can read the memoirs of Edwards and Brainerd without deep interest? I know of no Christian that does not read them with far greater interest than he would have done had they exhibited far less of the spirit of Christianity. And though Christians feel condemned by their high-toned piety, yet, for this very reason, they are not 'offended and grieved,' but love them the more. Though Christians are not up to the tone of piety exhibited by David and Paul, Edwards and Brainerd, yet they are highly delighted, and could walk together with them.

"Again, take the example of our Saviour. No Christian on earth is better pleased with any other. Though many of his friends have died and gone to heaven, whom he still loves, yet the Christian can say: 'Whom have I in heaven but thee, and there is none upon earth that I desire beside thee?' The tone of the Saviour's holy feeling is raised far above that of all His followers. Hence, according to the sentiment of the sermon, He could have had no followers on earth, and can have none now. All His disciples must have been '*displeased* with His warmth.' And the higher it rose 'above their temperature, the more they must have been *disgusted*.'

"Present to the mind of the Christian the holy character of God. Is not this subject far above the tone of the feelings of any man? Now, according to the sentiment of the sermon, if our affections are not brought to that point, we must feel 'uninterested, grieved, and offended.' According to the principle of his own sermon, brother Finney and his friends cannot walk with God, for they are not agreed. It must be acknowledged that God has an infinitely higher tone and degree of holy feeling than brother Finney. He is not 'up to it.' Consequently, on his principles, they cannot be agreed. God is displeased with him, and he with God. Brother Finney must '*necessarily*' be displeased with high and holy zeal in his Maker, which so infinitely transcends his own; and the 'farther it is above his temperature, the more he will be *disgusted*.' 'These are truths,' he observes, 'to which the experience of every man will testify, as they hold good upon *every subject*, and under all circumstances, and are founded upon principles that are incorporated with the very nature of man.' . .

. . . . . .

"The sermon in question entirely overlooks the nature of true religion. It says not one word by which we can distinguish between true and false zeal, true and false religion. If the tone of feeling can only be raised to a certain pitch, then all is well. The self-righteous, the hypocrite, and all who are inflated with pride, will certainly be flattered and pleased with such an exhibition, especially if they are very self-righteous and very proud. *False affections often rise far higher than those that are genuine;* and this every preacher, in seasons of revival, has had occasion to observe and correct. And the reason of their great height is obvious. There are no salutary checks of conscience—no holy, humble exercises to counteract them in their flight. And they court observation. 'A Pharisee's trumpet shall be heard to the town's end, when simplicity walks through the town unseen.' If the preacher is not extremely careful to distinguish between true and false affections, the devil will certainly come in and overset the work, and bring it into disgrace. False zeal and overgrown spiritual pride will rise up and take the management, and condemn *meekness and humility*, and trample upon all the Christian graces, because they are not 'up to it.'

"Matters of fact, which have passed under my own observation, might serve as an illustration. I have often seen it; and the preacher who has not been tried with this subject, and learned to correct it, has not got his first lesson.

"Leaving out of the question the *nature of true religion*, as brother Finney has done out of his sermon, there is a sense in which his theory perfectly accords with experience and matters of fact. So far as false zeal and false affections are concerned, the principle of the sermon is correct. A and B are very zealous, and extremely self-righteous; and being equally so, they can walk together, for they are agreed. Both having come up to the same tone of feeling with brother Finney in his sermon, now they are all agreed, and all pleased, having done all that the preacher required. Now the zeal of A 'strikes far above the tone of feeling' in his fellow, and both are 'displeased, grieved, and offended.' B does not come to the tone of A, and 'therefore he cannot be interested; it is enthusiasm—he is displeased with the warmth in which his affections refuse to participate; and the farther it is above his temperature, the more he is disgusted.' The Christian and the hypocrite may come up to the *same tone of feeling*, and yet they cannot walk together for *other* reasons. The character of their affections differs as widely as light and darkness; and the higher their affections rise, the wider the distance between them; and no tone or degree of feeling can possibly bring them together. Every effort of the preacher to unite them by raising the tone of feeling, will only increase the difficulty. This, too, accords with experience and matters of fact. Hence, those who adopt the same creed, and belong to the same communion, can have no fellowship. Though they are up to the same tone of feeling, and feel *deeply*, yet they cannot walk together, for they do not feel *alike*. Feelings which are not founded on *correct* theology cannot be *right;* they must *necessarily* be spurious, or merely animal.

"Without great care and close discrimination, the preacher will unwittingly justify all the quarrels and divisions in our churches. The church at Corinth valued themselves on their great spirituality and high attainments in religion. Now, on the principle of the sermon in question, their divisions and quarrels could be no evidence to the contrary, but much in their favour. Each one esteeming others worse than himself, would conclude that the whole difficulty lay in their not coming up to the tone of his own feelings. And this sermon would have confirmed them all in their good opinion of themselves. But *Paul* told them that the very contrary was true. 'For whereas there is among you envying, and strife, and divisions, are ye not carnal, and walk as men?' Without the same care, the preacher will condemn others for keeping the unity of the Spirit in the bond of peace, and for 'being of one accord and of one mind.' *That peace*, and harmony, and order, in which Paul so much rejoiced, will be disturbed, and broken, and trampled upon, by disorganizing spiritual pride, under a pretence that all are 'cold, and carnal, and stupid, and dead, and not up to the spirit of the times.' All who are thus inflated will take the advantage of this sermon, and be sure to construe all opposition to their own disorganizing movements and measures, into an evidence of superior piety in themselves. And all false converts, and others inflated with spiritual pride, will join them, if great care be not taken to discriminate between true and false zeal, and to give the distinguishing marks of both. Spiritual pride will often court opposition, and glory in it, and sometimes adopt the sentiment: 'The more opposition the better.' . .

"All who are acquainted with the history of facts on the subject, know that it was on the principles of the sermon in question that the revival was run out in the time of Edwards, and in Kentucky and Tennessee, about twenty years since. And all those ministers who do not discriminate between true and false zeal, true and false affections, in their preaching and conversation, and make that difference, and hold it up to the view of the world, if possible, clear as the sun, heartily approving of the one, and as heartily and publicly condemning the other, will turn out to be the greatest traitors to the cause of revivals. They become responsible, not only for the sentiment in question, but also for all the corruptions which prevail in consequence of this neglect. The neglect of ministers to correct these evils for fear of doing mischief, or of being denounced as carnal and cold-hearted, or as enemies to revivals, is extremely puerile and wicked. On the same principle, they must not attempt to correct intemperance and profane swearing in church members, lest they should be ranked among the wicked as infidels and enemies to Christianity. The sentiment in question would, if carried out into all its consequences, defend every abomination in religion that could be named. It would soon come to this: that the only evidence that ministers are cold, and carnal, and stupid, and dead, is, that they cannot approve of every art, and trick, and abominable practice in laymen, women, and children, in their attempts to promote a revival. And their approbation of all these abominations would be taken as a good sign, and as an evidence that they are *awake*. Whereas none but carnal and cold-hearted ministers would be influenced by such mean motives. It is only a trick of the devil to frighten the watchman of Israel from his post, that he may get possession of it himself; or, what he would like still better, by such base motives, to entoil and enlist him in his service, by compelling him to adopt his own measures. So did not Paul. His two epistles to the Corinthians contain little else than a humbling disclosure of abominable practices and quarrels about men and measures in promoting a revival. So did not Edwards. Though he was denounced at first, he could not be frightened; but frightened his denouncers, some of them at least, into a public recantation. A *denouncing* spirit is that with which *real* Christians have no fellowship, and are bound to shun.

"Without regard to the admonition: 'Take heed to thyself,' the preacher will be in danger of trampling upon the divine direction: 'In meekness instructing those that oppose themselves.' 'The servant of the Lord must not strive, but be gentle unto all men.' 'Be kindly affectioned, be pitiful, be courteous.' He will be in great danger of condemning the 'meekness and gentleness of Christ,' under the names of 'carnal policy,' and 'hypocritical suavity of manner.' The preacher should be extremely cautious what he says against 'wisdom and prudence,' as a mark of 'puffing-up' in his brethren, lest he trample upon the authority of his Divine Master, in the precept given him upon the same point: 'Behold, I send you forth as sheep in the midst of wolves; be ye therefore *wise* as serpents, and *harmless* as doves.' His precept is founded on the fact, that wicked men may become more offended with what is *wrong in manner*, than with what is *right in matter*. Hence the preacher may lose their consciences, and the devil has gained the victory. If the wicked *will* oppose, it becomes us to be careful how we furnish them with successful weapons against us. If we regard the direction of Christ, even though they rage, we may still keep our hold upon their consciences; and so long as we can do this, we need not despair of the victory. But when the preacher has lost the wisdom of the serpent and the harmlessness of the dove, the contest will end in a sham-fight, and the sooner he quits the field the better.

"Paul would allow none to be teachers but those of 'full age, who by reason of use have their senses exercised to *discern* both good and evil.' Hence he would not license young converts to preach: 'Not a novice, lest being lifted up with pride he fall into condemnation, reproach, and the snare of the devil.' So far as his *message* was concerned, the apostle himself went forth 'saluting no man by the way,'—'not as pleasing men.' Aside from the simple truth of that message, no man was ever more yielding and flexible in manner and measures: 'Give no offence, neither to the Jews, neither to the Gentiles, nor to the Church of God;' 'Even as *I please all men* in *all things*, that they may be saved;' 'I am made all things to all men, that I might by all means save some.' Was this 'carnal policy?' and was Paul 'in a very *cold* state when he wrote that?'

"The wisdom of the measures adopted and recommended by Paul, appear from the fact, that sinners may be more offended with what is *wrong in manner* than with what is *right in matter*. If the preacher does not hold a balance between conscience and depravity, he can do nothing. The very fact that the unrenewed heart is so opposed to God and the Gospel has, by some, been assigned as a reason for stirring up all its opposition. Whereas, aside from the simple exhibition of divine *truth*, Paul adopted a method directly the opposite. If the vigilance of human depravity should exceed the vigilance of the preacher in his manner and measures, by this very means he will quiet the consciences of his hearers. Regardless of his manner, Paul would have lost his hold on the consciences of sinners, and needlessly and wickedly have sent his hearers to a returnless distance from the Gospel. This made him exceedingly careful 'lest he should hinder the Gospel of Christ.' Since mankind *will* oppose, we should be careful not to put weapons of successful defence into their hands. While they oppose, we should be careful to keep their consciences on our side.

"A powerful religious excitement, badly conducted, has ever been considered by the most experienced ministers and best friends of revivals, to be a great calamity. Without close discrimination, an attempt to raise the tone of religious feeling will do infinite mischief. This was the manner of false teachers: 'They zealously affect you; but not well.' It will be like that of Paul before his conversion, and like that of the Jews who were never converted, 'a zeal of

God, but not according to knowledge.' The driving will become like the driving of Jehu: 'Come, see my zeal for the Lord!' The storm, and earthquake, and fire, are dreadful; but God is not there.

"The design of these remarks is to shew the infinite importance of distinguishing between true and false zeal,—true and false affections.

"On reading the sermon in question, I was reminded of the repeated complaints which, for some time past, I have heard from the most judicious, experienced, and best revival-ministers in the west; the substance of which is as follows:—'There are various errors in the mode of conducting revivals in this region which ought to be distinctly pointed out. That on the prayer of faith. This talking to God as a man talks to his neighbour, is truly shocking—telling the Lord a long story about A or B, and apparently with no other intent than to produce a kind of stage effect upon the individual in question, or upon the audience generally. This mouthing of words—those deep and hollow tones, all indicative that the person is speaking into the ears of man, and not to God. I say nothing of the nature of the petitions often presented; but *the awful irreverence of the manner!* How strange that good men should so far forget themselves, as evidently to play tricks in the presence of the great God!'

"'I have often been struck with this circumstance in the mode of preaching, that nothing was heard of the danger of a spurious conversion. For months together, the thought never seemed to be glanced at, that there was any such thing as a satanic influence in the form of religion; but only as openly waging war against all religion. Such a character as an enthusiastic hypocrite, or a self-deceived person, seemed never to be once dreamed of. The only danger in the way of salvation was *coldness, deadness, and rank opposition*. On no occasion did the eye ever seem to be turned to another quarter in the heavens.'

"The last paragraph contains the thought to which I allude. The sermon in question bears striking marks of the same character. It is an important part of a preacher's duty in a season of powerful revival to discriminate between true and false conversion. Without this, every discerning Christian knows that the work will rapidly degenerate. The most flaming spiritual pride will be taken for the highest moral excellence, and will rise up and take the lead.

"Preachers who have not guarded well this avenue in seasons of powerful excitement, have always done more to arrest, and disgrace, and run out revivals, than all the cold-hearted professors and open enemies of religion together. It was this neglect in some zealous preachers that run out the revival in the days of Edwards, and which led him to write his Treatise on the *Religious Affections*. . . . . .

"It is of the highest importance that the preacher present to his hearers the distinguishing marks of true religion, the graces of the Spirit, in all their native loveliness; and, at the same time, that he detect and expose every counterfeit. Having done this, he may labour with all his might to *bring them up to the highest possible tone*. He may exhort them to the exercise of 'love, joy, peace, long-suffering, gentleness, goodness, faith, meekness, temperance; and to be kindly affectioned one to another, with brotherly love, in honour preferring one another. That they walk with all lowliness and meekness, with long-suffering, forbearing one another in love, endeavouring to keep the unity of the Spirit in the bond of peace. That they let nothing be done through strife or vain-glory; but in lowliness of mind let each esteem others better than themselves. Let all bitterness, and wrath, and anger, and clamour, and evil-speaking, be put away from you, with all malice: and be ye kind one to another, tender-hearted, forgiving one another, even as God for Christ's sake hath forgiven you. Likewise, ye younger, submit yourselves unto the elder. Yea, all of you, be subject one to another, and be clothed with humility.' He may exhort them 'to put on, as the elect of God, —and be covered all over with these shining graces, —bowels of mercies, kindness, humbleness of mind, meekness, long-suffering, forbearing one another: even as Christ forgave you, so also do ye. And, above all things, put on charity, which is the bond of perfectness.' He may set their hearts all on fire with that heavenly Form,—'so pure, so peaceable, so gentle and easy to be entreated, full of mercy and good fruits, without partiality and without hypocrisy,'—that is, 'so long-suffering, so kind, envieth not, is not puffed up, doth not behave itself unseemly, seeketh not her own, is not easily provoked; thinketh no evil, rejoiceth not in iniquity, but rejoiceth in the truth; beareth all things, believeth all things, hopeth all things, and never faileth.' These are the prevailing characteristics of a revival of religion. Their absence cannot be compensated by flaming zeal.

"Nor is it sufficient that these and all other Christian graces be exhibited, and their counterfeit exposed, in theory alone. For so hypocrites will claim them all as their own. Profession is not principle. 'By their fruits ye shall know them.' 'Who is a wise man? Let him shew out of a good conversation his works with meekness of wisdom.'

> 'Easy indeed it were to reach
> A mansion in the courts above,
> If watery floods, and fluent speech,
> Might serve instead of faith and love.'

"The most important part of the preacher's duty, is to exhibit the evidence of their existence in the heart by corresponding actions in the life; and this, too, by being 'ensamples to the flock,' and by carefully copying the example of his Divine Master, 'beseeching them by the *meekness* and *gentleness* of Christ.'

"As the time would fail me to complete the subject, Edwards may, in part, supply this deficiency in brother Finney's sermon. I would therefore take this opportunity to recommend to all young converts a careful perusal of his account of the revival in New England, *fourth part*, and what he says on the marks of true humility and spiritual pride, of which the following is a brief abstract:—

"Spiritual pride disposes one to speak much of the faults of others, and with bitterness, or with levity. and an air of contempt. Pure Christian humility rather disposes a person to be silent about them, or to speak of them with grief and pity. Spiritual pride is very apt to suspect others. An humble saint is most jealous of himself. The spiritually proud person is apt to find fault with others that are low in grace, and to be much in observing how cold and dead they be, and crying out of them, and sharply reproving them for it. The humble Christian has so much to do at home with his own heart, that he is not apt to be very busy with the hearts of others; and is apt to esteem others better than himself, and to take most notice of what is good in them, while he takes most notice of what is wrong in himself. In his clearest discoveries of God's glory, and in his most rapturous frames, he is most overwhelmed with a sense of his own vileness, and feels the deepest self-abasement.

"It is a mark of spiritual pride when any are disposed to speak of what they see amiss in others in the most harsh, severe, and terrible language,—saying of their opinions, or conduct, or advice—of their coldness, their silence, their caution, their moderation, and their prudence, that they are from the *devil* or from *hell*—that such a thing is devilish, or hellish, or cursed, and the like; so that the words *devil* and *hell* are almost continually in their mouths, and especially when such language is used towards ministers of the Gospel, and others whose age or station entitles them to particular respect. Humility leads the Christian to treat others that are in fault with meekness and gentleness, as Christ did His disciples, and particularly Peter, when he had shamefully denied Him.

"Spiritual pride disposes to affect singularity in manner and appearance, for the purpose of attracting observation. Humility disposes the Christian to avoid everything which is likely to draw upon him the observation of others, and to be singular only where he cannot be otherwise without the neglect of a plain and positive duty. Spiritual pride commonly occasions a certain stiffness and inflexibility in persons in their own judgment and their own ways. Humility inclines to a yielding, pliable disposition. The humble

Christian is disposed to yield to others, and conform to them, and please them in everything but sin.

"Spiritual pride disposes persons to stand at a distance from others, as better than they. The humble Christian is ready to look upon himself as more unworthy than others; yet he does not love the appearance of an open separation from visible Christians, and will carefully shun everything that looks like distinguishing himself as more humble, or in any respect better than others.

"The eminently humble Christian is clothed with lowliness, mildness, meekness, gentleness of spirit and behaviour, and with a soft, sweet, condescending, winning air and deportment. Humility has no such thing as roughness, or contempt, or fierceness, or bitterness, in its nature, which things are marks of spiritual pride; as are also invectives and censorious talk concerning particular persons for their opposition, hypocrisy, delusion, pharisaism, and the like.

"Spiritual pride takes great notice of opposition and injuries that are received, and is often speaking of them. Humility disposes a person rather to be, like his blessed Lord when reviled, dumb, not opening his mouth. The more clamorous and furious the world is against him, the more silent and still will he be.

"Spiritual pride leads those who are reproached, to be more bold and confident, and to go greater lengths in that for which they are blamed. Humility leads to improve the reproaches of enemies as an occasion of serious self-examination.

"Spiritual pride leads to a certain unsuitable and self-confident boldness before God and man. Humility leads to the opposite.

"*Assuming* is a mark of spiritual pride,—putting on the airs of a master, to whom it belongs to dictate. Humility leads the Christian to take the place of a learner, to be 'swift to hear, slow to speak.' The eminently humble Christian thinks he wants help from everybody, whereas he that is spiritually proud thinks everybody wants his help. Christian humility, under a sense of others' misery, entreats and beseeches; spiritual pride affects to command and warn with authority.

"If young ministers had great humility, it would dispose them especially to treat aged ministers with respect and reverence as their fathers, notwithstanding that a sovereign God may have given them greater success than they have had.

"It is a mark of spiritual pride to refuse to enter into discourse or reasoning with such as are considered carnal men, when they make objections and inquiries. Humility would lead ministers to condescend to carnal men, as Christ has condescended to us, to bear with our unteachableness and stupidity, and still follow us with instructions, line upon line, precept upon precept, saying: 'Come, let us *reason* together;' it would lead to a compliance with the precept: 'Be ready always to give an answer to every man that asketh you a *reason* of the hope that is in you with *meekness* and fear.'

"Such are some of the marks of spiritual pride and true humility pointed out by President Edwards. The abstract is given as much as possible in his own words. The whole of what he says on the subject deserves the most serious consideration.

"The friends of religion have been so much gratified with that beautiful hymn by Newton, that I shall venture to insert it in my letter:—

'TRUE AND FALSE ZEAL.

'Zeal is that pure and heavenly flame
The fire of love supplies;
While that which often bears the name,
Is self in a disguise.

True zeal is merciful and mild,
Can pity and forbear;
The false is headstrong fierce, and wild,
And breathes revenge and war

While zeal for truth the Christian warms,
He knows the worth of peace;
But self contends for names and forms,
Its party to increase.

Zeal has attained its highest aim,
Its end is satisfied,
If sinners love the Saviour's name,
Nor seeks it aught beside.

But self, however well employed,
Has its own ends in view;
And says, as boasting Jehu cried:
"Come, see what I can do!"

Dear Lord, the idol self dethrone,
And from our hearts remove;
And let no zeal by us be shewn,
But that which springs from love.'

Your affectionate brother,
ASAHEL NETTLETON."

"REV. DR. SPRING."

The publication of the foregoing letters subjected Dr. Nettleton to great reproach. Many, however, who were at that time disposed to blame him, have long since been convinced, not only that he was actuated by a conscientious regard to the honour of God, and the good of Zion, but that he evinced great wisdom and foresight.

There were those at that period whose views accorded with his own, and who entirely approved of his course: indeed, they were the views entertained by the Congregational ministers generally in New England, and by a large proportion of the Presbyterians in the United States.

The Rev. Dr. Porter of Catskill, in a letter dated June 14, 1827, and published in the pamphlet which contains Dr. Nettleton's letters to Mr. Aikin and Dr. Spring, says: "Whatever might have been Mr. Finney's design, it is perfectly clear to my understanding, that the principle laid down and advocated in his sermon opens the door for the introduction of all those extravagances so often witnessed in religious conferences and prayer-meetings, and that Mr. Nettleton's remarks on said sermon are in point; and that they have no severity beyond the demands of sober truth. Mr. Nettleton has done what a faithful minister of the Gospel, and a friend to revivals of religion, and one who has had so much experience in them, was in duty bound to do." In the same letter he says: "In respect to Mr. Nettleton's remark on Mr. Finney's sermon, Dr. Griffin is willing to have it said and published, that he considers the remarks '*just what they should be.*' He also mentions the names of a number of other distinguished ministers, whose views he knew to agree with his own, as Drs. Hyde, Shepard, Spring, Blatchford, M'Auley, and Messrs. Tomb. Prime, Lyman, Rogers," &c.

"He was," says Dr. Humphrey, "in the truest sense, a Christian philosopher; and his philosophy was strictly Baconian. It consisted in observing phenomena and recording facts. I have long thought, and it is still my deliberate conviction, that he understood the whole subject of revivals better than any man with whom I ever conversed or laboured. He had studied it more profoundly. Indeed, no man could well be a more perfect master of his business or profession. Neither Cæsar nor Napoleon ever studied the art of war with greater assiduity, than he did the heavenly art of winning souls to Christ.

"In his own management in times of revivals, by preaching and personal intercourse, nothing was more deserving of being studied and imitated, than his *thoroughness, caution, and discrimination.* In these respects there was a heaven-wide difference between Dr. Nettleton and some of the most noted of his professed imitators. Being thoroughly 'rooted and grounded in the truth' himself, his presentations of it were clear, pungent, and searching. His revival topics were systematically and admirably arranged. In his discourses he began at the beginning. A full believer in the total depravity of the human heart, he arraigned sinners, whether young or old, as rebels against God; and made the threatenings of the law thunder in their ears, as but few preachers have power to do. With him, acting as an ambassador of Christ, there was no such thing as compromise. The rebels must 'throw down their arms,' and submit unconditionally, or he would give them no hope of pardon. Hundreds, if not thousands, can witness what a terrible dissector he was of the 'joints and the marrow.' At the same time that he shewed the impenitent they were lost, he made them feel that they had 'destroyed themselves.' It was difficult to say which he made plainest—their danger or their guilt; their immediate duty to repent, or the certainty that, without being drawn and renewed by the Spirit of God, they never *would* repent. It was in vain for them to retreat from one refuge to another. He was sure to strip them of all their vain excuses, and deliver them over to their consciences, to be dealt with according to law and justice. He preached what are called the hard doctrines—such as divine sovereignty, election, and regeneration—with great plainness, discrimination, and power. His grand aim was to instruct, convince, and persuade; to this end his appeals were constantly made to the understanding, the conscience, and the heart. The passions he never addressed, nor were his discourses at all calculated to excite them. Any outbreak of mere animal feeling he was always afraid of, as tending to warp the judgment and beget false hopes. His grand aim was to instruct his hearers as thoroughly, and point out the difference between true and spurious conversion so clearly, as to make it difficult for them to get hopes at all without good spiritual evidence on which to found them. Knowing how apt persons are to cling to their hopes, whether good or bad, he depended much more upon holding them back, till they had good evidence, than upon shaking them from their false foundations."

While he was himself an eminent example of discretion, he considered this a prime qualification in a minister of Christ. When the Rev. Dr. Cornelius was Secretary of the American Education Society, he submitted to Dr. Nettleton a list of qualifications to be possessed by those who should be encouraged to enter the ministry. It read thus:—"1. Piety. 2. Talents.

3. Scholarship. 4. Discretion." "Change the order," said he; "put discretion next to piety.

The following is an extract of a letter written to a theological student in 1826: "It is very important to a young preacher that he avoid a censorious spirit, and that he always speak kindly to those who are held in reputation among Christians. If he labour among such, he had better forego the prospect of doing *present* good, than lose the confidence of these men. I can think of times in the early part of my ministry, when I had no doubt that a given course would be blessed to the conversion of many souls. I might have been mistaken. At any rate, acquiescence in the judgment of my brethren did secure their confidence; and I have been astonished to find them so generally willing to allow me to adopt my own course. The truth is, all Christians are imperfect; and all our exertions to do good are attended with more or less imperfection. Good measures will be often *innocently opposed* for the want of experience only. The same measures may be very good, or very bad in different places, and under different circumstances. The question has often been proposed in the public prints: 'What is the best mode of dealing with anxious souls?' Much may be said and written to profit; but, after all, we might as well ask and answer the question: 'What is the best method of treating all manner of sicknesses and all manner of diseases among the people?' We may talk about the best means of doing good; but, after all, the greatest difficulty lies in doing it with a proper spirit. *Speaking the truth in love. In meekness instructing those that oppose themselves. With the meekness and gentleness of Christ.* I have known anxious sinners drop the subject of religion in consequence of a preacher addressing them in an angry tone. Mankind, it is true, will be sure to find fault with everything that awakens their fears; but we should endeavour so to conduct, as to keep their consciences on our side in spite of all their opposition. Take care and not give them just cause to complain."

In a letter to the same individual, written in 1827. speaking of the measures introduced in the western revivals, he says: "It is said that God has blessed these measures to the conversion of sinners. The same may be said of female preaching; and it may be asked in reference to that: 'How can that be wrong which God has blessed to the conversion of a soul?' I answer: It is an acknowledged fact, that profane swearing, opposition to revivals, mock conferences, have all been overruled to the conviction and conversion of sinners. And shall we not encourage and defend these things? The man who defends the principle in question appears bad in argument, and worse in practice.

"There is, no doubt, a kind of prudence which has ruined thousands for ever. But the preacher who condemns *prudence, in toto*, will soon be forsaken by her inmate. Prov. viii. 12. He may drive at the understandings and consciences of his hearers with all his might; but there is a point of prudence beyond which he cannot pass without loosing his entire hold on both. Zeal without prudence will defeat its own end. Zeal untempered with love and compassion for souls, will soon degenerate into harshness and cruelty of manner and expression, which will have no other effect on an audience than ranting and scolding, and even profane swearing. The result in morals will be what the children of this world denominate 'penny-wise,' and 'pound-foolish.' It is like cutting off the heads of hundreds to save the life of one man."

Some of his movements in going from place to place, appeared to his brethren at times somewhat strange, because they saw not, and he was not in the custom of telling, all his reasons. But his constant purpose was to keep the congregation where God was working, humble, sensible of dependence, and prayerful.

While Dr. Nettleton thus testified for the truth in matters of practice, where the cause of truth seemed likely to be injured, he jealously noticed also every appearance of error in doctrine, lesser or greater. An instance of this we find in the following letter, addressed to the Rev. Dr. Woods of Andover, dated May 6, 1829 :—

"You have, doubtless, read Erskine on the *Unconditional Freeness of the Gospel.* The writer doubtless wishes to promote the cause of religion. But the tendency of the work, I do think, is directly to defeat that object.

"In the early part of my ministry, the sentiments of Hervey and Marshall I found, in many places, meeting and checking the progress of conviction in some sinners, and giving false peace to others. I have found some studying Marshall's *Gospel Mystery of Sanctification*, and trying to believe it; but conscience, awakened by the Spirit of God, would not suffer them to rest in a belief that their sins were pardoned, while they had no evidence of a change of heart. I was invited to a house to converse with an interesting young lady who had been long anxious for her soul.* Many efforts had been made to give her consolation, but in vain. 'What do you think of this book?' said she. 'It is Marshall on *Sanctification*, and was recommended to be by ——; and if I dared believe it, I should think I was a Christian.' 'I am glad you dare not believe it. There is some part of it, at least, which you ought not to believe,' was my answer. I perceived that her conscience was more orthodox than the author. She gave it up; her convictions increased, and soon terminated in hopeful conversion. The faith which Marshall required did not commend itself to her conscience. Believing that her sins were pardoned, against the dictates of conscience and the Bible, seemed to her like believing a lie to make it true. How to reconcile this, I suppose Marshall found to be a 'mystery.' Hence the title of his book; hence, too, the more the conscience is awakened to perform its office, the more difficult divines of this description find it to deal with sinners. The great object, they think, is to give sinners peace, and all their efforts are directed to this single object. When the sinner begins to see his character and condition in some measure as it really is—when the Word of God begins to take effect, and conscience to perform its office, every effort is made to counteract the very means which the Spirit of God employs to bring the sinner to a reconciliation.

"Erskine agrees substantially with Marshall in his views of faith;—it consists in believing that our sins are pardoned. He has built his system upon Hervey

* See p. 99.

and Marshall, with this wonderful improvement, that we are not required to believe a lie to make it true; for *the sins of all mankind are pardoned, whether they believe it or not.* Pardon is *universal and unconditional. The atonement is itself the pardon, and is unaffected by man's belief or unbelief;* while, in all their rebellion and infidelity, *it is lavished upon the mass of the guilty without discrimination. The use of faith is not to remove the penalty, or to make the pardon better; for the penalty is removed, and the pardon is proclaimed, whether we believe it or not; but to give the pardon a moral influence, by which it may heal the spiritual disease of the soul. Mankind are sanctified by their belief of the pardon.* I cannot but notice how one error grows out of another. The definition of atonement is, 'THE ACTUAL REMOVAL OF SIN.' If so, then it must include pardon *irrespective of character*, antecedent to faith, or repentance, or conversion, and, of course, limited to the elect; and faith consists in believing that our sins are pardoned, and that we are of the elect. But to avoid this difficulty, limited atonement becomes unlimited; and so the atonement is made for all mankind. Therefore *pardon is lavished upon all mankind.* This is the most plausible scheme of universalism that I have ever seen. If mankind can only be made to believe that their sins are pardoned, this will make them *love God —restore the key-stone of the arch—sanctify them—give peace of conscience, and justify them.* Now, all this being taken for granted, without one text to prove it, and with the whole Bible against him, ('He that believeth not is condemned already, and the wrath of God abideth on him,' &c.,) he adopts every method in his power to make all his readers believe that their sins are pardoned. To doubt this must be a great crime. Unbelief is the greatest sin; and the more conscience awakes to perform its office of conviction, the more guilty and criminal is the sinner for listening to its admonitions. When the Spirit of God is convincing of sin, and the commandment comes and sin revives; and when the sinner sees and feels that he is lost, and needs pardon, he tries to take it off by convincing him that it is all false alarm. If he does not believe that his sins are pardoned before he has one thought of repentance, or of asking it, the poor man makes God a liar: 'He that believeth not,'—*i. e.*, that his sins are pardoned,—'hath made Him a liar.'

"The evil produced by such a book, from the pen of one who has already acquired a reputation as a writer and a Christian, cannot be calculated in this world. Here are false views of faith, of the atonement, of pardon, and of justification, which he makes to consist in a sense of pardon,—there is no such thing as evidence of a change of heart,—but believing that our sins are pardoned will produce that change, make us love God, and thus give *peace* and *confidence*, and *restore the key-stone of the arch!*

"I cannot but express my full conviction, that the sentiments contained in that book are more directly calculated to prevent conviction of sin, and to put a stop to genuine revivals of religion, than anything which has ever been published."

It will be seen by this letter, that Dr. Nettleton did not sympathize with the language used by both Hervey and Marshall in dealing with sinners about faith. The error, in this respect, of *Hervey* was, that he defined faith to be a persuasion "that Christ died *for me*," and pressed the sinner to begin at once with this persuasion as to his individual case. *Marshall* speaks to the same effect. Both of them, however, were thoroughly Calvinistic divines. Dr. Nettleton's own discovery of salvation (as the reader may remember) was in seeing the glorious and gracious character of God. It was not while believing anything about his own interest that his soul felt peace arise, but while believing and contemplating the glory of God in the face of Jesus. It seems to have been his case, as of very many others, that in the act of looking stedfastly at God's glory, as it is specially seen in the cross of Christ, his soul was led by the Spirit into peace almost imperceptibly. They saw the obstacles to their return gone—they perceived barriers broken down—they found their own resistance to God's righteousness had given way—and so they sailed into the haven of rest. No sooner did they "*know God's name*," than a secret "*confidence*" sprung up in their souls.

Besides, *Marshall and Hervey* seem too anxious to get the anxious souls whom they address brought at once to peace, as if the individual's present comfort of mind were the primary matter. This, at least, is evidently Dr. Nettleton's impression of their writings. But he forgets that these men of God wrote with a special object in view,—namely, to clear up what had been greatly obscured—the sinner's free warrant to go to the mercy seat at once. They were engaged, in their day, in dispelling the mists which some had tried to cast around the free and full Gospel. Both of them held uncompromisingly all the doctrines of grace. It is by no means just or fair in Dr. Nettleton to convey the impression that, substantially, they were at one with Thomas Erskine, the writer of *Unconditional Freeness of the Gospel.* This author is not only altogether opposed to the leading doctrines of Calvinism, but is very far from sound in his general views; though he has stated, very interestingly, some of the natural effects produced on the human soul by our believing the love of God. The general tendency of his works is never to be compared with that of the excellent and much blessed writings of Hervey and Marshall.

It was well, however, that such a man as Dr. Nettleton was found so jealous over the truth; and specially was it well that he so earnestly contended against every tendency to lightness or superficiality, at a time when error was beginning to make some impression.

The following, also, is from a letter addressed to Dr. Woods, and dated June 18, 1834. Speaking of a certain class of divines, he says: "They admit that there is *a tendency, or propensity to sin*, in the very constitution of the human mind;" but they *deny that this tendency is sinful.* They also admit that "every effect must have a cause, and that this cause must be prior to the effect."

"Now, I observe that the objections which they allege against the views of their opponents, lie equally against their own. It will be no easier for the sinner to repent and believe against this propensity to sin, than it was while it was called a 'sinful propensity.' Changing the name of a lion into that of a lamb, will not alter its nature. This propensity to sin, they admit, does all the mischief; and will it do any the less, in consequence of being called an 'innocent or harmless propensity.' Or will the sinner be any more likely to be on his guard, and to watch and fight against it? Directly the reverse. But why object to calling an 'infallible tendency or propensity to sin, a sinful propensity?' 'Then,' say they, 'regeneration must consist in removing it.' But suppose you give it any other name,—*e. g.*, *evil*, *bad*, *vile*, *vicious*, *pernicious*, *or dangerous*, then, also, regeneration must consist in removing it. Go one step farther, and call it *calamitous*, we should still think that regeneration consisted in removing this *calamitous* propensity to sin. Venture one step farther, and allay the fears of sinners entirely. Call it an innocent propensity, and then it need not be removed by regeneration. And yet one would be at a loss to see how their scheme can be made consistent with itself. One would think that an infallible tendency to sin would need to be removed in regeneration, or that regeneration could never take place. If 'every effect must have a cause, and this cause must be prior to the effect,' then no sinner ever did, or ever will put forth a holy choice until this infallible tendency to sin be removed, and succeeded by an infallible tendency to holiness; unless an infallible tendency to sin can be the cause of a holy choice. This latter opinion they seem to have adopted. They discard the principle that 'like produces like,' and assume another,—viz., that a 'fountain can,' and actually doth, 'send forth, at the same place, sweet water and bitter.' 'Men *do* gather grapes of thorns, and figs of thistles.' We have heard the new philosophy, that all trees are by nature alike, neither good nor bad, until they bear fruit. And then, the fruit is not good, but the tree is good only *because* the fruit is good, and *vice versa.* 'Make the tree good, and the fruit will be good,' said our Saviour; 'for the tree is known by the fruit.' Make the fruit good, and the fruit will be good, says the new philosophy; for the fruit is known by the fruit. Nothing is good or bad but fruit. There can be nothing in the tree *itself,* back of the fruit, but what is common to all trees,—'*pura naturalia.*'

"But how do they dispose of this 'propensity to sin,' in pressing the obligations of sinners?

"1. They give this propensity a soft name, deny its sinfulness altogether, and do not even call it bad or dangerous.

"2. They put into the mouth of the sinner an excuse for retaining his propensity to sin in all its strength.

"3. They call upon him to exercise no other *repentance of faith* than that which is consistent with the existence of this infallible tendency or propensity to sin in all its strength.

"4. They adopt, for his accommodation, a new theory of regeneration. 'It has been said by some, that regeneration consists in removing this sinful bias which is anterior to actual volition.' This they deny. But whether we call this propensity *sinful,* or not, all orthodox divines, who have admitted its existence, have, I believe, united in the opinion, that regeneration does consist in removing it. This, certainly, was the opinion of Edwards; and it constituted the principal difference between him and Dr. John Taylor. It was, also, the very quintessence of his Treatise on *Religious Affections.* Until this tendency to sin be removed, it is absolutely certain that true repentance never can begin. It is turning from the love to the loathing of sin. 'The heart,' says Edwards, 'can have no tendency to make itself better, until it first *has a better tendency.*' No sinner ever did, or ever will make a holy choice prior to an inclination, bias, or tendency to holiness. On the whole, their views of depravity, of regeneration, and of the mode of preaching to sinners, I think, cannot fail of doing very great mischief. This exhibition overlooks the most alarming features of human depravity, and the very essence of experimental religion. It is directly calculated to prevent sinners from coming under conviction of sin, and to make them think well of themselves while in an unregenerate state. It flatters others with the delusion, that they may give, or have given their hearts to God, while their propensity to sin remains in all its strength. Entertaining this delusion, they cannot be converted. Every sinner under deep conviction of sin knows this statement to be false so far as his own experience is concerned. The progress of conviction is ordinarily as follows: Trouble and alarm, 1. On account of outward sins. 2. On account of sinful thoughts. 3. On account of hardness of heart, deadness and insensibility to divine things,—tendency, bias, proneness, or propensity to sin, both inferred and felt. And this the convicted sinner always regards, not merely as calamitous, but as awfully criminal in the sight of God. And the sinner utterly despairs of salvation without a change in this propensity to sin. And while he feels this propensity to be thus criminal, he is fully aware, that if God, by a sovereign act of His grace, does not interpose to remove or change it, he shall never give his heart to God, nor make one holy choice. If the sinner has not felt this, he has not yet been under conviction of sin, or felt his need of regeneration.

"Those who adopt the views I am considering, exhort the sinner to do that only which leaves his propensity to sin in all its strength. Hence conversions are made as easy as you can turn your hand. It is only to resolve, and the work is done. They do, in effect, tell their hearers and their readers, what the most godly Christians certainly find it the most difficult to believe, that their propensity to sin, however strong it may be, is not criminal, but only calamitous—that they need not be alarmed at this awful propensity to sin—that they need not, for God does not, regard it with displeasure—that they can neither change it themselves, nor are required to do it—and that they need not ask, or even expect God to do it for them. Such a sentiment, however abhorrent to the ear and to the heart of piety, is, nevertheless, perfectly congenial with the feelings of all the most hardened in sin; and unless their consciences are more orthodox than such preaching, they will never be converted. Every step in the progress of conviction and conversion is in direct opposition to these sentiments. I know that converts may be made by hundreds and by thousands on these principles, with perfect ease; for so it has been in former times among the *Christians* and others in New England, as I have had full opportunity to know. *But piety never did, and never will descend far in the line of such sentiments.* Were I to preach in this manner, I do solemnly believe, that I should be the means of healing the hearts of awakened sinners lightly—of crying, Peace,

peace! when there is no peace—and of throwing the whole weight of my ministerial influence on the side of human rebellion against God."

The following extracts are taken from letters written at different times, and to different individuals:—

Speaking of the *character of infants*, he says: "For one I do solemnly believe, that God views and treats them in all respects just as He would do if they were sinners. To say that animals die, and therefore that death can be no proof of sin in infants, is to take infidel ground. The infidel has just as good a right to say, because animals die without being sinners, therefore adults may. If death may reign to such an alarming extent over the human race, and be no proof of sin, then it may reign to any extent in the universe, and be no proof of sin. Consequently, what Paul says: 'Death by sin, and so death passed upon all men, for that all have sinned,' cannot be true.

In another letter, speaking of the consequences of denying *the depravity of infants*, he says: "It is to deny that they need redemption by Christ, and regeneration by the Holy Spirit; or, if they do need redemption, it must be redemption from something which is not sin in any sense; and if they need regeneration, it must be a change of something which is not sinful in any sense. If the soul be innocent, it can be redeemed from nothing, and can never join the song of the redeemed: 'Unto Him that loved us and washed us from our sins in His own blood.' If the soul be innocent, it can be regenerated only for the worse."

Speaking of the theory which *accounts for the fact that sinners do not love God, by supposing that His character is not clearly seen*—that divine things are too remote and unreal to call forth the affections of their hearts—he says: "When brought near and real they will draw forth the opposition of the heart. You may destroy the sinner's earthly plans—break up all his interest in the concerns of time—fill his mind with all the solemn realities of death, judgment, and eternity—bring him under the most powerful convictions of sin—and the selfish principle may be more active this very moment than ever, in building up a righteousness, or in quarrelling with God about the terms of salvation. It is sometimes taken for granted, that if the sinner had clear views of the character of God, he would love Him. But facts prove the contrary. Sinners in the last stages of conviction, who have lost all interest in the concerns of time,—sinners, too, on a dying bed, who care nothing for the world, feel more opposition than ever. At this very crisis, when time, with all its concerns, has dwindled into nothing, the sinner for the first time discovers the appalling truth, that the *carnal* mind is enmity against God. The selfish principle—the carnal mind—with all its enmity against God, remains in full strength, until slain, or taken away by the act of the Holy Spirit. 'Even when we were dead, hath quickened us together with Christ.'"

In another letter, speaking of the theory, that "*God prefers, all things considered, holiness to sin in all instances in which the latter takes place*," he says: "If this be so, the question arises, Why does not God place holiness in the lieu of sin in a given case? The answer is: 'God cannot sustain the greatest amount of holiness in the universe, without that influence which results from the existence of sin and its punishment.' He needs, therefore, the influence which will result from the punishment of this sin. This is God's reason for not placing holiness in the lieu of this sin, though He desires it, in itself considered, and all things considered. He cannot do it without putting it out of His power to sustain the greatest amount of holiness. And yet 'He *sincerely* desires that the sinner would do it without divine influence.' Now, suppose the sinner should do it. According to this theory, he would put it out of God's power to sustain the greatest amount of holiness. Consequently, if the theory be true, God *sincerely desires that sinners would put it out of His power to sustain the greatest amount of holiness.*

"It is supposed, that if this theory is not true, sin must be excellent in itself. Is there no other alternative? If God brings *light out of darkness, order out of confusion, and good out of evil,* are darkness, confusion, and evil, good in themselves? May they not, by contrast, shew light, order, and good, to better advantage? So '*our unrighteousness may commend the righteousness of God.*'"

The foregoing extracts, which might be greatly extended, will serve to give the reader some idea of Dr. Nettleton's theological views.

It is well known that, within the last quarter of a century, there has been considerable controversy in New England respecting the best mode of stating and defending the doctrines of Calvinism. On the one hand, it has been maintained, that these doctrines, in the sense in which they have been commonly received, are inconsistent with sound philosophy, and that they ought to give place to more rational views. On the other hand, it has been maintained, that the explanations proposed, in some instances at least, amount to a virtual denial of the doctrines themselves, and to the adoption of dangerous errors. The points of controversy relate principally to the decrees and government of God, the moral agency of man, the nature of holiness, and the doctrines of native depravity, regeneration, and election. The reader who wishes to make himself acquainted with the manner in which these points have been discussed in America, is referred to the periodicals and pamphlets which contain the discussion, and which have been extensively circulated in the Christian community.

In this controversy Dr. Nettleton took no public part. But he did not regard it with indifference. On the contrary, he watched its progress with the deepest interest, and with an eye fixed on its bearings upon Christian experience and revivals of religion. It is evident, from the foregoing extracts from his sermons and letters, that his views of the Calvinistic doctrines were such as were maintained by the orthodox ministers of New England, at the beginning of the present century. The new views, therefore, which were put forth as improvements, he did not receive. They did not appear to him to be improvements. On the contrary, he believed them to be erroneous, and of dangerous tendency. From the first promulgation of them he was grieved and alarmed; and his sorrow was rendered the more intense by the fact, that some of the advocates of these views were brethren with whom he had laboured in revivals, and been on terms of the most endearing intimacy. The pain of Whitefield was not greater when his friend and brother, John Wesley, avowed his hostility to Calvinism, than was that of Dr. Nettleton when these brethren, whom he tenderly loved, began to maintain and propagate opinions which seemed to him to be unscriptural, and to be likely to injure the cause of revivals.

His strength had been spent in revivals. It had been his constant aim to elevate their character by sedulously guarding against everything that was suited to mar their purity, or weaken their power over the consciences of men ; and it was his settled conviction, that the purity of revivals depends greatly on the faithfulness with which the doctrines of the Cross are preached. He had observed, that when the standard of orthodoxy is lowered, the danger of delusion is increased, and the character of revivals is injured. He was "well aware that popular excitements, without doctrinal instruction," (or with false doctrinal instruction,) "may be called revivals ; and that zeal without knowledge may glory in the multiplication of its converts. But such excitements are no blessing to the Church."

It was the full conviction of Dr. Nettleton, that all genuine religious experience is based on correct views of the doctrines of grace ; and, consequently, that the *religious experience of those whose views of these doctrines are defective, or essentially erroneous, will be, in like degree, defective or spurious.* He felt, as we have seen, the great importance of exhibiting clearly the doctrines of the Cross in revivals of religion ; and hence he regarded those theological speculations which seemed to him to obscure, or utterly to subvert these doctrines, as directly tending to corrupt revivals, and, in this way, to destroy the souls of men. The opinions above referred to seemed to him to have, some of them in a greater, and some in a less degree, this dangerous tendency.

Such being his convictions, he could not hold his peace. It was, indeed, painful to him to disagree with his brethren; but he felt himself laid under solemn obligations to maintain what he believed to be the truth, and to bear testimony against what seemed to him to be dangerous error, whatever sacrifice it might cost him. Accordingly, he said to one of his brethren: "Such is my conviction of the tendency of these views to corrupt revivals, and produce spurious conversions, that if all New England should go over, I should prefer to stand alone."

But while he was thus decided in the maintenance of his own religious opinions, he entertained the kindest feelings towards those of his brethren from whom he felt compelled to differ. He was, as has been already remarked, grieved that their influence should be exerted to promote what he considered the cause of error; and he felt it to be his duty to expostulate with them. With some of them he maintained repeated and long discussions. But he never engaged in bitter and angry controversy. He always treated his brethren with kindness. He never impeached their motives, nor depreciated their talents, nor aspersed their characters by loading them with reproachful epithets. And his brethren never doubted the sincerity of his heart, however much they may have been grieved by the alarm which he felt and expressed at their supposed errors.

One of these brethren made him a visit at a period during his last sickness, when, in his own view, and that of his friends, he was near the close of life. The interview was tender and affectionate. It revived the recollection of many past scenes of thrilling interest. Nothing was said in regard to theological differences. Two days after this interview, Dr. Nettleton wrote to this brother the following letter:—

"My dear Brother,—I thank you for your visit, and the sympathy which you manifested in my affliction. The sight of your face revived many tender recollections. There were many things which I wished to say to you, but my strength would not permit. How long I am to linger on these mortal shores, I know not. But, as you are aware, I consider myself near to the eternal world; and I wish to say, that my views of the great doctrines which I preached twenty-five years ago, have not altered. They appear to me more precious than ever. I wish also to say, that I have the same views of some of your published writings, which I have often expressed to you in years past. I need not tell you that I love you. You know that I have ever loved you. You know also that I have been grieved and distressed that you should have adopted and publicly maintained sentiments which I cannot but regard as eminently dangerous to the souls of men. I impeach not your motives. I judge not your heart. I would cherish the hope that your own religious experience is at variance with some things which you have published; particularly on the subject of self-love, and the great doctrine of regeneration. It does seem to me I experienced all which you make essential to regeneration; while, as I now fully believe, my heart was unreconciled to God. And this is the reason which leads me to fear, that what you have written will be the means of deceiving and destroying souls. I say this with the kindest feelings, and with eternity in view. Receive it as my dying testimony, and as an expression of my sincere love. Farewell, my brother! We shall soon meet at the judgment-seat of Christ. God grant that we may meet in heaven.—Your affectionate friend and brother,

"ASAHEL NETTLETON."

"EAST WINDSOR, *January* 19, 1843."

This letter is inserted here, not to prove that Dr. Nettleton was right in his theological views, and his brethren wrong; but to correct two false impressions which were sought to be made to some extent on the public mind: the one, that Dr. Nettleton felt a bitter hostility toward those brethren from whom he differed; the other, that, in the near prospect of death, his views underwent an important change in respect to the tendency of those speculations which had caused him so much solicitude. Neither of these impressions is correct, as this letter fully evinces. He never entertained unkind feelings towards his brethren. And his views of Christian doctrine remain unaltered to the last. The great truths which he maintained through life, were his stay and solace amid the pangs of dissolving nature, and in the near prospect of an eternal retribution. He, doubtless, now knows what is truth on those points respecting which he and his brethren differed. They also will soon know. They and he will soon meet at the judgment-seat of Christ; and let every reader unite in the prayer, that they may meet in heaven.

CHAPTER XIII.

HIS INTELLECTUAL SHREWDNESS—ANECDOTES—HIS CHARACTER AS A CHRISTIAN MAN.

Dr. Nettleton possessed a clear, vigorous, and discriminating mind—a mind adapted to investigation, and well disciplined by study. The course of his life, particularly in the first years of his ministry, was such as to prevent him from cultivating a very extensive acquaintance with books. But his mind was ever active, and constantly engaged in search of truth. Amid his abundant labours, he found some time for reading; and the books which he read were well selected, and thoroughly studied. He made no pretensions to great scientific attainments, nor to any very extensive acquaintance with general literature; but his mind was well stored with biblical and theological knowledge. Few men ever possessed a more thorough acquaintance with the Bible, or were capable of expounding it in a more interesting manner. During his last protracted illness, it was a feast to sit by his bedside and hear him open the Scriptures. His expositions were so clear and natural, and were enlivened by such vivid and striking illustrations, and interspersed with such weighty practical remarks, as to render them not only exceedingly entertaining, but in a high degree edifying.

Dr. Nettleton was a profound divine; and in every species of theological discussion he was perfectly at home. "With his little duodecimo Bible, or his Greek New Testament, always in his hand," says a friend, "he was one of the most independent thinkers I have ever known." With the common objections and cavils against the doctrines of the Gospel, he was very familiar; and for skill in stopping the mouths of gainsayers, and in speaking a word in season to persons of every description, he was highly distinguished.

A few anecdotes in illustration of this remark, may be here inserted.

1. Being accosted by a *Universalist*, who wished to engage in a discussion on the doctrine of future punishment, he said to him: "I will not enter into any dispute with you at present; but I should be pleased to have you state to me your views, that I may have them to think of." The man accordingly informed him, that, in his opinion, mankind received all their punishment in this life, and that all would be happy after death. Dr. Nettleton then asked him to explain certain passages of Scripture,—such as the account of a future judgment in the 25th chapter of Matthew, and some others; merely suggesting difficulties for him to solve, without calling in question any of his positions. After taxing his ingenuity for some time in this way, and thus giving him opportunity to perceive the difficulty of reconciling his doctrine with the language of inspiration, he said to him: "You believe, I presume, the account given by Moses of the deluge, and of the destruction of Sodom and Gomorrah?"—"Certainly," he replied.

"It seems, then," said Dr. Nettleton, "that the

world became exceeding corrupt, and God determined to destroy it by a deluge of water. He revealed His purpose to Noah, and directed him to prepare an ark, in which he and his family might be saved. Noah believed God, and prepared the ark. Meanwhile, he was a preacher of righteousness. He warned the wicked around him of their danger, and exhorted them to prepare to meet their God. But his warnings were disregarded. They, doubtless, flattered themselves that God was too good a being thus to destroy His creatures. But, notwithstanding their unbelief, the flood came, and, if your doctrine is true, swept them all up to heaven. And what became of Noah, that faithful servant of God? He was tossed to and fro on the waters, and was doomed to trials and sufferings for three hundred and fifty years longer in this evil world; whereas, if he had been wicked enough, he might have gone to heaven with the rest.

"And there were the cities of Sodom and Gomorrah, which had become so corrupt that God determined to destroy them by a tempest of fire. He revealed His purpose to Lot, and directed him and his family to make their escape. 'And Lot went out and spake to his sons-in-law, saying, Up! get ye out of this place, for the Lord will destroy this city. But he seemed as one that mocked to his sons-in-law.' They did not believe that any such doom was impending. They, doubtless, flattered themselves that God was too good a being to burn up His creatures. But no sooner had Lot made his escape, than it rained fire and brimstone from the Lord out of heaven, and they all, it seems, ascended to heaven in a chariot of fire; while pious Lot was left to wander in the mountains, and to suffer many grievous afflictions in this vale of tears; whereas, if he had been wicked enough, he might have gone to heaven with the rest." After making this statement, he requested the man to reflect on thêse things, and bade him an affectionate adieu.

2. A *Restorationist* once attacked him, and quoted these words of the Apostle Peter in support of his doctrine: "By which, also, He went and preached to the spirits in prison." Dr. Nettleton observed to him, that the time was specified, in the next verse, when Christ preached to these spirits in prison. It was, "When once the long-suffering of God waited in the days of Noah. It was by His Spirit, which dwelt in Noah, that He preached to those who are now spirits in prison."—"No," said the man; "that cannot be the meaning of the passage. The meaning is, that Christ, after His crucifixion, went down to hell and preached to the spirits in prison." "Be it so," said Dr. Nettleton; "what did He preach?"—"I do not know," he replied; "but I suppose He preached the Gospel." "Do you think," said Dr. Nettleton, "that He preached to them anything different from what He preached on earth?"—"Certainly not," said he. "Well," said Dr. Nettleton, "when Christ was on earth, He told sinners, that if they should be cast into prison, they should not come out thence till they had paid the uttermost farthing. If He went down to hell to preach to the lost spirits there, He, doubtless, told them, You must remain here till you have suffered all that your sins deserve. What influence, then, would His preaching have towards releasing them from the place of torment?"

3. An *Antinomian* complained to him, that ministers

dwelt so much, in their preaching, on the demands of the law. "Believers," said he, "are not under the law, but under grace." "Is it not the duty of believers," said Dr. Nettleton, "to repent?"—"Certainly," he replied. "Of what is it their duty to repent?" said Dr. Nettleton. The man saw at once the precipice before him. If he said, 'Of sin,' he perceived that the next question would be: What is sin but a transgression of the law? and if believers are not under obligations to obey the law, what can there be for them to repent of?

This is a specimen of the manner in which he often demolished, at a stroke, the errors of men, and caused the light of truth to flash instant conviction on their minds.

4. Falling in company with a *violent opposer of religion*, who professed to be a Universalist, and who also denied the inspiration of the Scriptures, he said to him: "I will not dispute with you; but I presume I can tell you how you came to adopt your present sentiments. I suspect you have seen the time when the Spirit of God was striving with you—when you felt that you was a sinner, and that you must repent or perish. But your wicked heart resisted these convictions. You loved your sins, and were unwilling to renounce them. Your conscience told you that you must pray, or you would be lost; but your heart replied, I will not pray, nor will I be lost. Hence you undertook to convince yourself that God will not punish the wicked. But I do not think you have yet quite silenced your conscience. You still have some forebodings of future misery. You are sometimes afraid, at least, that the Bible is true, and that there

is a day of judgment, and a world of woe. But if you wish entirely to silence your conscience, you are in a fair way to do it. Continue to flatter yourself, and to resist the truth, and God will help you to succeed. Thus it is written: 'For this cause God shall send them strong delusion, that they should believe a lie, that they all might be damned, who received not the love of the truth, but had pleasure in unrighteousness.'"

This address proved an arrow in the man's heart. He saw himself to be a lost sinner, and soon became a hopeful subject of renewing grace.

5. A *caviller* once said to him: "How came I by my wicked heart?"—"That is a question," said he, "which does not so much concern you as does another,—viz., How you shall get rid of your wicked heart. You have a wicked heart which renders you entirely unfit for the kingdom of God, and you must have a new heart, or you cannot be saved; and the question which now most deeply concerns you is, How you shall obtain it?" "But," said the man, "I wish you to tell me how I came by my wicked heart."—"I shall not undertake to do that at present," said Dr. Nettleton; "for if I could do it to your entire satisfaction, it would not help you in the least towards obtaining a new heart. The great thing for which I am solicitous is, that you should become a new creature and be prepared for heaven." As the man manifested no wish to hear anything on that subject, but still pressed the question, how he came by his wicked heart, Dr. Nettleton told him that his condition resembled that of a man who is drowning, while his friends are attempting to save his life. As he rises to the surface

of the water, he exclaims, "How came I here?"— "That question," says one of his friends, "does not concern you now. Take hold of this rope." "But how came I here?" he exclaims again.—"I shall not stop to answer that question now," says his friend. "Then I'll drown," replies the infatuated man, and, spurning all proffered aid, sinks to the bottom."

6. A *stupid worldly man* once said to him: "You know, Mr. Nettleton, that when we would do good evil is present with us."—"Yes," he replied, "and that is a bad case; but it is worse when we would *not* do good, and evil is present with us."

7. A man once asked him: "How shall I get a *disposition to pray?*"—"I wish to know, in the first place," he replied, "whether you are sincere in asking the question; for, if you are not, it will be of no use for me to answer it, because you will not follow my directions." "I am sincere," said the man; "I really wish to know how I can get a disposition to pray."—"It seems, then," said Dr. Nettleton, "that you have already got a disposition to get a disposition to pray. How did you get that? And why is it not just as easy to have a disposition to pray, as to have a disposition to get a disposition to pray?" In this way he shewed the man that he deceived himself in supposing that he was sincere in asking the question.

8. A young female, who had been for some time in a state of religious anxiety, said to him: "What do you think of *the doctrine of Election?* Some say it is true; and some say it is not true, and I do not know what to think of it."—"And what do you wish to think of it?" said Dr. Nettleton. "I wish," said she, "to think that it is not true."—"Suppose, then," said

Dr. Nettleton, "that it is not true. *The doctrine of repentance* is true. You must repent or perish. Now, if the doctrine of election is not true, what reason have you to believe you ever shall repent?" After a moment's reflection, she replied: "If the doctrine of election is not true, I never shall repent." Her eyes were then opened upon her true condition. Every refuge failed her. She saw that she was entirely dependent on the sovereign grace of God; and, there is reason to believe, she was soon brought out of darkness into God's marvellous light.

A certain individual said to him: "I cannot get along with the doctrine of election."—"Then," said he, "get along without it. You are at liberty to get to heaven the easiest way you can. Whether the doctrine of election is true or not, it is true that you must repent, and believe, and love God. Now, what we tell you is, that such is the wickedness of your heart, that you never will do these things unless God has determined to renew your heart. If you do not believe that your heart is so wicked, make it manifest by complying with the terms of salvation. Why do you stand cavilling with the doctrine of election? Suppose you should prove it to be false, what have you gained? You must repent and believe in Christ after all. Why do you not immediately comply with these terms of the Gospel? When you have done this, without the aids of divine grace, it will be soon enough to oppose the doctrine of election. Until you shall have done this, we shall still believe that the doctrine of election lies at the foundation of all hope in your case."

A woman, who was known to be a great opposer

of the doctrine of election, said to him one day: "You talked to me yesterday as if you thought I could repent." "And can you not?" said he.—"No, I cannot, unless God shall change my heart." "Do you really believe," said he, "that you cannot repent unless God has determined to change your heart?"—"I do," said she. "Why, madam," said he, "you hold to the doctrine of election in a stricter sense than I do. I should prefer to say, not that *you cannot*, but that you *never will* repent unless God has determined to change your heart."

To a man who manifested great opposition to the doctrine of election, he once said: "If I should go to heaven, I feel as if I should wish to say in the language of the apostle: 'Who hath saved us, and called us with an holy calling. Not according to our works, but according to His own purpose and grace, which were given us in Christ Jesus, before the world began.' Now, if we should meet in heaven, and I should make use of this language, will you quarrel with me there?"

9. To a young woman who had long been *thoughtful, but not deeply impressed*, and who seemed to continue from week to week in the same state of mind, he said one day: "There are some who never will become true believers. Christ said unto the Jews: 'Ye believe not, because ye are not of my sheep.' Perhaps this is your case; and I tell you now, that if you are not one of Christ's sheep, you never will believe on Him; and I hope it will ring in your ears." And it did ring in her ears. From that moment she found no peace, till, as she hoped, her peace was made with God.

A young female, who had been for some time under distress of mind, said to him one day: "I know not what to do next."—"Next!" he replied, "next to what?" She instantly saw the worthlessness of all her prayers and strivings, and replied: "Next to nothing!"

10. "Do you believe," said an Arminian to him one day, "that *God influences the will?*"—"I do," he replied. "How do you prove it?"—"I prove it by this passage of Scripture: 'For it is God that worketh in you both to will and to do.'" "But that does not mean," said the Arminian, "that God influences the will; and now, how do you prove it?"—"I prove it," said Dr. Nettleton still, "by this passage: 'For it is God that worketh in you both to will and to do.'" "But that, I say, does not mean that God influences the will." "And what does it mean?" said Dr. Nettleton.—"It means," said the Arminian, "that God gives us a gracious power to will and to do." "Then it does not mean," said Dr. Nettleton, "that *God works in us to will and to do!*"

11. In one place, where he was labouring in an interesting revival of religion, there was a man of considerable influence who was a member of the Church, but whose principles and practices were a great reproach to religion. He opposed all religious meetings except on the Sabbath. At the same time, he made no objection to balls and parties of pleasure, but encouraged his children to attend them. Two of his daughters one evening, without his knowledge, went to hear Dr. Nettleton preach. Finding that they had gone, he repaired to the place, and interrupted the meeting by ordering his daughters to return immediately home.

Then addressing the preacher, he said: "Mr. Nettleton, will you call and see me to-morrow morning at nine o'clock?"—"I will, sir," he replied. Accordingly, at the time proposed, he was at the house. "Mr. Nettleton," said the man, "I do not approve of night meetings."—"Neither do I approve of balls," said Dr. Nettleton; "I think their influence upon young people is bad." "I do not approve of such meetings as yours," said he.—"Oh!" said Dr. Nettleton, "it is to *religious* meetings that you object, when people meet together to worship God. If I understand you, you feel no opposition to meetings of young people for amusement, if they are held in the night, and continue all night. Did you ever take your children from the ball-room?"—"The command," said he, "is, Six days shalt thou labour." "Did you ever quote that command," said Dr. Nettleton, "to prove that it is wrong to attend balls and parties of pleasure?"

Then, assuming a solemn and affectionate mode of address, he said to the man: "My dear sir, you are a member of the Church, but you must not wonder if you are regarded by your acquaintance as, in heart, the enemy of religion, unless you pursue a more consistent course of conduct. While you uphold balls, and oppose meetings for religious worship, you will find it difficult to make anybody believe that you have the least regard for the religion which you profess." This address brought tears into the man's eyes; and whatever may have been his feelings, there was, after this, a decided change in his outward deportment. He suffered his children to attend religious meetings; nor do I know that he ever afterwards openly opposed them.

12. He once fell in company with two men who were

disputing on the doctrine of the *Saints' perseverance.* As he came into their presence, one of them said: "I believe this doctrine has been the means of filling hell with Christians." "Sir," said Dr. Nettleton, "do you believe that God knows all things?"—"Certainly I do," said he. "How, then, do you interpret this text:* '*I never knew you?*'" said Dr. Nettleton. After reflecting a moment, he replied: "The meaning must be, I never knew you as Christians." "Is that the meaning?" said Dr. Nettleton.—"Yes, it must be," he replied; "for certainly God knows all things." "Well," said Dr. Nettleton, "I presume you are right. Now, this is what our Saviour will say to those who, at the last day, shall say to Him, Lord, Lord, have we not eaten and drunken in thy presence? &c. Now, when Saul, and Judas, and Hymeneus, and Philetus, and Demas, and all who, you suppose, have fallen from grace, shall say to Christ, Lord, Lord! He will say to them, I never knew you—I NEVER *knew you as Christians.* Where, then, are the Christians that are going to hell?"

Said an individual to him: "Do you believe in the doctrine of the saints' perseverance?"—"It is my opinion," he replied, "that that doctrine is taught in the Bible." "I should like, then," said the individual, "to have you explain this passage, Ezek. xviii. 24: '*When the righteous turneth away from his righteousness and committeth iniquity, and doeth according to all the abominations that the wicked man doeth, shall he live? All the righteousness that he hath done shall not be mentioned: in his trespass that he hath trespassed, and in his sin that he hath sinned, in them shall he die.*'"

* Matth. vii 23.

Said Dr. Nettleton: "You have imposed upon me a hard task. That is a difficult text to explain; and what renders it the more difficult is, that the commentators are not agreed as to its meaning. Some have supposed, that by a righteous man in this passage, is meant a self-righteous man." "I do not believe that," said the individual.—"Neither do I," said Nettleton; "for, in that case, it would seem to teach, that if a self-righteous man should persevere in his self-righteousness he would be saved. Some have supposed, that by a righteous man is meant one who is apparently righteous." "I do not believe that," said the individual.—"Neither do I," said Dr. Nettleton; "for, in that case, the text would seem to teach, that if a hypocrite should persevere in his hypocrisy, he would be saved. You suppose, do you not, that by a righteous man in this passage, is meant a true saint?"—"Certainly I do." "And you suppose, that by a righteous man's turning away from his righteousness, is meant falling away, as David did, and as Peter did?"—"Certainly." "And you believe that David and Peter are now in hell?"—"No, by no means. David and Peter repented, and were restored to the favour of God." "But," said Dr. Nettleton, "when the righteous turneth from his righteousness—in his trespass that he hath trespassed, and in his sin that he hath sinned, *in them shall he die*—IN THEM SHALL HE DIE. Now, if David and Peter did turn from their righteousness, in the sense of this passage, how can we possibly believe that they were saved?" The individual now found the labouring oar in his own hands; and after attempting for some time unsuccessfully to explain the difficulty in which he found his own doctrine involved, Dr. Nettleton said to him: "If there is any difficulty in explaining this text of Scripture, I do not see but you are quite as much troubled with it as I am."

13. A man once said to him: "*I sincerely desire to be a Christian.* I have often gone to the house of God, hoping that something which should be said might be set home upon my mind by the Spirit of God, and be blessed to my salvation." "You are willing, then, are you not," said Dr. Nettleton, "that I should converse with you, hoping that my conversation may be the means of your conversion?"—"I am," he replied. "If you are willing to be a Christian," said Dr. Nettleton, "you are willing to perform the duties of religion; for this is what is implied in being a Christian. Are you willing to perform these duties?"—"I do not know but I am." "You are the head of a family. One of the duties of religion is family prayer. Are you willing to pray in your family?"—"I should be," he replied, "if I were a Christian. But it cannot be the duty of such a man as I am to pray. The prayers of the wicked are an abomination unto the Lord." "And is it not," said Dr. Nettleton, "an abomination unto the Lord to live without prayer? But just let me shew you how you deceive yourself. You think you really desire to be converted. But you are not willing even to be convicted. Just as soon as I mention a duty which you are neglecting, you begin to excuse and justify yourself, on purpose to keep your sin out of sight. You are not willing to see that it is a heinous sin to live in the neglect of family prayer. How can you expect to be brought to repentance until you are willing to see your sinful-

ness? And how can you flatter yourself that you really desire to be a Christian while you thus close your eyes against the truth?"*

A young lady, who was under concern of mind, said to him: "I certainly do desire to be a Christian. I desire to be holy. I would give all the world for an interest in Christ."—He replied: "What you say will not bear examination. If you really desire religion for what it is, there is nothing to hinder you from possessing it. I can make a representation which will shew you your heart, if you are willing to see it." "I am," said she.—"It will look very bad," said he; "but if you are willing to see it, I will make the representation. Suppose you were a young lady of fortune; and suppose a certain young man should desire to obtain your fortune, and should, for that reason, conclude to pay his addresses to you. But he does not happen to be pleased with your person. He does not love you, but hates you. And suppose he should come to you, and say: I really wish I could love you; but I do not. I would give all the world if I could love you; but I cannot. What would you think of that young man?"

14. A person once said in his presence, that to

* Dr. Griffin (in the revival of 1799) tells of some who, before conviction became deep and powerful, attempted to exculpate themselves of the plea of inability, and, like Adam, to cast the blame on God by pleading: "The *nature* which *thou gavest* me beguiled me" These persons would say: "They would be glad to repent, but *could* not,—their *nature* and *heart* were so bad." They overlooked that their "nature and heart" were *themselves!* In the progress of conviction they speedily, in general, forsook their refuge of lies, and were filled with a sense of utter inexcusableness. In every case, as soon as their enmity to God was slain, this plea utterly vanished. Their language then was: "I wonder I ever should ask such a question as, 'How can I repent?' My only wonder now is, that *I could hold out so long.*"

inculcate upon sinners *their dependence on God for a new heart,* is suited to discourage effort, and to lead them to sit down in despair. He replied: "The very reverse of this is true. Suppose a number of men are locked up in a room, playing cards. Some person informs them that the roof of the building is on fire, and that they must make their escape, or they will perish in the flames. Says one of them: 'We need not be in haste, we shall have time to finish the game.' 'But,' says the person who gave the alarm, 'your door is locked.'—'No matter for that,' he replies; 'I have the key in my pocket, and can open it at any moment.' 'But I tell you that key will not open the door.'—'Won't it?' he exclaims; and, rising from the table, flies to the door, and exerts himself to the utmost to open it. So sinners, while they believe that there is no difficulty in securing their salvation at any moment, quiet their consciences, and silence their fears. But when they are taught that such is the wickedness of their hearts, that they never will repent unless God interposes by His regenerating grace, they are alarmed, and begin to inquire, in deep distress, what they shall do to be saved."

15. A young man, of liberal education and of a clear and vigorous mind, having just read Edwards' *Treatise on the Will,* said to him: "The reasoning is conclusive. It is impossible to controvert it. It amounts to absolute demonstration." To which he assented. "Then," said the young man, "I am not a free agent, and am not accountable for my conduct." —"That does not follow," said Dr. Nettleton. "I admit your premises, but I deny your conclusions; and, moreover, you do not believe it yourself. If you

did, you would not fear to blaspheme your Maker. But you dare not do it. You know you are a free and accountable agent."

16. To a young man who professed to be an *atheist*, he said: "You are not so sure as you pretend to be, that there is no God. You dare not go alone, and kneel down, and, in a solemn manner, offer a prayer. If there is no God, you will incur no danger by so doing; and yet you dare not do it. This shews that you are afraid that there is a God who cannot be deceived, and who will not be mocked."

In conversing with opposers of religion, while he was very plain and faithful, he was never harsh in his manner; but always kind and affectionate, in obedience to the divine injunction: "In meekness instructing those that oppose themselves, if, peradventure, God will give them repentance to the acknowledging of the truth." And not a few of the open enemies of religion were, through his instrumentality, hopefully converted to Christ.

17. Dr. Tenney, of Wethersfield, says of him in a letter: "I have felt he was a remarkable man—fitted to draw forth the often-repeated saying of a venerable president of a distinguished college respecting him: '*A wonderfully wise man!*' He was distinguished for a ready, clear, correct, and far-reaching perception or discernment. Almost as by intuition, he discerned individual characters, and seemed to see the precise truth fitted to reprove or benefit them. At once he seemed to learn the state of a church and people; and to see doctrines and errors, and all their bearings and tendencies; and to bring them instantly to what he regarded as the supreme test,—the Word of God. In

the Scriptures he was mighty. He had evidently studied the Word of God much, and deeply, and seemed to perceive the exact purport and design of a verse, a paragraph, or larger portion; and to see its precise application and force. He entered so much into the very meaning and spirit of the Word of God, that on almost any passage he would so naturally and strikingly present the meaning as to appear singularly original. Conversing at one time in my study with a number who had for a considerable period indulged hope, but who were disposed to hesitate and delay in professing religion, he turned to Luke viii. 45, 48, and briefly stated, that the diseased woman *feared and trembled* (after she had been healed by touching Christ in the crowd) when she perceived that Christ would bring her and the miracle to public view. And well she might tremble, said he, for she had been *stealing* a cure, and meant to conceal herself in the multitude; and now she expected reproof from Christ; but when she confessed the whole, *before all the people*, He said to her: 'Daughter, be of good cheer, thy faith hath made thee whole; go in peace.' He then guarded the converts against concealing among the multitude what Christ had done for them, or fearing His rebuke if they confessed Him before all the people.

"To a man of education, and of a very proud spirit, who, under some seriousness of mind, had a private interview with Dr. Nettleton, and said at its close, Mr. Nettleton, I will thank you not to speak of my case to any one, for it is doubtful yet what the result may be;' he at once replied: 'I agree with you perfectly, that it is best your case should not be known; and I engage to keep it entirely to myself; and if you will do the same, it will not be known. It is, as you say, very doubtful how the case will turn. You may soon give up the subject, and lose your soul.' Under this remark, the man was soon so deeply distressed that he cared not if the whole world knew it; and very soon he found peace."

18. "When a person once asked me with a supercilious air: 'Do you, according to the Assembly's Catechism, believe that God has *foreordained whatsoever comes to pass?*' Dr. Nettleton, coming up at that moment, said to him in reply: 'Mr. P——, do *you* believe that *God* worketh *all things after the counsel of His own will?*'"

19. He made the following remarks on *Infant Depravity:*—"If infants sustain the same relation to the moral government of God as brute animals, then they can no more be the subjects of prayer, of regeneration, of redemption by Christ, or of salvation, than brute animals.

"Those who deny that infants are sinners, have devolved on them the Herculean task of defending the justice of God in bringing suffering and death upon millions of beings who are perfectly innocent. Those who admit the doctrine of infant depravity, have no difficulty on this subject.

"How old must a child be before he can be said to belong to the human race? When a child dies, how old must he be before it can be said of him that his death was *by sin?*—in other words, before he can be considered as included in the following declaration of the apostle: 'By one man sin entered into the world, and death by sin, and so death passed upon *all men*, for that *all have sinned.*'"

20. He said in regard to *Eternal Punishments:* To believe against personal interest requires an honest heart. Without it the mind will exert itself to evade the truth. It often requires but little evidence to lead to the adoption of a pleasing sentiment; while the most conclusive evidence fails to produce conviction of an unwelcome truth. *E. g.*, The word everlasting, when applied to the future punishment of the wicked, is by some explained to mean always a limited duration; but when applied to the future happiness of the righteous, it is readily admitted to denote endless duration. I know not that the latter was ever questioned. If a man were to undertake seriously to prove, that the word everlasting, when applied to the happiness of the righteous, denotes only a limited duration, and when applied to the punishment of the wicked, means an endless state of being, he would be pronounced a fool. And yet he would act no more irrationally than the man who adopts the opposite course of reasoning, by which so many profess to be convinced.

Hence we should exercise great caution in receiving doctrines which are pleasing to the natural heart; and equal caution in rejecting doctrines to which the natural heart is opposed.

21. We may add an anecdote that illustrates his practical wisdom in dealing with opposition:*—"He was once labouring in a village in Connecticut, where were strong indications of the beginning of a good state of things. Christians were engaged in powerful labour, and a spirit of violent opposition manifested itself among the ungodly. The pastor of the church was called to a distant part of the parish to

* Given in Dr. Belcher's *Clergy of America*.

officiate at a wedding, and Dr. Nettleton accompanied him. They rode together; and when they arrived at the house the pastor left his surtout-coat hanging over the back of his chaise. Nothing particular occurred during the ceremony; but when they were preparing to return home, it was discovered that the harness was cut in several places. This, after a time, was repaired, and they arrived at the pastor's house without accident. When he took his horse to put him into the stable, he found that the hair from the mane and tail of the animal had been shaved closely off. He brought his surtout into the study, which was then seen to have been torn from top to bottom into ribbons. The good pastor was greatly excited, and declared that he would find out the perpetrators of the outrage, and prosecute them to the utmost extremity of the law. When he had time to cool, Dr. Nettleton said to him: 'Brother, try on the surtout; it may not be injured so much as you suppose.' He did so, and so grotesque was his appearance that both burst into a hearty laugh. Dr. Nettleton saw that the time was now come to make an impression upon him, and said: 'Brother, it is evident that the Spirit of God is at work with this people, and this is a device of the adversary of souls to turn off their attention from the subject of religion. You may, I doubt not, find out the authors of this mischief, and punish them; but in doing it, you will raise a hubbub, there will be an end of the revival, and souls will be lost for ever. Now, my advice to you is this: keep your horse in the stable; feed him yourself; do not take him out even to water. Lay by your surtout in the bottom of your trunk, and do not mention these circumstances even to your wife. The wrongdoers will not dare to mention their mischief; and if we are silent, it will not be known, and they will lose their labour. The parish will continue in quietness, and we shall go on in our work without molestation. We shall thus defeat the adversary of souls, and gain a blessed victory for the Redeemer.' The pastor took his advice. No one ever heard of the occurrence from that time, and God blessed the church with a glorious outpouring of His Spirit. Such was the good doctor's method of dealing with persecutors."

That Dr. Nettleton was a man of more than ordinary piety, will be evident to all who have attentively perused the foregoing account of his life. His piety was deep, steady, operative, and consistent. Nor was it subject to those alternations of feeling which are sometimes witnessed in eminently good men. Some seem to be always in the possession of great spiritual enjoyment, or else in the mists of darkness. Dr. Nettleton's feelings were more uniform. He seems never to have been greatly elated, nor deeply depressed; but to have maintained generally a calm and peaceful frame of mind.

His piety was consistent. There was a beautiful symmetry in his Christian character. The various graces of the Spirit were harmoniously blended and exhibited, each in its proper place, and in its due proportion. It is the nature of false religion to be deformed; and characteristic of all hypocrites, that they strain at a gnat and swallow a camel. But the Christian character of Dr. Nettleton was formed on principles which enter into all the minutiæ of a man's life. His opinions were not formed hastily, nor taken up upon credit, but were the result of deliberate and prayerful examination; and when formed they were rarely changed. He acted, not from passion, or any sudden impulse of the moment, but from principle; and could not be induced to swerve from the path of duty, either by flattery, or frowns, or any worldly motive. When entreated, by one in whom he had reposed great confidence, and whose friendship he highly prized, to give up his opposition to certain doctrines which he believed to be erroneous, and of dangerous tendency, he replied: "You might as well ask me to cut off my conscience and throw it away." He was not influenced by the principles and practices of others, any further than he was satisfied that they were conformed to the Word of God. He thought for himself, and formed his purposes in the fear of God, and with reference to the final judgment.

HUMILITY was a striking trait in the character of Dr. Nettleton. When a young man, he read in an old book this maxim: "Do all the good you can in the world, *and make as little noise about it as possible.*" This maxim had great influence in the formation of his character. He treasured it up in his memory, and believing it to be in accordance with the precepts of the Gospel, he made it a rule of conduct. Hence everything like ostentation he abhorred. Few men ever had greater temptations to the indulgence of pride. His great popularity as a preacher, and the almost unparalleled success which attended his labours, even while he was but a youth, constituted a source of great danger. Many of his fathers and brethren in the ministry trembled for him, lest he should be lifted up with pride. But he seems to have been remarkably delivered from the power of this temptation. Notwithstanding his great popularity, he seems not to have been elated. He was modest and unassuming, and always sensible that the success which attended his labours was not owing to any goodness in himself, but to the sovereign grace of God. He was aware of his danger. Once, when asked what he considered the best safeguard against spiritual pride, he replied: "I know of nothing better than to keep my eye on my great sinfulness."

Dr. Shepard of Lenox, says: "He would not suffer any one to commend his sermons or any of his public performances, or to speak of the success of his labours, if he could prevent it; and when any one attempted to praise him in view of the good he had done, it seemed directly to fill his heart with grief."

Mr. Cobb of Taunton, also says: "He was remarkably free from the love of applause. When any one spoke to him of the good he was doing, he would sometimes reply: 'We have no time to talk about that.' And frequently I have known him to turn pale and retire from the company, and prostrate himself before God as a great and unworthy sinner."

Dr. Nettleton was never married; having devoted himself to a missionary life soon after his conversion, he supposed it would be necessary for him to remain single. Both he and Mills entertained the opinion, that it would be inexpedient, if not impracticable, to take wives with them on a foreign mission; and they entered into an agreement on their first acquaintance, to hold themselves free from all matrimonial engagements. Afterwards, the course of life pursued by Dr.

Nettleton was such as to render it inconvenient, to say the least, to enter into the family state.

But he had a soul formed for friendship. He possessed a mild and amiable disposition, and rendered himself exceedingly agreeable in the society of his friends. No one could be long in his company without discovering the kindness of his heart. He never put on a morose, austere, or sanctimonious air. He was uniformly cheerful; but never suffered his cheerfulness to degenerate into levity. His conversational powers were good, and were agreeably and usefully employed. He was very successful in his attempts to interest young persons, and to secure their confidence and esteem. He would address them with such kindness and tenderness, and make his conversation so entertaining (and at the same time so instructive), that it could not fail to win their affection, and cause them to take pleasure in his society. He was very much in the habit of introducing poetry to enliven conversation, and gave it a useful direction. In a circle of young persons he would often read some striking passage from Cowper, or Milton, or Pollok, or Carlos Wilcox; and after commenting on the beauties of the poetry, he would, in a natural and easy way, lead their minds to the contemplation of some important truth suggested by the passage. Many a youth has in this way had his attention first arrested to the great concerns of eternity.

During his many preachings he received, as compensation, barely sufficient to defray his expenses. But he manifested no solicitude on that subject. At a meeting of ministers on one occasion, when he was present, an allusion was made by some one to the scanty support which he received, he replied, by simply repeating the following passage of Scripture, Luke xxii. 35: "When I sent you without purse, and scrip, and shoes, lacked ye anything? And they said, Nothing."

The thought of accumulating property never entered his mind. He seemed to dislike even to speak upon that subject. And yet, while even indifferent to his own personal comforts, he was most generous to others. On finding a godly person destitute of a Bible, or Psalm Book, or Hymn Book, he forthwith took care to supply the deficiency. When his "*Village Hymn Book*" met with unlooked-for success, and yielded a considerable income, Dr. Nettleton gave a donation of the whole profits of the first edition to the American Board of Commissioners for Foreign Missions. In after editions, he gave generously to various objects of usefulness; finishing all by bestowing a noble portion on a Theological Institute.*

LOVE TO THE SOULS OF MEN was another striking trait in the character of Dr. Nettleton. It has been remarked, that "the mind sometimes receives a bias in conversion, or the period of first love, which gives a particular direction to the whole course of future life." It may have been so in this case. In the period of his espousals to Christ the worth of the soul and the affecting condition of all unrenewed men, were powerfully impressed upon his mind, and awakened most intense desires for their salvation. He used to say to himself: "If I might be the means of the salvation of one soul, I should prefer it to all the riches and honours of this world."

* In this disinterestedness, as in many higher points, there seems to have been a remarkable similarity between Dr Nettleton and that man of God, already spoken of in Chapter II., whom God used to awaken so many in Scotland.

MEEKNESS was another trait in the character of Dr. Nettleton. The success of his labours greatly exasperated the enemies of religion, and awakened in their breasts the most malignant hostility. False reports, intended to destroy his character, were invented and industriously circulated; and in other ways he frequently met with personal abuse. But the malice of his enemies awakened only his pity. So far as is known, he was never known to manifest the least resentment towards those who slandered and abused him. When reviled, he reviled not again; when he suffered, he threatened not, but committed himself to Him who judgeth righteously. He felt himself laid under special obligations to pray for his persecutors; and, to the honour of divine grace let it be recorded, not a few of them were hopefully brought to repentance, and became some of his most ardent friends.

He never allowed himself to talk about the ill treatment which he received from his enemies, lest it should awaken wrong feelings in his heart. He was in the habit of inculcating upon young converts a spirit of meekness: and for this purpose he often brought before their minds the words of the apostle, 1 Pet. ii. 20, 21: "For what glory is it, if, when ye be buffeted for your faults, ye shall take it patiently? but if, when ye do well, and suffer for it, ye take it patiently, this is acceptable with God. For even hereunto were ye called: because Christ also suffered for us, leaving us an example that ye should follow His steps." He also, frequently referred to this passage, Prov. xxiv. 17, 18: "Rejoice not when thine enemy falleth; and let not thine heart be glad when he stumbleth; lest the Lord see it, and it displease Him." He evidently possessed, in an uncommon degree, that charity which suffereth long, and is kind; which envieth not; which vaunteth not itself, and is not puffed up; which doth not behave itself unseemly; which seeketh not her own; is not easily provoked, thinketh no evil; which beareth all things, believeth all things, hopeth all things, endureth all things.

He was not a perfect man. He had his failings. He was ready to acknowledge that he was a miserable sinner, and that his proper place was at the foot of the Cross. But his faults were better known to himself and his God, than to his fellowmen. It is true, he did not escape reproach. His great success as a minister of Christ brought upon him the maledictions of infidels and scoffers, and stimulated them to the most unremitted efforts to destroy his character; and many a time might he have said: "If it had not been the Lord who was on my side, when men rose up against me, then they had swallowed me up quick, when their wrath was kindled against me." Never for a moment were they believed by the ministers and churches of Connecticut; nor did they do him the least injury, except for a day, when sent after him, or sent *for* to the places where his preaching was blessed; and even then only till the friends of religion had opportunity to obtain correct information on the subject. It would be difficult to conceive the virulence with which some persons in New England oppose revivals of religion, without understanding, that in many places where the truth has been preached too faithfully to be endured in a state of disobedience, there is often a club of infidels or nothingarians, whose enmity is always made rampant by a revival of religion, and whose ridicule and misrepresentation are sure to be propagated by the irreligious and immoral.

He died in the full and firm belief of the doctrines which he maintained and defended while he lived.

CHAPTER XIV.

HIS LAST SICKNESS AND DEATH.

THE sickness of Dr. Nettleton in 1822, gave a shock to his constitution from which it never recovered. For a considerable part of the time during the remainder of his life he was exceedingly feeble, and at no time was he able to engage in arduous labour. Still he was not entirely laid aside. He preached, as we have seen, in many places, and in some with great success. Finding the climate of New England too severe for his enfeebled constitution during the winter months, he usually, for a number of years, spent them in the south; and by great care in avoiding excitement and excessive fatigue, he was able to enjoy a comfortable degree of health for most of the time, until the summer of 1841, when he began to be afflicted with urinary calculi, which soon confined him to the house, and subjected him to great bodily suffering. Finding no relief from medical prescriptions, and being reduced to that state in which it was evident he could live but a short time, on the 14th of February 1843, he submitted to the operation of lithotomy, by which he obtained partial relief, and hopes were entertained, for a season, of his entire recovery. But after a few months it became manifest that the disease was returning upon him. His sufferings again became exceedingly great, till, on the 8th of December 1843, he submitted to a second operation. For some time he appeared to be doing well, and hopes were again entertained of his recovery. But these hopes were not realized. He continued in a feeble state until the 16th of May 1844, when the powers of nature failed, and he resigned his spirit into the hand of God who gave it.

During his protracted and severe sufferings his piety was subjected to a new test. We have seen its efficacy in prompting him, while in health, to the most arduous and unremitted labours in the cause of Christ; and it was no less efficacious in sustaining him in the day of trial. For many months together his bodily pain was almost without intermission, and exceedingly great,—at times, indeed, excruciating. But he was strengthened to endure it with patience and resignation. During the whole of his sickness he was never heard to utter a murmuring word. He was often heard to say: "My sufferings are great, but they are nothing in comparison with what I deserve." A large part of the time during his sickness his mind was vigorous and active. He read many books during this period, particularly D'Aubigné's *History of the Reformation*, with which he was much delighted, Gaussen on *Inspiration*, Tracy's *History of the Great Awakening*, the entire works of the younger Edwards, much of the works of Emmons, a large part of the works of Andrew Fuller, besides many smaller works. What he read he read with great attention; and he would often make criticisms and comments on the things which he had read. But the Bible was the man of his counsel. He would often say: "There are many good books, but, after all, there is nothing like the Bible." And it never was so precious to him as at this period. Although he had made it his study for more than forty years, and had acquired a knowledge of it to which few attain, yet he found it an inexhaustible fund of rich instruction. He could adopt the language of the Psalmist: "*How sweet are thy words unto my taste! yea, sweeter than honey to my mouth! Thy testimonies have I taken as an heritage for ever; for they are the rejoicing of my heart. Thy statutes have been my songs in the house of my pilgrimage.*" . . . .

He not only read some portion of the Scriptures every day, but he devoted much time to a close and critical study of them. He usually kept his Greek Testament and his Greek Concordance by him, and diligently compared different parts of Scripture with each other in the original language, that he might be sure to get the precise meaning. I found him one morning with the Greek Testament in his hand. He said: "You will perhaps wonder that I should be reading this. You may suppose that a person in my situation would prefer to read the translation. But I seem to get nearer to the fountain when I read the original. It is like drinking water at the spring, rather than from a vessel in which it has been carried away. By reading the Greek I get shades of meaning which cannot be expressed in any translation." It was common for him to entertain his friends with comments and remarks on portions of Scripture; and these comments were exceedingly interesting and instructive. Many an individual has gone away from his bedside with a more lively sense of the worth of the Bible than he ever felt before.

He was not in the habit, during his sickness, of speaking very often of his own religious feelings; but it was manifest from the whole strain of his conversation, and particularly from the lively interest which he took in the truths of the Bible, that he generally enjoyed great peace of mind.

On one occasion, having expressed to me his apprehension that his disease was incurable, Dr. Tyler inquired of him the state of his mind. He expressed entire submission to the will of God—a willingness to be in His hands, and to be disposed of according to His pleasure. He spoke of the great deceitfulness of the human heart, and the danger of self-deception; but intimated that he had no distressing doubts and fears. He manifested an ardent attachment to the doctrines which he had preached, and seemed to derive from them great support in the near prospect of eternity; and he expressed a peculiar love for those of his brethren who had been decided in their adherence to the truth, and in their opposition to prevailing errors.

On another occasion he conversed very freely concerning his own spiritual state. He gave Dr. Tyler a more particular account of his conversion than he had ever done before.* It brought to his recollection so many tender scenes, that he was greatly affected, and wept abundantly. He spake of the doctrines of grace, and said, with great emotion: "I do not need anybody to tell me that they are true. I am fully convinced of their truth by my own experience.

One morning, as Dr. T. entered the room, he said to him, that these words had been running in his mind:

"Death will invade us by the means appointed;
Nor am I anxious, if I am prepared,
What shape he comes in."

---

* The same that is inserted in Chapter I.

In the course of the conversation he said: "More of my life is written in Bunyan's *Grace Abounding to the Chief of Sinners*, than anywhere else." He was a great admirer of the writings of Bunyan, and often referred to them in illustration of his own opinions.

On being asked whether he still entertained the same views of the errors, on account of which he had manifested so much solicitude, he spoke with great emotion, saying: "It is the bearing which these errors have upon the eternal interests of men which gives them all their importance in my estimation. It is in view of death, judgment, and eternity, that I have looked at them. If I had not regarded them as dangerous to the souls of men, I should have felt no solicitude respecting them."

At another time he wished me to read to him the following hymn in Wardlaw's collection:—

"Come let us join our friends above
That have obtained the prize,
And on the eagle wings of love
To joy celestial rise.

Let saints below in concert sing
With those to glory gone;
For all the servants of our King
In heaven and earth are one.

One family, we dwell in Him,
One church, above, beneath,
Though now divided by the stream,
The narrow stream of death.

One army of the living God,
To His command we bow,
Part of the host have crossed the flood,
And part are crossing now.

Each moment, to their endless home,
Some parting spirits fly;
And we are to the margin come,
And soon expect to die.

Dear Saviour, be our constant guide,
Then, when the word is given,
Bid death's cold stream and flood divide,
And land us safe in heaven."

He alluded to this hymn several times, with great interest, during his sickness.

On one occasion he spoke with great feeling of those who were hopefully converted in the revivals under his preaching, and said, the thought of meeting them in the future world was often exceedingly interesting. "But," said he, "I have never allowed myself to be very confident of arriving at heaven, lest the disappointment should be the greater. I know that the heart is exceedingly deceitful, and that many will be deceived. And why am not I as liable to be deceived as others?"*

* Dr Nettleton fully believed that assurance of an interest in Christ is a privilege held out to all believers. He thus speaks in a sermon on 2 Cor. xiii 5: "He who is a true Christian may know it; that is, he may obtain satisfactory evidence of the fact

"This is evident from several examples recorded in the Scriptures *Job* could say: 'I know that my Redeemer liveth, (he was assured that Christ was *his* Redeemer,) and that He shall stand at the latter day upon the earth. And though after my skin, worms destroy this body, yet in my flesh shall I see God Whom mine eyes shall behold, and not another' He felt assured that he should behold Christ for *himself*, as his portion, with his own eyes, in his own body raised from the dead *Paul* could say: 'I know whom I have believed, and am persuaded that He is able to keep that which I have committed unto Him against that day' In respect to his Christian race and his warfare, the event was not to him uncertain 'I therefore so run, not as uncertainly; so fight I, not as one that beateth the air.' He could say, also, in connexion with some of his *Corinthian* brethren: 'For *we know* that if our earthly house of this tabernacle were dissolved, we have a building of God, a house not made with hands, eternal in the heavens' And thus, also, the Apostle *John* could say: 'Beloved, now are we the sons of God, and it doth not yet appear what we shall be; but we know that when He shall appear, we shall be like Him, for we shall see Him as He is' Here the apostle's assurance is twice asserted. 'Now are we the sons of God; and, 'We know that we shall be like Him' Again: 'We *know* that we have passed from death unto life, because we love the brethren.' 'And hereby we *know* that we are of the truth, and shall assure our hearts before Him.'"

Perhaps we read this account of Dr. Nettleton's state of mind with something of disappointment. We may have expected to find him saying with Paul: "*Henceforth there is laid up for me a crown of righteousness, which the Lord, the righteous Judge, shall give to me at that day.*" And our expectation of this is founded on our knowledge of his firm faith in Jesus, not of his long life of devoted service. Paul cast behind him in such an hour all thought of his services, experiences, high office, attainments, and betook himself to the sinner's sure ground, "*the beginning of our confidence,*" (Heb. iii. 14,)—namely, "*I know whom I have believed.*" Why do we not find *Dr. Nettleton* doing the same?

Now, not forgetting the sovereignty of divine grace in this respect, we can see some explanation of the matter in calling to mind Dr. Nettleton's past course. He had, along with every sound minister of the Word, urged on his hearers the certainty, that wherever real faith existed, holy fruits would attend it. But in his extreme jealousy of self-deception, (as it seems to us,) he had gone further, and had cast doubt upon any hope which was not built upon such a measure of holiness as could be easily discerned by the person himself, along with this direct looking to and resting upon Christ. And hence, in his own case, he seems to have sought for larger evidence of holiness following in his faith than he could perceive in himself. The absence of this complete evidence (which his very tenderness of conscience kept him from discerning) had the effect of preventing him taking all the joy he might have had from a simple and direct looking to the Saviour. We are ready to think that, but for this tendency, he might have fully followed the footsteps of some of the flock at such an hour; he might have felt as one of our Scottish forefathers, David Dickson, who said: "I have taken all my good deeds and all my bad deeds, and have cast them together in a heap before the Lord, and have fled from both to Jesus Christ; and IN HIM *I have sweet peace.*"

Speaking of the opinion entertained by some, that none are ever actuated by any other principle than self-love, he said: "I should have no hope of being saved if I believed myself never to have been actuated by a higher principle."

He one day referred to the words of the apostle: "Despise not the chastening of the Lord, nor faint when thou art rebuked of Him." He observed, that there are two ways in which divine chastisements are improperly received. One is, *despising* them,—that is, making light of them—disregarding them, as a stubborn, disobedient child sometimes sets at defiance and treats with contempt the chastisement of his father. The other is, *fainting* under them,—that is, making too much of them, feeling as though they were too heavy to be borne, and greater than we deserve. "We ought," said he, "to feel that all our sufferings, however great, are *light afflictions*, infinitely less than we deserve."

When asked at one time if he did not sometimes get weary of life, he said: "It is wearisome. But I have sometimes heard persons express a desire to die, when it was painful to me. I desire to have no will on the subject." He felt that it was as much our duty to be willing to live and suffer, if such be the will of God, as to be willing to die. Asking for the hymn-book, he read the following stanza:—

"Be this my one great business here,
With holy trembling, holy fear,
To make my calling sure;
Thine utmost counsel to fulfil,
And *suffer* all thy righteous will,
And to the end endure."

It was very common for him, when inquired of respecting the state of his mind, instead of giving a direct answer, to point to some hymn, or some passage of Scripture, as indicative of his feelings.

On one occasion, finding him in very great pain, Dr. Tyler said to him: "I hope the Lord will give you patience." He replied: "I have need of patience." Dr. Tyler remarked, that when suffering severe pain, it was profitable to think of the sufferings of Christ. He said, that the words of Newton's hymn had been running in his mind all night:—

"Begone unbelief!
My Saviour is near,
And for my relief
Will surely appear.
By prayer let me wrestle,
And He will perform;
With Christ in the vessel,
I smile at the storm.

Determined to save,
He watched o'er my path,
When, Satan's blind slave,
I sported with death:
And can He have taught me
To trust in His name,
And thus far have brought me
To put me to shame?

Why should I complain
Of want or distress,
Temptation or pain?
He told me no less;
The heirs of salvation,
I know from His Word,
Through much tribulation,
Must follow their Lord.

Though dark be my way,
Since He is my guide,
'Tis mine to obey,
'Tis His to provide;
His way was much rougher
And darker than mine;
Did Jesus thus suffer,
And shall I repine?

His love in time past,
Forbids me to think
He'll leave me at last
In trouble to sink:
Though painful at present,
'Twill cease before long,
And then, oh! how pleasant
The conqueror's song!"

Dr. Tyler (his biographer afterwards) was much with him. Being one day in very great pain, he said to him: "I ought not to complain; but all that I have ever suffered in the course of my life is nothing in comparison with this. But it is nothing in comparison with what I deserve." "No," said I, "nor is it worthy to be compared with the glory that shall be revealed." He requested me to take from the shelf and hand to him the *Remains of Carlos Wilcox;* and with great interest he read the following lines:—

"But wherefore will not God
E'en now, from ills on others brought, exempt
The offspring of regenerating grace,
The children of His love? Imperfect yet,
They need the chastenings of eternal care,
To save them from the wily blandishments
Of error, and to win their hearts away
From the polluting, ruining joys of earth!"

Speaking at one time of his disease as that which, for many years, he had dreaded more than any other, he pointed to the following passage in the Life of Samuel Pearce, as expressive of his own feelings:—

"It was never till to-day that I got any personal

instruction from our Lord's telling Peter by *what death* he should glorify God. Oh! what a satisfying thought, that God appoints those means of dissolution whereby He gets most glory to himself! It was the very thing I needed; for of all the ways of dying, that which I most dreaded was by consumption, in which it is now most probable my disorder will issue. But, O my dear Lord! *if* by *this death* I can most *glorify thee*, I prefer it to all others, and thank thee that by this means thou art hastening my fuller enjoyment of thee in a purer world."

During his sickness he greatly enjoyed the society of his brethren in the ministry, and other Christian friends; and was often heard to say that he never loved his friends so well before. Every little favour shewn him seemed deeply to affect him and awaken emotions of gratitude. He would say: "Oh! how kind this is!"

On the first day of January 1843, which was the Sabbath, he sent the following note to the Seminary Church, with a request that it should be read at the communion:—

"The Rev. Mr. Nettleton sends his very affectionate regards to the members of this church, requesting an interest in their prayers, that God would sanctify him wholly in spirit, in soul, and in body, and prepare him for the solemn hour of exchanging worlds, whenever it shall come."

The next morning he was in an unusually happy frame of mind. After inquiring whether his note was received, he remarked with great animation, his eyes sparkling through the tears, that he loved the Church more and more. He expressed a peculiar affection for the students of the Seminary, and an ardent desire that they might become faithful ministers of the Gospel. He mentioned the great satisfaction which it had given him to hear of the prosperity and usefulness of those who had gone out from the Seminary. He then went on to expatiate on the importance of a high standard of ministerial character, on account of its great influence on the interests of the Church. He deprecated particularly, in the ministers of Christ, everything which savours of pride and self-sufficiency —everything which looks like ostentation, or a desire to attract notice to themselves. He loved to see ministers humble, meek, unassuming, steadily devoted to their work, and more anxious to glorify God, and save the souls of men, than to acquire popularity.

He often remarked, that a time of health was the time to prepare for death, and the time to give evidence of an interest in Christ. He said he had seen persons who, when in health, were very much devoted to the world; but who, when brought upon a sick-bed, were very religious; agreeably to the representation in Jer. xxii. 20, 23: "*Go up to Lebanon, and cry; and lift up thy voice in Bashan, and cry from the passages: for all thy lovers are destroyed.* I SPAKE UNTO THEE IN THY PROSPERITY; BUT THOU SAIDST, I WILL NOT HEAR: THIS HATH BEEN THY MANNER FROM THY YOUTH, THAT THOU OBEYEDST NOT MY VOICE. *The wind shall eat up all thy pastures, and thy lovers shall go into captivity; surely then shalt thou be ashamed and confounded for all thy wickedness. O inhabitant of Lebanon! that makest thy nest in the cedars,* HOW GRACIOUS SHALT THOU BE WHEN PANGS COME UPON THEE!"

Dr. Tyler thus narrates the closing scene:—A

short time before his death, when he was very ill, and when he thought it probable that he had but a short time to live, I said to him, you are in good hands. "Certainly," he replied. "Are you willing to be there?"—"I am." He then said: "I know not that I have any advice to give my friends. My whole preaching expresses my views. If I could see the pilgrims, scattered abroad, who thought they experienced religion under my preaching, I should like to address them. I would tell them that the great truths of the Gospel appear more precious than ever, and that they are the truths which now sustain my soul." He added: "You know I have never placed much dependence on the manner in which persons die." He spoke of a farewell sermon which he preached in Virginia, from these words: "*While ye have the light, walk in the light.*" He told the people, that he wished to say some things to them that he should not be able to say to them on a dying-bed. And he would now say to all his friends, "While ye have the light, walk in the light." While making these remarks, there was a peculiar lustre on his countenance. I said to him, I trust you feel no solicitude respecting the issue of your present sickness. He replied with emphasis: "No, none at all. I am glad that it is not for me to say. It is sweet to trust in the Lord."

During the last twenty-four hours of his life he said but little. In the evening of the day before his death, I informed him that we considered him near the close of life, and said to him, I hope you enjoy peace of mind? By the motion of his head he gave me an affirmative answer. He continued to fail through the night, and at eight o'clock in the morning he calmly fell asleep, as we trust, in the arms of his Saviour. May all his friends remember his dying counsel: "WHILE YE HAVE THE LIGHT, WALK IN THE LIGHT."

> "Farewell! dear brother; may thy mantle rest
> Upon the youthful prophets of our God
> Farewell! now rest, amid the blessed band
> With whom thou once didst worship here below.
> And oft didst take sweet counsel. There are seals
> Thy ministry attesting, and the crowns
> Of thy rejoicing, through eternal days.
> There numbers beyond number of the sav'd
> Together sing Redemption's endless song"

APPENDIX.

No. I.—P. 55.

Mr. Davenport's Career.

There is a good account of him, and the disorders he introduced, in an old pamphlet, containing nine sermons by the Rev. Joseph Fish, pastor of a church in Stonington, preached in 1763. Mr. F. seems to have been a sound and faithful minister of the Gospel. He was the pastor of a large and flourishing church which had shared richly in the revival of 1740. But his parish was one of the theatres of Davenport's operations, —the result of which was, as he informs us in his preface, that not less than two-thirds of his congregation withdrew from his ministry, and formed themselves into separate societies. The sermons were preached twenty years after these separations took place; and their object was to make the youth of his flock acquainted with the scenes through which their church and society had passed. As this pamphlet is but little known at the present day, and as the facts which it contains are well worthy to be preserved, it may be useful to make a few exracts:—

"About twenty-three or twenty-four years ago, there was the most wonderful work of God that ever was known in this part of the world, both for the extent and visible appearance of it. It seems there was a general thoughtfulness about religion prevailing in the minds of the people, before they made it manifest by word. The ministers of Christ were stirred up to preach with uncommon zeal and solemnity; and the people were as ready to hear with unusual attention, while the things of eternity were charged home to the conscience.

"The work went on gloriously. The standing ministers (there being no other then in the land) became more abundant and fervent in their labours, as they saw their people were attentive to hear. Nor did they labour in vain. Scarce a sermon could be preached but the hearts of the people, more or less, would be touched, and some deeply affected. While we were thus engaged in religion, a new and surprising scene opened upon us,—even such religious operations and appearances as engaged both the careless and the serious to come and see and hear for themselves. In these strange operations there was a marvellous mixture of almost everything *good and bad*, truth and error, chaff and wheat. For while the Spirit of God wrought *powerfully*, Satan raged *maliciously*, and acted his old subtle part to deceive. This happened—or, at least, was carried to the highest pitch—under the preaching and ministrations of a wonderful, strange, good man, (the Rev. James Davenport of Long Island,) who visited these parts in the time of our religious concern and awakening,—a young man of undoubted real piety—fervent zeal for God—love to souls—and ardent desire to advance the Redeemer's kingdom; but (thus it was permitted) a man, while with us, under the powerful influence of a *false spirit* in a great part of his conduct, as *many* then told him, and as he himself did afterwards acknowledge with deep abasement. Satan, taking the advantage of his zeal in religion, transformed himself into an angel of light, and hurried him into extremes; yea, artfully carried him beside the truth and duty, and beyond the bounds of decency.

"The things promoted by him that were evidently and dreadfully wrong, are such as these:—He not only gave an unrestrained liberty to *noise and outcry*, both of *distress and joy*, in time of divine service, but promoted both with all his might. . . . . . Those persons that passed immediately from great distress to great joy and delight, (which, 'tis true, have their place in religion,) after asking them a few questions, were instantly proclaimed *converts*, or said to have *come to Christ;* and upon it the assembly were told that a number—it may be *ten* or *fifteen*—have come to Christ already, who will come next? But (I desire to speak it with sorrow) numbers of such *converts*, in a little time, returned to their old way of living—were as carnal, wicked, and void of Christian experience as ever they were. Again: He was a great favourer of *visions, trances, imaginations, and powerful impressions* upon the mind in others; and made such inward *feelings* the rule of his conduct in *many respects;* especially if the impression came with *a text of Scripture*, which he looked upon to be *opened* to him at such a time, and in such cases pointing out his duty, which he would accordingly pursue. Upon such powerful impressions and openings of Scripture, he went to Boston, strongly persuaded that multitudes in *that great city* (to use his own expressions) would be converted by his preaching there. But, as Mr. Edwards rightly observes, such circumstances attending religious affections are no sure sign that they are *gracious*, or truly religious. He was a great encourager—if not the first setter up—of public *exhorters;* not restricting them to the Gospel rule or order of *brotherly* exhortations; but encouraging *any lively zealous* Christians (so reputed) to exhort *publicly*, in full assemblies, with all the *air and assurance* of ministerial authoritative exhorting; although they were exceeding *raw and unskilful* in the word of righteousness, and altogether unequal to the solemn undertaking. However, they being very warm and zealous, spake *boldly and freely*, [which qualities of speech, by the way, Mr. Edwards judiciously observes, are no sure signs of gracious, religious affections,] and so were highly esteemed, had in admiration, and preferred before *the letter-learned rabbis, scribes, and pharisees, and unconverted ministers;* which *phrases* the good man would frequently use in his sermons, with such peculiar *marks*, not only of *odium*, but of *indication*, as served to beget a jealousy in many of the people's minds, that *their* ministers were the letter-learned, unconverted teachers which he aimed at. And thus the exhorters came into credit among multitudes of people, who chose rather to hear them than their old teachers; which served directly to puff them up with spiritual pride, and fitted them for the daring undertaking which followed.

"By these means the standing ministers began to fall in their credit and esteem among the people; especially among such as were reckoned the foremost Christians; many of whom, with the bloated exhorters, began to treat their ministers with such assurance, haughtiness, and contempt, as plainly spoke their sentiments, that they knew more and better how to teach than they; especially if the ministers opposed them, or only questioned whether they were right. And thus the sèeds of discord and disunion were sown, and a foundation laid for after separations. But what tended more effectually than all that has been said, to prepare the way for separation, was this that followed: This zealous good man, from a sense, hopefully at first, of the eminent danger of an unconverted ministry, both to themselves and the people, was betrayed by the false spirit, into that bold, daring enterprise of going through the country to *examine* all the *ministers* in private, and then publicly to declare his judgment of their spiritual state. And this he did whenever he could be admitted to examine them. Some that he examined [though for aught that appeared, as godly as himself] were pronounced, in his public prayers immediately after examination, to be *unconverted*. And they who declared this design and practice of his to be unscriptural, and so refused to be *examined* by him, were sure to suffer the same fate; they were condemned by him as Christless; or [which amounted to as much with the populace] he would declare that he had reason to fear they were unconverted; in which cases he could ordinarily have no other ground or reason for his fear, than that of their refusing submission to his *tribunal*. Many good people, thinking highly of Mr. Davenport, as though he was authorized from Heaven to proceed in this manner, and, at the same time, having great regard for their own ministers, seemed even as much concerned lest they should not stand the trial, [when examined,] as if they were going before the Judge of all the earth.

"Now, the counsel of this strange man, *which he counselled in those days, was* [like the counsel of Ahithophel] *as if a man had inquired at the oracle of God*. Multitudes of honest good people believed everything that he *said*, and had such a veneration for all that he *did*, that if they could *quote* the *word and example* of Mr. Davenport, 'twas enough with *them* to justify any of the wild, unscriptural notions and ways which they, through weakness, had run into; so that a minister could not gainsay or correct them, under the price of his reputation. The things which I have mentioned [to which solemn testimony to the work of God that was carried on in the land, by the outpouring of His blessed Spirit in those things that were really and properly *God's* work; and said that he doubted not but that *he*, though [as he added] most unworthy, had been made an instrument for the saving good of many souls; but declared with all humility and openness of heart, that in many things—such as above—he had grievously erred. He told us how the Lord had led him to a sight of his errors, and convinced him fully that he had been under the powerful influence of the false spirit; though, in the time of its operation, he verily thought 'twas the Spirit of God in a high degree. Thus the good man [no longer the noisy, boisterous, rash, and censorious Davenport, but the meek, humble, and yet the *fervent* man of God] confessed, bewailed, and *warned* against the errors which he had unhappily spread and promoted.

"How great and how happy the change! But how is he now received and hearkened to by those zealous people, who, in the time of his wildness and false zeal, were ready to adore him? Why, verily, they that were not convinced of their own, and his former mistakes, were far from being pleased by his present conduct. They saw that he was turned *against them*,—that is, against some of their darling principles and ways; and thought that he *was now become their enemy* in those things wherein he only told them the truth. They now looked upon him to be cold, dead, and lifeless,—that he had got away from God, and joined, in a great measure, with the world of opposers, and *carnal ministers*. In a word, they were sadly disappointed, sorely vexed, or disquieted in their spirits, grievously offended, [that is, numbers of them;] and, on the whole, they all rejected his message."—Pp. 114-128.

No. II.

The Cumberland Presbyterians.

"Scenes, in some measure similar to those in the days of Davenport, have been repeatedly exhibited since that time.

many more might, doubtless, be added] were such manifest ERRORS, that even the carnal and ungodly world could not but see and know they were wrong. And so herein they agreed with some judicious good people and discerning ministers who opposed them as such. And for this reason the good and the bad were ranked together, and frequently run upon by those who were zealous for these things, and declared to be *opposers* of the work of God, and on the *enemy's* side. He that speaks to you being an eye and ear-witness to *all*, or the *substance* of what has been related, is the more free in declaring these things unto you. . . . . .

"Having gone on a year or more [if I mistake not] in the practices above stated, he was, by the gentle treatment and earnest expostulation of some pious and judicious ministers, put upon serious reflection, and close examination of his strange conduct in the things which have been related, and others similar to them; and after some months' deliberation, and earnest seeking to the Father of lights, he was deliberately, clearly, and fully convinced of his errors. The mask was thrown aside—the delusions of Satan appeared to him in their own horrid light—and the dreadful consequences of his awful mistakes filled him with deep concern. He was made sensible of the injury he had done to *ministers and churches*,—how he had broke the order of the Gospel, by causing divisions and offences; and, on the whole, that he had brought reproach on the glorious work of God, and endangered the souls of men. For these things he was deeply abased—humbled himself before the Lord, and lay in the dust. Hereupon he returned, and visited many of the places where he had so grievously erred and offended, to see if he might, by any means, repair the damage he had done. When he came to this town, it was with such a mild, pleasant, meek, and humble spirit, broken and contrite, as I scarce ever saw exceeded, or even equalled. He not only owned his fault in private, and, in a most Christian manner, asked forgiveness of some ministers whom he had before treated amiss, but, in a large assembly, made a public recantation of his errors and mistakes; and particularly mentioned and declared against *some*, if not *all* that I have exposed in this narrative, as well as others that I have not mentioned. He gave a full and such assurance, haughtiness, and contempt, as plainly spoke their sentiments, that they knew more and better how to teach than they; especially if the ministers opposed them, or only questioned whether they were right. And thus the sèeds of discord and disunion were sown, and a foundation laid for after separations. But what tended more effectually than all that has been said, to prepare the way for separation, was this that followed: This zealous good man, from a sense, hopefully at first, of the eminent danger of an unconverted ministry, both to themselves and the people, was betrayed by the false spirit, into that bold, daring enterprise of going through the country to *examine* all the *ministers* in private, and then publicly to declare his judgment of their spiritual state. And this he did whenever he could be admitted to examine them. Some that he examined [though for aught that appeared, as godly as himself] were pronounced, in his public prayers immediately after examination, to be *unconverted.* And they who declared this design and practice of his to be unscriptural, and so refused to be *examined* by him, were sure to suffer the same fate; they were condemned by him as Christless; or [which amounted to as much with the populace] he would declare that he had reason to fear they were unconverted; in which cases he could ordinarily have no other ground or reason for his fear, than that of their refusing submission to his *tribunal.* Many good people, thinking highly of Mr. Davenport, as though he was authorized from Heaven to proceed in this manner, and, at the same time, having great regard for their own ministers, seemed even as much concerned lest they should not stand the trial, [when examined,] as if they were going before the Judge of all the earth.

"Now, the counsel of this strange man, *which he counselled in those days, was* [like the counsel of Ahithophel] *as if a man had inquired at the oracle of God.* Multitudes of honest good people believed everything that he *said*, and had such a veneration for all that he *did*, that if they could *quote* the *word and example* of Mr. Davenport, 'twas enough with *them* to justify any of the wild, unscriptural notions and ways which they, through weakness, had run into; so that a minister could not gainsay or correct them, under the price of his reputation. The things which I have mentioned [to which returned to their old way of living—were as carnal, wicked, and void of Christian experience as ever they were. Again: He was a great favourer of *visions, trances, imaginations, and powerful impressions* upon the mind in others; and made such inward *feelings* the rule of his conduct in *many respects;* especially if the impression came with *a text of Scripture*, which he looked upon to be *opened* to him at such a time, and in such cases pointing out his duty, which he would accordingly pursue. Upon such powerful impressions and openings of Scripture, he went to Boston, strongly persuaded that multitudes in *that great city* (to use his own expressions) would be converted by his preaching there. But, as Mr. Edwards rightly observes, such circumstances attending religious affections are no sure sign that they are *gracious*, or truly religious. He was a great encourager—if not the first setter up—of public *exhorters;* not restricting them to the Gospel rule or order of *brotherly* exhortations; but encouraging *any lively zealous* Christians (so reputed) to exhort *publicly*, in full assemblies, with all the *air and assurance* of ministerial authoritative exhorting; although they were exceeding *raw and unskilful* in the word of righteousness, and altogether unequal to the solemn undertaking. However, they being very warm and zealous, spake *boldly and freely*, [which qualities of speech, by the way, Mr. Edwards judiciously observes, are no sure signs of gracious, religious affections,] and so were highly esteemed, had in admiration, and preferred before *the letter-learned rabbis, scribes, and pharisees, and unconverted ministers;* which *phrases* the good man would frequently use in his sermons, with such peculiar *marks*, not only of *odium*, but of *indication*, as served to beget a jealousy in many of the people's minds, that *their* ministers were the letter-learned, unconverted teachers which he aimed at. And thus the exhorters came into credit among multitudes of people, who chose rather to hear them than their old teachers; which served directly to puff them up with spiritual pride, and fitted them for the daring undertaking which followed.

"By these means the standing ministers began to fall in their credit and esteem among the people; especially among such as were reckoned the foremost Christians; many of whom, with the bloated exhorters, began to treat their ministers with

Of these (says Dr. Miller of Princeton, in a letter to Dr. Sprague) I have neither time nor inclination to speak of more than one. The case to which I refer is that of the remarkable revivals which took place in the years 1800, 1801, and 1802, in the western country, and more particularly within the bounds of the Synod of Kentucky. My impression is, that the most enlightened and sincere friends of vital piety, who had the best opportunity of being intimately acquainted with the revivals referred to, believe them to have been a real work of the Holy Spirit; or, at least, to have been productive of a number of genuine conversions. But that this work of grace was attended, and finally overshadowed, disgraced, and terminated, by fanaticism and disorders of the most distressing character, will not, probably, now be questioned by any competent judges.

"This excitement began in Logan county in Kentucky, but soon spread over all the state, and into the neighbouring states. Besides increased attention to the usual seasons and the ordinary means of religious worship, there were, during the summers of the years just mentioned, large *camp meetings* held, and a number of days and nights in succession spent in almost unceasing religious exercises. At these meetings hundreds—and, in some cases, thousands—of people might have been heard and seen at the same time engaged in singing and prayer—in exhortation and preaching—in leaping, shouting, disputing, and conversing, with a confusion scarcely describable. This wonderful excitement may be considered as standing related, both as cause and effect, to several other deplorable irregularities. A love of excitement and agitation seemed to take possession of the people. They began to suppose, that when these were absent, nothing was done. A number of hot-headed young men, intoxicated with the prevailing element of excitement, and feeling confident of their own powers and call to the work, though entirely destitute of any suitable education, assumed the office of public exhorters and instructors. These were soon afterwards licensed to preach,—a majority of the presbytery hoping, that though not regularly qualified, they might be useful. When once this door was opened, it was found difficult to close it. Candidate after candidate of this character, and on this plan, were licensed, and subsequently ordained, until this description of ministers threatened to become a majority of the whole body. As might have been expected, a new source of trouble now appeared. A number of these raw and ignorant young men, and a few of the older ministers, began to manifest a great laxness as to their theological opinions. And a new Presbytery having been set off, consisting chiefly of those who were friendly to the new opinions and measures, it became a sort of mint for issuing, in great abundance, similar coin. Candidates were freely licensed and ordained who declined adopting the Confession of Faith of the Presbyterian Church in the usual form. They were received on their declaring: 'That they adopted that Confession only so far as they considered it as agreeing with the Word of God.' On this plan it is manifest that subscription was a piece of solemn mockery. Persons of all conceivable sentiments might freely enter at such a door. The consequence was, that Arminians and Pelagians actually entered the Presbyterian Church, and went on rapidly to multiply, until the decisive measures of the Synod of Kentucky, and of the General Assembly, arrested the progress of the evil. By means of the measures referred to, these disorderly intruders, with their pertinacious adherents, were finally separated from the Synod of Kentucky. A majority of them formed the body known by the name of the 'Cumberland Presbyterians,'—now consisting of a number of presbyteries professing to adopt the presbyterian form of government, but avowedly embracing semi-Pelagian principles in theology. Another, but similar portion, formed a new body, denominated 'Christians,' and sometimes 'New Lights,' or 'Stoneites,' (from the name of their principal leader,) and became a kind of enthusiastic noisy Socinians; while the remainder, under the same lawless impulse, took a third course, and fell into all the fanatical absurdities of 'Shakerism.'

"In this case, indeed, as in some of those before recited, several of the ministerial brethren more advanced in life, who had lent their names and their influence to these deplorable disorders, became, after awhile, sensible of their mistake, acknowledged their fault, and were restored to the bosom of the Presbyterian Church; but, as in former cases, not until mischief, then beyond their control, had been consummated.

"The mournful results of their course had been predicted; and they were entreated to guard against the division and corruption to which it could not fail of leading. But they would not be prevailed upon to pause, until the Church had been rent in pieces—until heresies of the grossest kind had been engendered and embodied—and until they had effectually scattered in that country the seeds of deep and extended ecclesiastical desolation. No intelligent Christian, it is believed, who has any adequate acquaintance with the course of the events in question, has any doubt that these revivals, on account of their sad accompaniments, *left the churches in the west in a far worse state than they were before.*"

No. III.

Mr. Finney's Career.

Dr. Nettleton and his friends spoke decidedly, but in a very brotherly and charitable tone, of Mr. Finney's movements; and a few years shewed that they were not wrong. Mr. Finney's doctrines soon deviated from the truth as much as his measures did from scriptural order and wisdom. At this day no orthodox body of Christians could receive him into their pulpit. No doubt he published works that contained rousing and startling truths; but even truth was given forth alongside of much error which counteracted all. And now he seems to be drifting no one can tell whither. In a volume of lectures on theology, published a few years ago, he utters such irreverent statements as these: "It is *God's duty* to govern; *His conscience* must demand it." He adjusts whatever he finds in the Bible to his own preconceived metaphysical determinations, instead of submitting his metaphysical musings to the test of unerring wisdom. He *assumes* (not offering one argument in proof of his position) that "A sense of obligation is inconsistent with a sense of entire inability;" although, for ages, the very opposite has been held, and been felt to be true, by the churches of Christ. He imposes on the unthinking reader by *half-truths*; and crowns his errors by maintaining, that "*no man* is responsible for *his feelings*, but only for his *intention!*" And thus he arrives at the possibility of *never sinning*, and that "men are saved by returning back to *personal holiness!*" As for *moral excellence*, he has found out that it lies in *happiness*; duty is degraded by him to the position of being the chief way to the highest happiness; and love to God and man mean no more than seeking the highest happiness of both! But the conscience and the consciousness of every man, even apart from the Word of God, contradict him at every step. "If the light that is in thee be darkness, how great is that darkness!" In the *British and Foreign Evangelical Review*, September 1853, there is a full review of his aberrations as a writer.

Not long since, the following statement was made by a minister in America, whose information and character are alike such as entitle him to be depended on:—"A class of evangelists arose, of whom the Rev. C. G. Finney was a distinguished leader, who adopted Pelagian, or Semi-Pelagian views of doctrine, and introduced a system of measures adapted to produce excitement. The consequence was, that great excitement was produced, and multitudes of converts were proclaimed. But a large proportion of these proved to be like seed sown on stony places. *Moral desolation succeeded these excitements. Some of these evangelists have lost their character, and most of them have lost, in a great measure, their influence. Very few of them would now be invited to preach in those places where their labours were said to be so remarkably successful.* This is true of Mr. Finney himself. If our English brethren who are giving Mr. Finney their countenance and support, are not making work for repentance, many of the most sound and judicious ministers of this country will be greatly mistaken. I am happy to be able to state, that, in the Presbyterian and Congregational Churches generally, in our country, the '*New Measure System*,' as it has been called, has gone into disrepute, and revivals are becoming more like those which were witnessed at the beginning of the present century."

No. IV.

Thoughts on Revivals, by Dr. Nettleton.

Against revivals many objections are urged. It is said they are mere excitements, which have in them nothing of the nature of true religion, and that they ought not to be ascribed to the Spirit of God. In support of these allegations is alleged:—

1. Their suddenness, and the fact that such numbers profess to be converted in so short a time.

Answer. The influences of the Spirit are compared in the Scriptures to the rain: "He shall come unto us as the rain, as the latter and the former rain unto the earth." Would you object to the rain, and say, it cannot be rain, because it sometimes comes suddenly and in so many drops? We are given to understand that a nation will be born in a day.

2. The great distress which exists in revivals is urged as an objection against them.

Answer. It is not religion which causes the distress, but a conviction of the want of it. Is it surprising that sinners should be distressed when they are brought to realize that they are exposed to eternal destruction? When a person's body is in pain, he is in distress; and his friends often sigh and weep. And is the soul of less consequence than the body? Are heaven and hell trifles? Were not sinners pricked in the heart on the day of Pentecost? And was not the jailer of Philippi distressed when he fell down before Paul and Silas?

3. It is said that it is only that persons are terrified by alarming preaching.

Answer. Why were they not terrified before? They have often heard the same truths. They have heard, perhaps for years, the most alarming preaching, and remained unmoved. Why are they alarmed now if they are under no influence from on high? Besides, the very same truths which fill sinners with alarm, often, after a season, fill them with joy unspeakable and full of glory. How is this to be explained?

Does the same preaching, of itself, cause, in the same mind, sorrow and joy?

But have not sinners reason to be terrified? When persons have no fear of God before their eyes, it is a mark of great depravity. Was not Felix terrified under the preaching of Paul?

If the results witnessed in revivals are the result of human influence only, believing what I do of the nature of these results, I should feel under obligation to awaken all my hearers. I should not expect to be saved myself, if I failed to do it. Are you willing to grant that ministers have so much power? Are they able to change the enemies of God into His friends? —to cause them to love what they hated with perfect hatred?

But the objection might have been made against the revival on the day of Pentecost, as well as against modern revivals. It might have been said, that the people were terrified—that Peter frightened them.

4. It is said that what we witness in revivals is all the effect of sympathy.

Answer. What begins them? Are the first cases of awakening to be attributed to sympathy? But it not unfrequently happens that numbers are awakened about the same time, without any knowledge of each other's feelings, or of the awakening of any other individuals.

But suppose sympathy does have an influence after a revival has commenced; cannot God make use of it as a means of promoting the work, as well as any other means? The Psalmist says: "Many shall see it and fear, and shall trust in the Lord." When sinners see others anxious for their souls, it is to them powerful preaching, and God can bless it to their conviction and conversion.

5. It is said that it is all enthusiasm.

Answer. If the distress of sinners is greater than the case demands, then call it enthusiasm. But if the sinner is in danger of losing his soul, not to be distressed is blockish stupidity. Is it rational to brave the terrors of the Almighty, and to slumber on the brink of eternal perdition?

6. It is said, the sudden joy manifested in revivals is irrational, and cannot be the effect of divine influence.

Answer. What shall we find to answer these expressions in the Bible?—"The peace of God that passeth all understanding;" "Rejoicing with joy unspeakable and full of glory;" "All joy and peace in believing;" "Called out of darkness into marvellous light;" "Having the day-star arise in our hearts." Would not a criminal, who should be reprieved on his way to the gallows, rejoice? Besides, were not the same effects witnessed in the days of Christ and the apostles? Did not Zaccheus come down from the tree, and receive Christ joyfully? Did not Peter's hearers, on the day of Pentecost, receive the Word with joy? When Philip preached in Samaria, was there not great joy in that city?

7. It is said, many who are zealous for a season, turn back, and become worse than before.

Answer. True. And so it was in the time of Christ. "Many went back and walked no more with Him." Does this prove that Christ had no true disciples? It was so likewise in the days of the apostles. John says: "They went out from us, but they were not of us; for, if they had been of us, they would, no doubt, have continued with us."

That the objection may be valid, it must be shewn that all who profess to be the subjects of revivals apostatize. But this cannot be shewn. There are precious fruits that abide.

8. The question is sometimes asked, If revivals are the work of God, why do they not exist among other denominations? and why am not I taken?

Answer. This objection lies with equal force against the Christian religion. Not more than one-fifth part of the world is evangelized. Jews, Mohammedans, and Pagans, might say: If yours is the true religion, why does not God convince us of its truth?

But revivals do exist in other denominations. All evangelical denominations have been favoured with them in a greater or less degree.

If I were to find serious praying people generally opposed to revivals, and all the impenitent and profane in favour of them, it would alter the case. But praying people pray for them, and rejoice in them.

They are, doubtless, the work of God, or the work of the devil. If they are the work of the devil, I believe all will acknowledge, that there is more praying, and more apparent religion in the devil's kingdom, than there is out of it.

To all who oppose revivals, I would say: Beware! lest you be found fighting against God.

A revival of religion is well described in the parable of the sower. There are four kinds of hearers, represented by the seed which fell by the way-side, among thorns, in stony places, and on good ground. . . . .
. . . .

Should a number of those who think they have experienced religion, turn back, it will not disprove the reality of religion. Because there was a Judas among the apostles, does it prove that Christ had no true disciples? Because some seed fell on stony places, does it prove that none fell on good ground?

When those who profess to have experienced religion apostatize, how common it is for the wicked to triumph!—but what does it prove?

1. That those who thus triumph have no religion; and that they are glad others are going to hell with them.

2. That they are in very great danger. If others have been deceived, they may well imagine that the danger of being lost is imminent.